Hawaii: An Informal History

GERRIT P. JUDD IV

HAWAII

An Informal History

MAUI HISTORICAL
SOCIETY MUSEUM

HALE HOIKEIKE

COLLIER BOOKS

NEW YORK, N.Y.

A Collier Books Original

First Edition 1961

Collier Books is a division of The Crowell-Collier Publishing Company

For my Father

Contents

By the same author

Members of Parliament 1734-1832
Horace Walpole's Memoirs
Dr. Judd, Hawaii's Friend

Hawaii: An Informal History

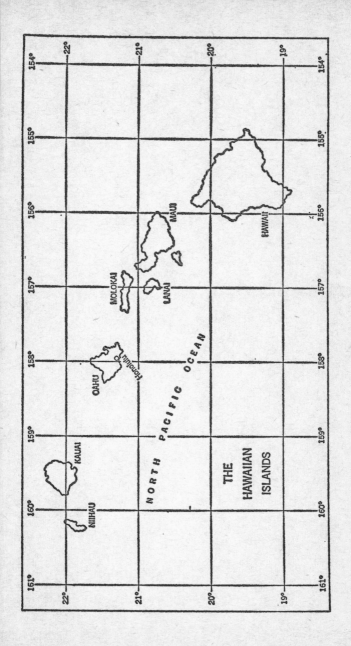

THE
HAWAIIAN
ISLANDS

Chapter 1

The Land

HAWAII HAS a history. More than that, Hawaii has a distinctive history. The Islands are much more than a fabled vacation land. They are, and have been, the recipient and carrier of vigorous historical movements. The net result is not only the fiftieth American state, but a community which, in reflecting the main vital tendencies of the globe-encircling past, makes a unique contribution to American civilization.

Going to Hawaii for the first time is a memorable experience. By air, Honolulu is only a few hours from the West Coast. The plane ride high above the cloud line is smooth and uneventful, almost boring because it is so serene. Despite excitement among the newcomers (*malihinis*, strangers), the old-timers (*kamaainas*, native born) ignore the unchanging vista of clouds and bright blue sky. They read, or doze a little, and wait for the passage of time. Toward the end of the journey the captain announces the arrival over the loudspeaker. Reshuffling of possessions begins, along with craning of necks. The aircraft slants downward. A few clouds brush its sides and wings, but the sunlight persists. The engines change tone, and the ship of the skies seems to coast along without effort, occasionally shuddering slightly as it slices through minor turbulence. Glimpses of land flash by, soft green and brown, edged by a white and blue ribbon of beach and sea. It is hard to see much as the plane banks and turns for the landing. Seconds later the white runway of the airstrip is rushing by. In minutes the passengers file down the stairway toward the terminal building of Honolulu International Airport, which is west of Waikiki Beach and near Pearl Harbor.

The newcomer walking in the brilliant sunlight notices at once the soft and persistent blowing of the trade winds, their force broken by the jagged green hills—much higher than those of San Francisco—which lie across the island like a verdant spine. As the days pass he deludes himself into thinking that he can forget the trade winds, as they ceaselessly agitate the leaves with a sound that is a combination of a hiss and a murmur. They are as much a part of Hawaii as the sunlight

13

and warmth and lush semitropical vegetation. He deludes himself because few can forget them, just as few can forget Hawaii.

Meanwhile the newcomers and old-timers sort themselves out. The old-timers become centers of a cluster of warmhearted welcomes, smiling broadly and ducking their heads to receive fragrant flower necklaces (*leis*). The wise ones among them reward the flower-givers with a kiss. The newcomers glance about nervously, and stare with a certain awe at bulletin boards announcing flights to and from the Orient. In the taxi they stare with unbroken fascination at the furrowed hills rising on the mountain or inland side (*mauka*), or turn to the seaward side (*makai*), for a glimpse of the waves or a longer look at a passing freighter or naval vessel. In short order they pass through Honolulu's downtown business district, which, except for its vegetation, looks much like that of any other American city of the same age. They then head for one of the hotels fringing the world-famous beach at Waikiki.

The first impressions multiply and end in a blur. The traffic is brisk, but the drivers are courteous and slow down to yield the right of way. From time to time they stop, as in London, at the crosswalks to let the pedestrians saunter across the street. In this way the tourist has a chance to stare some more at the modernistic buildings, reminiscent of southern California, or at the passers-by, many of them Orientals or crossbreeds in Hawaii's racial melting pot. He sees some strikingly beautiful Japanese girls, lithe and long-legged in trim American clothing, Filipino boys with long hair and flamboyant aloha shirts, an occasional Polynesian with light-brown skin and gentle features, along with a few aged Orientals, wrinkled and stooped, and an occasional group of young servicemen trying to look like sophisticated world travelers. But these are only glimpses, for the traffic starts again, and it will be days or even months later before the tourist can catalogue his impressions.

It is particularly exciting to see Hawaii for the first time at night. Instead of green hills with brown patches and occasional houses, the tourist sees clusters of lights, many apparently twinkling, as the airplane glides in for the landing. If he is lucky he has a good look at the Waikiki area and the hills in back of Diamond Head, where the lights are like incandescent diamonds studded with jewels of many colors. But like the daytime landing it is all too swift. In minutes it is all over, the plane comes to its final stop, and the newcomer stands in anticipation and bewilderment waiting to disembark. Those arriving by night see less than the daytime traveler, but they have seen some special things invisible by day. Not only have they seen the city's lights, looped like an endless necklace up and down the hills, but as they alight at the airport they may look upward and see the stars. No description of this panorama, without the actual experience of witnessing it, can be wholly credible. The stars seem larger and nearer than they appear to be in more northerly latitudes, as if they were glittering baubles set in a black velvet dome. If there is moonlight so much the better. Moonlight in Hawaii, and even the moon rising red from the sea, are both as beautiful as they are in Miami, and some people say even more so. A particularly good way to see moonlight in Hawaii is to sit at night on the beach at Waikiki, faintly lit with slow-burning torches set in poles, with the lights of the city flickering at your back and the waves flashing with white foam at your feet. Look upward, then, and watch the moonlight filter like quicksilver through the palm fronds. Take a good look. There is nothing more beautiful anywhere in the world, even in Ceylon, reputedly the world's second most beautiful place. All this awaits the traveler who arrives for the first time at night.

Experienced travelers say that the best way to go to Hawaii is by ship. Many of them, of course, traveled extensively this way in the days before airplane flights became commonplace. Like old-timers of all varieties, they are creatures of habit who genuinely prefer the old ways. On the other hand they have a strong argument in their favor. Arrival by plane is over in a matter of minutes. It happens so quickly that after a glimpse or two the traveler finds himself on the ground. By way of contrast, arrival by ship is leisurely, a pace more in keeping with Hawaii's general life-rhythm, which is far less swift and exhausting than that of colder northern areas.

Ordinarily landfall comes just after dawn. To the crew, of course, it is just another day. Not so for the new visitor, whose only breakfast is a cup of coffee hastily gulped so that he will not miss anything on the way to port. With other excited passengers he stands at the rail on the port side watching the sheer, indented cliffs and valleys of the island of Molokai as the ship steams westward. Toward the top of the high hills the rising mist of the morning meets the cloud line, and occasionally there is a rainbow. The light greens of the hilltops turn to lighter green and brown toward the drylands and scrub forest near the shore. If the new arrival is fortunate, someone familiar with the Islands is nearby to explain that the tiny low-lying peninsula at the base of a towering and almost impassable cliff contains the Kalaupapa settlement. Here a very few Islanders, mainly elderly people, receive treatment for Hansen's disease, formerly called leprosy. Here the heroic Father Damien labored in conditions which were grim but subject to much irresponsible exaggeration by later writers. (Hansen's disease is now extremely rare and kept under control without undue difficulty.)

At this point the ship turns southward and enters the Molokai Channel. The newcomer gazes for a moment at the wide beaches of Molokai's west end, then hurries to the starboard side of the ship. Here he sees Oahu's windward (*koolau*) coast, the green lowlands with the huge craggy mountains at their back. This landscape is much more rich and variegated than the Molokai plains, where algarroba (*kiawe*) forests merge with pineapple fields on the plateau. The ship passes Makapuu and some rocky beaches, where the surf is rough and angry, then turns westward again past Koko Head and Diamond Head.

On its slow progress toward the dock at Aloha Tower, the ship commands an unsurpassed view of Waikiki Beach and the city of Honolulu stretching upward to the hills. Return visitors answer questions patiently and point out important landmarks. But little of this the newcomer remembers. He is preoccupied instead with native boys (*kanakas*) diving for coins, which they put in their mouths for safekeeping, and with the faint sound of music coming across the water. As the ship edges into the berth the music is loud and clear, the throbbing melody of "Aloha Oe" (Greetings to You), Hawaii's most famous song. This music, along with the *leis* and the wildly waving crowds, creates an atmosphere of almost unbearable excitement. A number of people weep. In many ways the old-timers are right when they insist on going to Hawaii by ship. After this leisurely introduction the newcomer may then go ashore to seek his first detailed impression of Hawaii and its people.

Leaving Hawaii is another matter. The sunlight is still there, and the trade winds still blow, but this time the ship heads eastward past Diamond Head and eventually into the open sea. The band still plays, but this time "Aloha Oe" becomes a song of sadness and farewell. As the ship passes Diamond Head many passengers throw their *leis* overboard, as a token of their hope to return. For some old-timers, the present writer included, this is an experience almost too overwhelming to bear. Perhaps in leaving the Islands it is better to take a plane, and get the matter over with as quickly as possible.

Within a few days after his arrival almost every tourist buys a guidebook of some sort about Hawaii. Here he satisfies his curiosity with a fairly standard set of statements and statistics. Honolulu on the island of Oahu (not on the island of Hawaii), he finds, is 2,395 miles southwest of San Francisco. The Islands as a whole lie near the center of the Pacific Ocean and deserve their popular name of the "Crossroads of the Pacific." They are indeed isolated, being about 2,000 miles from any major body of land. Specifically, they extend from about latitudes 18°55′N. to 23°N. and from about longitudes 154°40′W. to 162°W. In point of sober fact they are in the North Pacific, just below the Tropic of Cancer, and therefore not really part of the South Seas group, although the original native inhabitants were an offshoot of the Polynesian settlements in the South Pacific. The southernmost point of the Islands is almost 1,200 miles north of the equator.

In geographic terms the Hawaiian Islands form part of a series of islands about 2,000 miles long, like great stepping stones flung in a northwesterly arc. But the extreme geographic limit of the seven main islands is less than 350 miles. The area of the twenty islands comprising the present State of Hawaii is 6,435 square miles, slightly larger than the combined area of Connecticut and Rhode Island.

The Hawaiian Islands are volcanic in origin, built up from the sea bed by successive flows of lava and extended somewhat by the slow accumulation of coral. They are, in fact, the tops of a gigantic mountain range. The geologic process which produced them is impressive to contemplate, as successive layers of lava thrust themselves upward about 15,000 feet from the ocean floor to sea level and reached maximum height at the mountain of Mauna Kea (White Mountain, so called because of the snow on its summit) on the island of Hawaii, which is 13,784 feet high, the highest island mountain in the world. Volcanic flows on this island still continue, so that one part of the Hawaiian Islands is still in process of formation.

Mauna Loa (Long Mountain), also on the island of Hawaii, is the world's largest volcano, rising to a height of 13,675 feet. With Kilauea on its southeastern slope about 4,000 feet above sea level, it is one of Hawaii's two remaining active volcanoes. Kilauea is Hawaii's newest and most active volcano, and in recent years it has become fashionable for tourists to gather near its crater whenever there is an eruption. The sight is fascinating at night. Even by day it is awe-inspiring to watch the lava bubbling crimson-red and spraying upward in high fiery fountains. The point of most intense heat is bright yellow.

These colors stand in sharp contrast to the light greens and browns of the surrounding vegetation, and to the light blue sky streaked with clouds. At times this lava, which reaches a heat of 2,000°F. or more, flows outward and down the slope at speeds up to thirty-five miles per hour, incinerating everything in its path. But even here there is a natural compensation, for the disintegrating lava in time produces extraordinarily fertile soil. A feature of Hawaii's volcanoes is the fine glossy fibers spun by the breeze as the drops of lava fly through the air and outward from the crater. These are called Pele's hair, Pele being the ancient and much-feared goddess of the volcano.

The island of Hawaii is the most easterly and southerly of the Hawaiian group. It is also the largest of the Hawaiian Islands, with an area of 4,021 square miles, comprising over three fifths of the land surface of the fiftieth state. The Big Island, as it is familiarly called, is roughly shaped like a triangle, with sides ninety, seventy-five, and sixty-five miles long. The Kona (in Hawaiian, south or southwest) coast on the leeward side of the island has extraordinarily fertile soil, good beaches, and some of the best fishing in the world.

About twenty-five miles northwest of the island of Hawaii, across Alenuihaha Channel is the island of Maui, the second largest island in the group. Maui consists of two mountains connected by an isthmus about six miles wide. The easterly mountain is the world's largest extinct volcano, Haleakala (literally, the House of the Sun), which covers nineteen square miles and rises to a height of 10,025 feet. Westward of Maui are the smaller islands of Molokai and Lanai.

About thirty miles northwest of Molokai and Lanai is Oahu, the third largest but most important island of the group, the site of the city of Honolulu (literally, Sheltered Port). Oahu has the best natural harbors in the state of Hawaii, the most famous being the naval base of Pearl Harbor. Waikiki (literally, Quick Water) on the leeward, or south, side of the island is Hawaii's best all-around beach. (Other beaches have more sand, but Waikiki is the best for swimming.) The surf rolls in majestically for a quarter of a mile. The beach itself is sheltered from the wind, and in this heavenly spot it seldom rains for more than a few minutes. Oahu is also famous for its extinct volcanoes, among them Diamond Head, Koko Head, and Punchbowl. Two mountain ranges cross the island in a north-westerly direction, rising to a maximum height of 4,030 feet. A distinctive feature of these mountains is their numerous towering cliffs. The most celebrated cliff is the windswept Pali (in Hawaiian, precipice), which connects Honolulu's Nuuanu Valley to the Koolau district on the windward side of the island. It is 1,186 feet high. The Pali was the site of a famous battle won by the native king Kamehameha I. At present it has a winding roadway used by hundreds of commuters who live on "the other side of the island" and work in Honolulu.

About sixty-five miles northwest of Oahu is the island of Kauai, the fourth largest in the group, roughly circular with a diameter of just over thirty miles. Kauai is geologically the oldest island of the group. Because of its regular and abundant rainfall it has long been known as the Garden Isle. Kauai is especially noted for its fern grottos and for Waimea Canyon, sometimes called the Little Grand Canyon or the Grand Canyon of the Pacific.

Niihau, the smallest and westernmost of the major islands in the group, lies about seventeen miles southwest of Kauai. This privately owned island is only sixteen miles long and six miles wide. It is the least known of all the Hawaiian Islands, at present inhabited by some 250 pure-blooded Hawaiians, living much as they did before the coming of the first foreigners. Niihau has no police or law courts, and communicates with Kauai by carrier pigeon. It was the only island to vote against statehood in 1959.

The Islands are, as a whole, mountainous, with hundreds of pleasant valleys merging with the lowlands of the coastal areas. Some of the more remote valleys, thinly inhabited, are unbelievably lovely havens. Some are almost inaccessible save by sea, such as the valleys of Wailau and Pelekunu on the north coast of Molokai.

Although in the tropical zone, the Islands have a mild and moderate climate because of the surrounding ocean and the refreshing winds. From March through December the easterly and northeasterly trade winds blow steadily. But in the first three months of the year there are occasional southerly (*kona*) storms, when rain, accompanied by warm and slightly discomforting winds, soaks the leeward side of the various islands. At sea level Hawaii's annual mean temperature is 74.9°, and the temperature varies little from month to month. In Honolulu the mean temperature for August, the hottest month of the year, is 78.4°, and the mean temperature for the coldest month, January, is 70.1°. Further, in any given month there is little difference between the temperature in the daytime and at night. The absence of seasons, that is, the continuous summer weather, sometimes disturbs newly arrived residents.

On the other hand, within the Islands there are a number of climatic variations. The windward sides of the various islands are somewhat cooler and wetter than the more pleasant leeward areas. The temperature drops and the rainfall increases in the higher elevations. In the winter months snow falls on the summit of Mauna Kea and Mauna Loa on the island of Hawaii, and sometimes also on Haleakala, Maui, and Hualalai, Hawaii. From time to time, incredible as it may seem, skiing enthusiasts have tried out their skill on these subtropical peaks.

The rainfall also varies considerably, from an annual average of forty feet at the summit (5,080 feet) of Mount Waialeale on Kauai (one of the wettest places in the world) to twenty inches only a few miles away. There is generally more rain in January, February, and March than in the other months. Some parts of the Islands are dry indeed, among them a desert on the southern part of the island of Hawaii, as well as the plains of Maui, Lanai, and Molokai. But, as it so happens, the rainfall in these plains is just enough to produce Hawaii's magnificent pineapple crops, which require little water.

In the favored leeward sections the rain is ample but intermittent. Rain clouds form quickly in the narrow valleys and race toward the coast with their "liquid sunshine." Yet it seldom rains for long, and soon the sunshine reappears to dry the streets and stimulate the vegetation, although it is not unusual for rain to fall while the sun is still shining. Sometimes these little rainstorms are so sharply delimited that it rains on only one side of the street. In such circumstances rainbows are common.

Because of its isolation comparatively few varieties of vegetation and animal life are native to Hawaii. By far the greater part are imports. In any case, the present vegetation is lush. The surrounding seas yield an astonishing variety of edible fish. Probably Hawaii's most famous fish is a tiny creature with the fantastically long name of *humuhumunukunukuapuaa* (literally, trigger fish with a snout like a pig), featured in a popular song. There are no snakes in Hawaii.

For all these reasons, and more, Hawaii deserves its well-known nickname, the "Paradise of the Pacific."

Chapter 2

The People

THE HAWAIIANS themselves believed that they came from Tahiti, and overwhelming evidence supports this view. The English missionary William Ellis, after his tour of the Islands in 1823, mentioned a "native belief that the first inhabitants were created on the islands, descended from the gods . . . or, that they came from a country which they called Tahiti. . . ." He added: "The accounts they have of their ancestors having arrived in a canoe from Tahiti are far more general and popular among the people."

The native antiquarian David Malo, born in Hawaii in 1795, corroborated this statement. He wrote: "It is thought that this people came from land near Tahiti and from Tahiti itself, because the ancient Hawaiians at an early date mention the name of Tahiti in their chants, prayers, and legends."

Much evidence confirms this belief. The stone adzes of the first native settlers in Hawaii are of a sort found in only one other area, that of the Tahitian group. Further, in their physical type, language, and way of life the Hawaiians resemble the natives of Tahiti more closely than other peoples of Polynesia.

The natives first came to Hawaii about 950 A.D. Genealogies of the Hawaiian chiefs to 1900 extend back thirty or forty generations, although the earlier parts of these genealogies are often mythical, as, in common with those of other primitive peoples, they connect the early chiefs with the gods. Nonetheless, an estimated twenty-five years per generation would extend the genealogies back as far as 900 A.D.

Confirmation of this estimate comes from a remarkable scientific technique first developed in 1948; namely, radiocarbon dating. Imagine a group of natives roasting fish or a pig in an open fire. They eat, sing, talk, make love, and go their various ways. The fire dies out and the ashes cool. How is it possible to date this incident? The answer is a by-product of the present nuclear age, for there is a variant (isotope) of carbon known as carbon-14 which is radioactive and disintegrates at a known rate. Through scientific measurements of the amount of carbon-14 remaining in an object investigators can calculate about when the incident took place.

A radiocarbon test of charcoal taken in 1950 from the first (lowest) level of debris in a cave on Oahu dated the fire at 1004, with an estimated margin of error of 180 years before or after this year. The radiocarbon test is an approximation, for scientists have to allow for possible contamination and other factors, but within reasonable limits it is accurate. Another charcoal sample taken in 1957 from the first level of debris on a site on the island of Hawaii was dated at 957, plus or minus 200 years. Further radiocarbon tests may yield even more exact information.

The Hawaiian genealogies state that for a few generations the earliest chiefs made trips back to Tahiti. But for reasons which are obscure these early voyages stopped. Linguistic analysis, especially the amount of change in vocabulary (glottochronology), gives striking confirmation of this native tradition. The linguists estimate that after they reached Hawaii the natives lived in isolation for about 1,000 years, until the first coming of the white foreigners (*haoles*) toward the end of the eighteenth century.

Dr. Kenneth P. Emory of Honolulu's Bishop Museum, a foremost expert on the origins of the Hawaiian people, concludes that Tahitian chiefs organized the early voyages to Hawaii, for chiefs alone would have had the resources to equip and staff these remarkable overseas expeditions. He has demonstrated, on the basis of archaeological and other information, that a more primitive people, later called the *Menehunes* (dwarfs or elves), did not precede the expeditions organized by these Tahitian chiefs. The *Menehunes*, he concludes, were really the common people of Tahiti called *Manehunes*, brought along by the chiefs. Neither Ellis nor Malo, so he points out, mention the earlier arrival of the *Menehunes*, and the tradition about them given in the standard histories of Hawaii rests on the later work of a Hawaiian historian Kamakau which, in any case, is suspect from internal evidence. Dr. Emory's research is a brilliant example of how archaeological, linguistic, and other forms of analysis, reinforced by radiocarbon dating, may revise many interpretations once believed to be authentic.

Linguistic studies by Dr. Emory and other scholars trace the Polynesians, including, of course, the Hawaiians, to Indonesia. In the transit eastward the original words of prehistoric Indonesia tended to become simplified. *Rain*, in Old Indonesian *huzan*, became *usa* in the islands to the west of Polynesia, *uha* in Tonga, and *ua* in eastern Polynesia and Hawaii. *Canoe*, in Indonesia *vangkang*, became *vangaa* in the western islands, *waka* in Polynesia, and *waa* in Hawaii. The natives also took with them the names of various islands. Savaii, the biggest of the Samoan Islands, became Hawaii, the Big Island of the Hawaiian group.

These complicated linguistic and other techniques lead to fairly firm conclusions. About 1500 B.C., three centuries before the fall of Troy celebrated by Homer, peoples of various origins settled a western part of Polynesia. In isolation they moved eastward to Tonga, Samoa, Tahiti, and Easter Island, southward to New Zealand, and northward to Hawaii. A few canoes or rafts may have had slight contact with Peru. In their isolation inbreeding produced a remarkable uniformity of appearance and blood groupings among the natives, as well as an equally remarkable uniformity in their way of life.

Such cold facts demand interpretation, for it is well to remember that in the Pacific the distances are immense and the land masses minute by comparison. It is 2,700 miles from Raiatea in the Tahitian group to Hawaii, and 2,600 miles from Samoa to Hawaii, with only a few small islands and atolls in between. In addition, occasional violent storms sweep through these desolate open stretches of water. No other voyages of exploration and settlement in world history have demanded more courage and skill.

The Polynesians, of course, lived close to the sea. Anyone who has visited a Polynesian settlement can testify that the natives are practically amphibious, as used to the sea as the Eskimo is to the snow. They depended on the sea for fish, a staple in their diet, and over the centuries they had accumulated much sea-lore, some of it inherited from previous migrations. Nonetheless, these long voyages across almost unbroken water are awe-inspiring.

They had seaworthy ships—canoes, some of them almost 100 feet long, carved with stone tools from tree trunks and shaped to glide through the waves. Many canoes also had an outrigger for stability and carried sails of woven coconut fiber or other materials. Polynesians also built large double canoes with a platform and cabin on the connecting beams, the forerunner of the catamarans now daily dashing through the surf at Waikiki. Some of these vessels could make twenty knots, a speed which flabbergasted European sailors on the eighteenth century voyages of exploration. Presumably the "long voyages" took place in these large double canoes.

In time the Polynesians developed extraordinary navigational skills. They steered by the sun and at night by the stars. They identified over 150 stars and knew which ones remained in the same latitude and how they changed position from month to month. In addition they calculated their course from the generally steady trade winds. They watched carefully the pattern of the waves, since turbulence might mean the presence of land ahead. They also scanned the skies for cloud masses which might indicate a far-off mountain, and they kept a sharp outlook for migrating birds.

To survive these grueling voyages they fished along the way. They took with them coconuts for food and liquid, and carefully caught water from occasional rainstorms. Aside from provisions they brought with them dogs, swine, and chickens. All three were regularly eaten in Hawaii. They also brought for cultivation in their new home such plants as breadfruit, bananas, yams, sugar cane, and a starchy tuber called taro. The presence in prehistoric Hawaii of the sweet potato indicates some contact with South America, but it is apparent—the author of *Kon-Tiki* to the contrary—that such contact was not extensive.

One may picture these sturdy double canoes, alone or in a fleet, moving swiftly across the warm water. One may hear the steady slapping noise of the waves against the hulls and the steady murmur of the wind through the rigging. The human beings aboard were gaunt and intent, searching the horizon for some sign. In many cases the suffering from thirst and hunger was intense. Then some hopeful portent appeared—a tiny bird or a fresh green twig, possibly a patch of rough sea or a cluster of clouds. Eager voices broke the silence. And if it was really land there followed a warm glow of anticipation and rapture, followed by prayers to the gods. This happy ending occurred often enough. But sometimes the land never appeared, and the craft sailed aimlessly on until all the living creatures aboard fell into faintness preceding death.

The leaders of the great migration established a tribe-clan system of government, common among primitive peoples, and in this case directly inherited from Central Polynesia. The class structure resembled a caste system. At the top were the chiefs (*alii*), a noble, privileged order, who ruled the common people, the *makaainana* (literally, those who live on the land). A group of experts (*kahunas*), including priests and navigators, formed a kind of professional class to help the chiefs. At the bottom of the social pyramid were the slaves (*kauwas*), an obscure and apparently not numerous group. Largely because of the simplicity of the economy there was no middle class.

The greatest of the chiefs acquired the status and power of a king (*alii aimoku,* literally, chief of the district or island) because of rank and ability. Ordinarily the king ruled with the help of two great officers, the chief priest (*kahuna nui*) and the counsellor (*kalaimoku*).

Because of the geography of Hawaii there was a tendency to form kingdoms on the four largest islands, Hawaii, Maui, Oahu, and Kauai. The smaller islands, such as Molokai and Lanai, were sometimes independent, sometimes the battle-grounds of inter-island warfare, and sometimes held by one of the larger kingdoms as tributary communities. The Islands did not become a unified kingdom until the time of Kame-hameha I (the Great), who ruled in the years 1795-1819.

In theory the will of the king was the supreme law of the land. In practice, customs (for example, those related to fish-ing rights and religious observances) limited his authority somewhat. But upon occasion the rulers could be arbitrary and oppressive. The various Hawaiian traditions distinguish be-tween a number of good and bad kings.

A distinctive and impressive feature of the administration was the taboo (in Hawaiian, *kapu;* literally, forbidden or sacred), highly developed in Polynesia and common among primitive peoples throughout the world. This system provided a religious sanction for the daily rules of life and for the structure of both society and government. In essence it pro-ceeded from the Polynesian view that some parts of nature are sacred (including the masculine principle and life), and that some are profane (including the female principle and death). Some *kapus* were permanent. There were several sacred days each month for religious rituals. A commoner was forbidden to stand in the presence of a chief. Women were forbidden to eat pork, bananas, and some kinds of fish. They had to cook their food separately and eat apart from their male masters. In addition to these permanent prohibitions, the chiefs and priests occasionally imposed special *kapus.* In view of the volatile and whimsical temperament of the Hawaiians, many abuses resulted. The penalty for violating a *kapu* could be severe. A death sentence was not unusual, even if the offender had unknowingly broken one of the sacred rules. An amusing survival of this often cruel system appears in the many *kapu* signs posted as "no trespassing" warnings throughout the Islands today.

The *kapu* system was part of the general Hawaiian religion of nature worship. Each important act, such as building a house or preparing for war, had its own special rites. Regular places of public worship (*heiaus*) existed, consisting of un-roofed stone platforms surrounded by stone walls. Many such sacred places still stand in the Islands. Upon occasion human sacrifice was practiced.

The gods and goddesses were mainly personifications of nature, much like the pantheon of Homer. The main gods were Kane (Light and Life), Lono (Harvest), and Ku (War). In addition there was Pele, the goddess of the volcano, and Akua Paani, the god of sports. In the winter months during the tax-collecting season when warfare ceased in favor of games, it was customary to make an image of Lono, which the natives carried with great ceremony around the island.

The full strength of the native religion was used to sustain the position of the kings. In theory much like the feudalism of medieval Europe, the king owned all the land, which he distributed among the various chiefs. But there was no security of tenure. What the king gave he could take back, and did so upon occasion. Much like medieval serfs the common people farmed their own and their chief's property, and turned over to the chief a part of the produce. In time of war the commoners were obliged to furnish military service to their chiefs.

The main food of the Hawaiians consisted of fish and *poi* (taro paste). In fishing the Hawaiians were particularly adept, as they were in everything pertaining to the sea. They made strong nets and spears, as well as lines and bone-hooks, and they built large stone fish ponds in the coves and on the reefs. Even today one may occasionally see Islanders throwing their nets expertly into the sea or spear-fishing at night by torchlight. From the sea they also ate seaweed, rich in minerals. Another delicacy was a shellfish called *opihi*. Even today at *luaus* (feasts) in outlying areas the guests enjoy side dishes of sea-weed and *opihi*, along with rock salt and dried squid.

Poi, now canned and a regularly prescribed food for infants, deserves a dissertation in itself. It is the product of wet-land taro, laboriously cultivated in complex irrigated fields. After being cooked in an underground oven (*imu*), it was pounded to a thick paste with stones on a *poi*-board. Early travelers to Hawaii made much of the intricate rhythms produced by Hawaiian women at this familiar task. After being thinned with water, *poi* was let to stand a few days to ferment slightly, for fresh *poi* has a flat taste. Infants and invalids now often eat their *poi* thinned with a little milk. Without question *poi* is, like caviar and spinach, an acquired taste. But to the Islanders it is as perfect an accompaniment to fish as pork to beans or cheese to apple pie. In old Hawaii it was traditional that a taro patch forty feet square could feed a man for a year.

The ancient Hawaiians also ate quantities of chicken, dog, and pork, but these items were luxuries for the common people. They supplemented their diet with breadfruit, yams, bananas, and arrowroot.

Although modern taste is somewhat squeamish about roast dog, both pork and chicken cooked Hawaiian-style are a gastronomic delight. At a *luau* the cleaned pig is cooked whole in the *imu*, with the heat supplied by hot volcanic rocks and the whole covered with the long green leaves of the *ti* plant, then sealed with earth so that the aromatic flavor of the *ti* leaves blends with the meat. It is customary to add to the *imu* a few *laulaus* (literally, wrappings), consisting of fish and pork wrapped in *ti*-leaf packages. Considering the gigantic physiques of the Hawaiians, as reported by the early European travelers, it is apparent that their diet was balanced and ample.

In general, it was the task of the men (in Hawaiian, *kanes*) to fish, farm, and fight. The women (in Hawaiian, *wahines*) kept house, tended the children, and made tight-woven mats of *lauhala* (pandanus leaves), which are still used in the Islands for place settings.

Their clothing, made by the women, consisted of *kapa* (tapa) cloth made from the bark of mulberry trees which they brought with them on the "long voyages." Much of this cloth was dyed with tasteful designs of yellow, red, blue, and brown. In view of Hawaii's warm climate, the natives were far from overdressed. The men generally wore the *malo* (loincloth) and the women the *pau*, a skirt extending from the waist to the knees. Their unabashed nudity later shocked the missionaries. They also wore a variety of stone, wood, bone, and shell ornaments, and many were elaborately tattooed.

For their great chiefs the Hawaiians produced the best featherwork in the world. The golden cloak of Kamehameha the Great was made of an estimated 5,000 choice and tiny feathers said to have taken nine generations to assemble. Other cloaks were yellow and scarlet in color. One of these, in the possession of the family of the Earl of Elgin since 1792, is almost five feet long and fifteen feet around at its base. Other insignia of the reigning chiefs were the girdle and helmet of red feathers, along with the *kahilis*, long standards topped with feather plumes, generally similar to the royal emblems of the ancient kings of Persia.

In the popular mind one of Hawaii's most distinctive features is the "grass shack," which early European visitors compared to hay stacks or straw bee hives. These quaint houses were generally well built and consisted of a framework of posts and poles, tied together and covered with coarse grass (*pili*) or other vegetation. But it is possible to romanticize these constructions. The traveler Jacques Arago, who was in the Islands in 1819, described the royal house as "a miserable hut, built of straw, from twenty-five to thirty feet long, and from twelve to fifteen feet broad, the entrance to which is by a low and narrow door . . . walls of cocoa-tree leaves, well sewed together; the roof made of seaweed, much neglected, and presenting but a feeble defense against the wind and rain." The journalist and art collector, James Jackson Jarves, who arrived in 1837, was even less flattering. He wrote, "Conceive a thousand or more thatched huts, looking like geometrical haystacks, most of them low and filthy in the extreme, scattered higgledy-piggledy over a plain, and along the banks of a scanty river, surrounded in general with dilapidated mud-walls, and inhabited by a mixed population of curs, pigs, Shanghae [*sic*] poultry, and unwashed natives." Nonetheless these airy and generally sturdy houses probably served fairly well the needs of the native population.

The Hawaiians were a fun-loving people, given to games and frolic. They swam often in the sea and used surfboards to ride the waves. They arranged boxing and wrestling matches and foot races, particularly in the time of the winter festival. They also enjoyed bowling and dart-throwing games, along with *konane*, a form of checkers. A particularly favored sport was tobogganing on slopes covered with dried grass, either on sleds (*holuas*) or bunches of *ti* leaves.

Throughout the years they developed an extensive unwritten literature consisting of songs (*meles*), chants, genealogies, and stories. Like other preliterate peoples they had prodigious memories, and a large part of this rich body of poetry and tradition has now been recorded. Many Hawaiian legends are touching in their simplicity and earthy charm.

The Hawaiian language, which is soft and melodious, lent itself well to this body of literature. A variant of the Polynesian tongue, it contains over 20,000 words, many of which express a precise shade of meaning. Much of its musical quality comes from the fact that every syllable and every word ends in a vowel. The Hawaiian alphabet, as standardized by the missionaries early in the nineteenth century, consists of 12 letters. Of these, five are vowels, *a, e, i, o,* and *u* and seven are consonants, *h, k, l, m, n, p, w.* The consonants are pronounced as in English, except that some scholars insist on pronouncing the *w* as a *v.* On this point there is some dispute, but there is general agreement on the vowels: *a* as in *car, e* as in *vein, i* as in *marine, o* as in *own,* and *u* as in *rule.* In addition there are vowel combinations much like diphthongs: *ai* as in *mile, ao* and *au* as in *how, ei* as in *vein,* and *oe* as in *boy.* Otherwise every letter is sounded, and any number of vowels can appear together, as in *Hooiaioia,* for example, which means certified. Generally each word is lightly accented on the next to last syllable, but some words have no accent. By changing the accent one may often change the meaning. *Po'ho,* for example, means patch, but *poho'* means sink.

In the early days of contact with Europeans, *k* was rendered as *t* and *l* as *r.* In early publications, therefore, it is not unusual to find the traditional Hawaiian greeting of *Aloha* given as *Aroha,* and the famous beach at Waikiki as *Waititi.*

Anyone who has heard Hawaiians sing knows that they are superb vocalists, clear and rhythmic, and above all they sing for the pure joy of making music. Much of their ancient literature was chanted to the accompaniment of gourd drums. Before the coming of the foreigners they naturally lacked knowledge of the harmonies in the music of Western civilization, and some of the early missionaries complained that their singing was far from melodious. Hawaiians had much difficulty at first in learning to sing hymns. What now passes for Hawaiian music is actually an amalgam of the ancient songs with Western European harmonies, and, of course, much of it has been written by modern popular composers. But underneath the surface there is still a trace of the drum beats and chanting of the ancient times.

Along with music went the *hula,* which is actually a combination of a song and a dance. The *hula* was by no means merely an erotic invitation. It was a religious and physical exercise as well as a form of entertainment. As such it was highly stylized and full of symbolism, a graceful and delicate work of art as well as a robust and charming amusement.

It is hard to make an over-all judgment of the condition and way of life of the ancient Hawaiians, just as it is hard to evaluate the standards of any primitive people. The early missionaries condemned many native practices such as polygamy, infanticide, and human sacrifices, and deplored their many unhygienic habits. Mark Twain probably reflected a missionary viewpoint when in the 1860's he wrote of prehistoric Hawaii in his *Roughing It*:

"The king and the chiefs ruled the common herd with a rod of iron; made them gather all the provisions the masters needed; build all the houses and temples; stand all the expense, of whatever kind; take kicks and cuffs for thanks; drag out lives well flavored with misery, and then suffer death for trifling offenses or yield up their lives on the sacrificial altars to purchase favors from their gods for their hard rulers."

The learned antiquarian David Malo agreed, "Only a small portion of the kings and chiefs ruled with kindness; the large majority simply lorded it over the people."

Undoubtedly these and other similar accounts contain some truth. That warfare and a measure of oppression existed is undeniable. At the same time the English missionary William Ellis, who visited Hawaii in 1822, wrote:

"The inhabitants of these islands are, considered physically, amongst the finest races in the Pacific, bearing the strongest resemblance to the New Zealanders in stature, and in their well-developed muscular limbs. . . . They are also more hardy and industrious than those living nearer the equator. This in all probability arises from their salubrious climate."

In any case, when the first foreigners came in 1778, the Hawaiian Islands supported a population estimated at 300,000. Despite some abuses, they appear to have been generally prosperous and content and to have enjoyed a standard of living comparable to that of the European peasantry of the time.

Chapter 3

The First Foreigners

AT ONE TIME it was believed that Spanish voyagers of the Pacific chanced upon Hawaii on their regular trips between Panama and the Philippines. But in recent years the experts, who have sifted the evidence with care, have rejected this belief. At any event, even if a stray Spanish vessel had encountered Hawaii, nothing came of it, just as nothing came of the Viking discovery of North America in 1000 A.D. The first European to bring Hawaii into contact with Western civilization was Captain James Cook, in 1778.

Cook was one of England's greatest maritime explorers. Born in 1728, the son of a Yorkshire farm laborer, this kindly but aloof, self-educated mariner volunteered in the Royal Navy and distinguished himself in North America during and after the Seven Years (French and Indian) War. In three great voyages to the Pacific he disproved the existence both of an Antarctic land mass and of a navigable northwest passage through the western hemisphere from Europe to Asia. On his third voyage, on January 18, 1778, as he was proceeding from Tahiti (discovered by Samuel Wallis in 1767) to the mainland of northwestern America, he discovered the Hawaiian Islands.

Early that morning his expedition sighted Oahu and then Kauai. On the nineteenth he anchored off Waimea, Kauai. Soon a number of native canoes headed for the ships. The natives were amazed at the appearance of these large "moving islands," and at once established trade relations with the newcomers. "We were agreeably surprised," Cook wrote, "to find that they spoke in the language of Otaheite [Tahiti] and of the other islands we had lately visited. . . . Some small nails or bits of iron, which they valued more than any other article, were given them. For these they exchanged more fish, and a sweet potato."

Cook was impressed with the appearance of the natives, who, he commented, "were of a brown color, and though of the common size were stoutly made." He marveled at their aquatic skill. "It was very common to see women, with infants at the breast, when the surf was so high that they could not land in the canoes, leap overboard, and without endangering their little ones, swim to the shore through a sea that looked dreadful."

Above all Cook was impressed with the wonder which the natives showed at his arrival. "I never before met with the natives of any place so much astonished as these people were upon entering a ship. Their eyes were continually flying from object to object; the wildness of their looks and gestures fully expressing their entire ignorance about everything they saw, and strongly marking to us that they had never been visited by Europeans."

Cook's two ships spent two weeks in the area, mainly occupied in taking aboard provisions. He left some goats and swine on nearby Niihau but apparently did not suspect the existence of the other islands to the southeast. He had generally friendly relations with the natives, but one of his lieutenants shot and killed a Hawaiian who tried to steal a boathook. Cook named the group the Sandwich Islands, in honor of the Earl of Sand-wich, at that time the First Lord of the Admiralty, and then departed for the American Northwest.

Cook's first contact with Hawaii had one immediately tragic consequence, a portent of the later decline of the Hawaiian people because of contact with white foreigners. It is established beyond doubt that Cook's sailors introduced venereal disease to Hawaii in February, 1778.

News of Cook's arrival spread quickly to the other islands. When he returned on November 26 and anchored off Maui, he received respectful delegations from chiefs who believed that he was the god Lono, much as the Mexicans had believed that Cortez was a god 250 years before.

In January, 1779, the two ships of Cook's squadron anchored in Kealakekua (Pathway of the Gods) Bay, on Hawaii's Kona coast. Cook went ashore, where the *kahunas* proclaimed him as the god Lono in religious ceremonies at the *heiau*. Gifts were exchanged, and among other things Cook received several feather cloaks from the king of the island.

Despite these friendly and hospitable gestures friction broke out between the natives and the members of the British explor-ing expedition. On February 13 a native stole a pair of black-smith's tongs and received a severe flogging. That night some natives stole a large boat from one of the British ships.

Cook went ashore on the fourteenth with the intention of kidnapping the king and holding him until the boat was returned—a stratagem which had been successful elsewhere in Polynesia. A threatening crowd gathered. In a scuffle which followed Cook was hit with a club and stabbed. He fell into the water and died either of drowning or of the wounds which he had received. His violent death was another omen that har-mony would not result from the contact of the Hawaiians with foreigners.

Other foreigners soon followed, but meanwhile the Islands underwent an unprecedented and striking political transforma-tion. Kamehameha I (literally, The Lonely One) conducted a series of fierce wars which unified the Islands and created the Hawaiian Kingdom. Whether he deserves his title, the Great, may be and has been disputed. Nonetheless this brave and intelligent man had many good qualities, and his reign (1795-1819) has much historic importance because it coincided with the first full impact of the outside world on the Hawaiian community. His statue in front of Iolani Palace in Honolulu remains a symbol of the strength and dignity of Old Hawaii.

Kamehameha was born on the island of Hawaii, probably

in 1758, for tradition, corroborated by other evidence, connects his birth with the appearance of a new star, believed to have been Halley's comet. He was of a noble family and apparently grew up with the sense of command and self-confidence characteristic of the ruling *alii*. Lieutenant James King of Cook's expedition wrote in 1779 that Kamehameha had "as savage a looking face as I ever saw." But King added that his disposition "was good natured and humorous, although his manner showed somewhat of an overbearing spirit."

As a young man Kamehameha became involved in the civil wars which convulsed the Islands. One incident in this warfare has become a Hawaiian classic. During a campaign Kamehameha dashed ashore to attack some native fishermen, one of whom hit him on the head with a paddle with such force that the paddle splintered. When the fisherman, a commoner, was later captured, Kamehameha forgave him and instead admitted that his own assault had been wrong. Years later Kamehameha recalled the incident when he issued a decree known as the Law of the Splintered Paddle: "Let the aged men and women and little children lie down in safety in the road."

Standard histories of Hawaii make much of his conquests, and certainly a considerable amount of drama attaches to some of them. In 1790 an eruption of Kilauea killed part of a force opposing him, so that many concluded that the volcano goddess Pele was fighting on his side. In the spring of 1791 he won a great naval victory, with cannon supplied by Europeans and used on both sides. The climax of the wars came in 1795, the traditional year of Kamehameha's ascension to the throne of united Hawaii. After conquering Maui and Molokai, he invaded Oahu, landing in force at Waikiki. Advancing inland up narrow Nuuanu Valley, he routed the forces of his opponent Kalanikupule. Many of the troops opposing him had never heard cannon before and fled headlong. Some escaped, but others fell to their deaths over the high and steep *pali*. Kalanikupule evaded his pursuers but was later captured and executed.

There remained the westerly island of Kauai. A large fleet, which set out to conquer Kauai, was dispersed in a storm in 1796, and for many years Kamehameha delayed sending another expedition, for he was preoccupied with restoring order and prosperity to his other dominions. In 1809 he assembled another large fleet, including forty European-type sailing ships, but this armada never sailed. In 1810 the king of Kauai acknowledged Kamehameha's sovereignty, and the unification of Hawaii was complete.

Rather more important—and certainly much more disastrous—than the unification of Hawaii by Kamehameha the Great was the coming of white foreigners. In 1785-86 five foreign ships appeared, the first a small British brig. Two were part of the exploring expedition of the French mariner La Pérouse, who later disappeared mysteriously at sea after leaving Botany Bay, Australia, in 1788. The delay in the arrival of foreigners after Cook's discovery of Hawaii in 1778 was probably occasioned, not by the unfavorable circumstances of his death, but by the involvement of England and France in the American War of Independence, which lasted until 1783. After 1786 foreign ships visited Hawaii every year. In 1787 the British *Imperial Eagle* came to Hawaii and took aboard Hawaii's first emigrant, a native girl who agreed to become the servant of the captain's wife, and Hawaii's first foreign resident appeared, John Mackay, an Irish surgeon who settled in the island of Hawaii. In that year an attractive and prominent chief, Kaiana, took passage on a British trading vessel to China, where he was feted until his return by way of the American Northwest in 1788. It soon became known that Hawaiians made good sailors, and a number of them went to sea on foreign ships either voluntarily or because of kidnapping.

Before the fall of 1789 all the ships known to have come to Hawaii were British, except for those of La Pérouse. In the fall of 1789 the first American ship, the *Columbia,* appeared, having traveled from New England by way of Cape Horn. The *Columbia* was also the first ship of the United States to circumnavigate the globe. For the next generation, England being preoccupied with the wars against France, American ships predominated in Hawaii.

Further explanation for this situation is not far to seek. Cook's last voyage had demonstrated that furs from the American Northwest were a valuable commodity in China, and after 1783 ports under British control were normally closed to American shipping. Ingenious Yankees added these two facts together and solved the riddle of the China trade. The United States, still mainly a struggling, rural nation, had little or nothing to sell directly in Chinese ports. But by taking items such as hardware to the Pacific Northwest it was possible to obtain at low cost the luxurious furs, among them sea otter, which fetched a high price in China. The *Columbia* pioneered this long and profitable sea venture. With furs the Americans were able to buy the tea and silk so much in demand in the United States. In this way a threefold profit materialized, from hardware to furs to Chinese commodities, much like some of the celebrated Atlantic triangle trades of the eighteenth century.

It was, of course, a glamorous adventure to cruise down the South Atlantic, beat westward across Cape Horn, then sail north again to the chill winds and tall firs of Oregon. With a load of precious fur the ships headed southwest to Hawaii for provisioning and a rest for the crews in the balmy climate. Then they sailed westward to Shanghai (a city of a thousand sights and delights) and, with a new, precious Oriental cargo, southward past Borneo to the Cape of Good Hope, and north toward home after a voyage of three years. Under the circumstances, Hawaii became an ideal stopping point for these numerous voyages, as well as an ideal place to spend the winter during the actual fur-gathering in the Pacific Northwest.

John Boit, Jr., a young American mate, recorded his regret in leaving Hawaii in 1792. "Bore off and made all sail for the coast of China, and soon lost sight of these beautiful Isles, the inhabitants of which appeared to me to be the happiest people in the world. Indeed there was something in them so frank and cheerful that you could not help feeling prepossessed in their favor."

In the years 1792-94 the British explorer George Vancouver, for whom western Canada's Vancouver Island is named, made three trips to Hawaii. He had been on Cook's voyage. On reaching Hawaii in 1792 he communicated with the natives through a Hawaiian sailor who had come from England, having reached that distant spot on one of the earlier English voyages from Hawaii. Vancouver's mission was to adjust land disputes with Spain at Nootka in western Canada, to explore the coast from California to Alaska, and to survey the Sandwich (Hawaiian) Islands, then known as Owhyee.

Vancouver tried and failed to arbitrate the inter-island warfare of Kamehameha I. In 1794 he accepted the cession of the island of Hawaii to Great Britain. It is clear that the Hawaiian negotiators, unschooled in the niceties of European diplomacy, merely intended a British protectorate, similar to an alliance, in order to have help against their enemies, while retaining full control of their internal affairs. In any case the British government did nothing about the cession, and the main importance of the affair was to establish a vague but persistent tradition of British pre-eminence in Hawaii.

Of greater actual importance was the landing in Hawaii of sheep and horned cattle, which Vancouver brought from California in 1793 and 1794. The natives had never seen cattle before, and Thomas Manby, one of Vancouver's mates, has left an amusing description of the natives wildly scattering into the trees and sea when one of these "large hogs" cavorted along the beach. Kamehameha I wisely put a *kapu* on the cattle for ten years to insure their safety and propagation. Vancouver also left goats, geese, grapevines, vegetable seeds, and both orange and almond trees.

These additions were typical of the enrichment of the Hawaiian economy in these early years. In 1778, Cook had left some livestock (which perished) on Niihau, along with seeds of melon, pumpkins, and onions. The British Captain Charles Barkley brought turkeys in 1787. In 1803, Richard Cleveland and William Shaler introduced the first horses. Other additions about this time and later included guava, mango, eucalyptus, and the algarroba tree, which now grow wild and dominate many areas, the mynah bird and mongoose (from the Orient), coffee, and less pleasant imports such as the flea, mosquito, centipede, toad, and scorpion.

Aside from provisions and sailors, sandalwood was Hawaii's most important export in this early period. This sweet-smelling wood was in great demand in the Orient as a source of incense and perfume. From small beginnings it became a profitable export for about twenty years after 1810, until Hawaii's supply was exhausted. At its peak it made much profit and achieved much fame. In these days China's name for Hawaii was the "Sandalwood Islands." The sandalwood trade had its unpleasant aspects. It was a royal monopoly, and Kamehameha I did not hesitate to exploit the commoners engaged in cutting the sandalwood forests.

In general, Kamehameha I maintained order and equitable trade relations, and it is a tribute to his intelligence and character that he was able to do so. The last native attack on a foreign ship occurred off Niihau in 1796, before that area came under the jurisdiction of the united Hawaiian kingdom. In foreign affairs he was firm in handling a potentially dangerous situation. The first Russian ships came to Hawaii in 1804, as a by-product of the Russian fur trade in Alaska and California. In 1816 a Russian agent began to build a fort in Honolulu, but Kamehameha I stopped the construction. The Hawaiians later finished the fort, which was a familiar landmark during the nineteenth century and which still gives its name to Fort Street in downtown Honolulu. In 1817, when Russians built fortifications and raised their flag on Kauai, Kamehameha I drove them out of the Hawaiian Islands.

The Islands soon acquired resident foreigners. As early as 1790 three foreigners had settled in Hawaii: John Mackay, mentioned above, S. I. Thomas, and Isaac Ridler, who deserted from the *Columbia* in 1789-90. In 1790 the American sailors Isaac Davis and John Young took residence in Hawaii as advisers to Kamehameha I. By 1794 the island of Hawaii alone had eleven foreigners, including Europeans, Americans, and Chinese. At the end of Kamehameha I's reign in 1819 the Islands had about 200 foreigners, permanent residents as well as drifters, half a dozen of whom had escaped from the British penal colony in Australia.

The presence of foreign residents and the sporadic visits of sailors created problems for the Hawaiians beyond their capacity to solve. The times were rough, and the seafaring men and adventurers drawn to the Islands, a natural stopping point on the way to Oceania and China, were reckless and unprincipled. It was a common saying that sailors hung their consciences on Cape Horn as they entered the Pacific, and much lurid evidence corroborates the truth of this remark. In describing the generally debauched atmosphere, John Coffin Jones, Jr., an American trader in Honolulu, commented in 1821: "Till now I never knew the rascality of mankind, everyone here is ready to cut his neighbor's throat, truth never is spoken, treachery is the order of the day, I am disgusted with my fellow man."

The natives, who had lived so long in isolation from the other peoples of the world, had no natural immunity to the white man's diseases. Not only venereal disease introduced by Cook's men but measles, whooping cough, and smallpox killed thousands of Hawaiians. Many rushed into the sea or found a breeze to cool their fevers, and in so doing only aggravated their afflictions. The Islands lacked the regular services of white doctors, and native doctors lacked the knowledge to take any effective measures. There was, for example, an epidemic in 1804—possibly of cholera or the bubonic plague—which took the lives of untold thousands.

Like other natives of Polynesia, Hawaiians were helpless when it came to liquor introduced by the foreigners, either brandy or rum directly imported, or native spirits distilled with an iron pot and gun barrel or other tube. Hawaiian liquor, now being produced commercially, was distilled from a mash of *ti* leaves, which have a high sugar content. It was called *okolehao* (politely translated as Iron Bottom). When properly made and aged it is not unlike bourbon. In any case, the Hawaiians developed great fondness for liquor, which led to public debauches which horrified the missionaries. It would be unrealistic, of course, to accept all missionary testimony at face value, for they came to the Islands with built-in Puritan moral standards in many ways inapplicable to the ways of a primitive people. On the other hand, when well-educated and honest missionaries reported that they had seen whole Hawaiian villages drunk, including women and children as well as men, it is wise to discount modern antimissionary prejudices and accept the bulk of their testimony as generally reliable. Worldly novelists such as Herman Melville and Robert Louis Stevenson have left appalling accounts of native drunkenness in Polynesia, which corroborate the reports of the missionaries in Hawaii.

Concurrently with alcoholism and the ravages of new diseases, the Hawaiians underwent a mass psychological deterioration. The ships, firearms, and other articles of the better-educated sailors and traders overawed the natives and, as was happening with other primitive peoples of the world, made them distrust their own way of life. In effect, they acquired a community inferiority complex, which some anthropologists call social staleness or cultural fatigue. The immediate result was to produce in the Hawaiians a sense of shock which numbed them and in many cases deprived them of their will to live. Their tragic situation may be compared to that of the Mexicans in the time of Cortez and the Peruvians in the time of Pizarro. In any event, the traders and sailors in Hawaii were, with few exceptions, mainly interested in profit or vice, and made little effort to check the progressive deterioration of the native population.

Many Hawaiians fell into a dreamlike trance, in part compensated by liquor and sensuality. In such circumstances the chiefs, preoccupied with new luxuries such as tobacco and silk, could not adapt themselves or their bewildered people to the superior civilization which Cook's voyage had introduced. As Judge William Lee remarked in 1851, "Living without exertion, and contented with enough to eat and drink, they give themselves no care for the future, and mope away life, without spirit, ambition, or hope." By way of illustration, many adopted grotesque combinations and fragments of European clothing instead of their native *kapa* garments, as if seeking some pathetic status symbols in a frame of mind that they barely comprehended. Somewhat later, others behaved like school-children and spent their days delightedly playing with marbles or flying kites.

A climax in the demoralization process came in November 1819, when the new, young ruler, Kamehameha II, abolished the *kapu* system, and ordered the destruction of the *heiaus* and ancient idols. Although some natives resisted the change, others had for some time secretly disregarded them, in imitation of the white foreigners. The abolition of the *kapus,* involved as they were with the old native nature-religion, struck a crushing blow at the entire Hawaiian system of values. In the confusion which followed the natives lived in a condition of more or less aimless drift.

Meanwhile, the Hawaiian population declined, as for similar reasons the native populations in places such as Fiji and the New Hebrides were declining. The native Hawaiians, estimated at 300,000 at the time of Cook's discovery in 1778, fell to about 135,000 in 1820, about 85,000 in 1850, and 40,000 in 1890.

Much rubbish has been written about the alleged destruction of the Hawaiian way of life by the missionaries. The fact of the matter is that long before the first missionaries reached Hawaii in 1820, the Hawaiian people were well on the way to destruction as a result of forty-two years of contact with the pre-missionary foreigners. It is a cruel irony that the people which the dedicated if sometimes misguided missionaries tried to save had already been ruined before their arrival.

Chapter 4

The Missionaries

THE CALVINIST MISSIONARIES who came to the Hawaiian Islands in 1820 were part of a vigorous Protestant movement centered mainly in England and the United States during the early years of the nineteenth century. The forces which motivated this movement were complex, but their interaction produced a sort of spiritual imperialism which is too often underrated among critics who deplore the expansion of Europe into the colonial areas. The revival of religion after the Napoleonic Wars; the romantic movement which arose in part from disillusion with the failure of the French Revolution and which expressed itself as a revolt against the science and formal classicism of the eighteenth century; the humanitarian movement, which may be described as a variety of secular Christianity or as Christianity's secular aspect—these and other currents crossed and countercrossed to send Protestant missionaries all over the world in the 1800's.

In broad perspective the missionary movement was a latter-day counterpart of fervent medieval Christianity—for Calvinism was much like the medieval religious revivals. There is a direct line of inheritance, then, extending from the missionaries of the nineteenth century to the monks and priests who converted Scandinavia toward the end of the Dark Ages, to the Cistercians who established their sheep ranches on the many remote wastelands (frontiers) of the thirteenth century, or to the members of several religious orders who accompanied farmers, traders, and miners to the unexploited lands of eastern Europe (for example, Bohemia), about the same time.

The missionary movement in America took its immediate origins in the strong Calvinist impulses and values which had motivated many of the original settlers of the seventeenth century, particularly those who went to New England. Indeed, in dedication and uncompromising singleness of purpose the American missionaries to Hawaii closely resembled the Pilgrims of the New World 200 years before, and in many cases the missionaries were direct descendants of these earlier Pilgrims.

The American evangelists often shared the wild religious enthusiasm of frontier revivalism, for in these lonely areas warmhearted religion provided both poetry and ethics to a population in transit across a wilderness as large as the old Roman Empire. At the same time this religion was transforming itself in conformance with other major tendencies of the time. In place of the dour Calvinism of the past, saturated with older concepts such as predestination and original sin, a new liberal Calvinism was rising which taught, in humble terms, the goodness of mankind along with man's free will to find his own salvation. In many places the new Calvinism came into sharp conflict with the old, and set off hot and prolonged controversies. But the new Calvinism harmonized well with, and at the same time reinforced, the growing American spirit of self-reliance, based on the frontier and other experiences, and expressed in the bright new image of the dignity of the individual. As such, liberal Calvinism assisted the evolution of American democracy, for the suffrage is a badge of man's dignity.

Liberal Calvinism also harmonized well with the growing American (and English) movements for social reform. For if man has inner worth he should certainly not be enslaved, and free men should certainly not be flogged on land and at sea or brutalized in jails and asylums. The brave and earnest work of Dorothea Dix in reforming the asylums and prisons of Massachusetts and elsewhere, and the abolitionist movement led by firebrands such as William Lloyd Garrison and the quieter but more effective Tappan brothers, all found nourishment and encouragement in the new Calvinism with its fervent humanitarian emphasis. It should be noted in passing that this outburst of social reform, accompanied as it was by the rise of democracy, was a new phenomenon in the English-speaking world.

In sum, American revivalists—such as the fiery and handsome Charles Grandison Finney, later president of Oberlin College—released a mighty humanitarian impulse. Finney's converts, who included more than one missionary to Hawaii, set out not only to evangelize the world but to reform its secular abuses. The American Protestant missionaries to Hawaii came, then, not only to save souls but to bring to the natives such amenities of Occidental civilization as roads, schools, and hospitals—in effect to transplant New England folkways as a whole to the Pacific.

In this respect the American missionaries resembled the English. A spokesman of the London Missionary Society, which sent a mission to the South Pacific in 1797, stated, "Nothing in my opinion can pave the way for the introduction of the gospel but civilization—and that can only be accomplished among the heathen by the arts."

The sponsor of the mission to Hawaii was the American Board of Commissioners for Foreign Missions, known by abbreviation as the ABCFM, a non-denominational but mainly Congregational and Presbyterian body of Boston, founded in 1810. The American Board sent missions to India (1813), Ceylon, and the Cherokee Indians of Tennessee (1816). It sent its first missionaries to Hawaii in 1820, and in later years sent missions to Palestine (1821), Turkey (1826), China (1830), and Oregon (1835).

The instructions of the Prudential (Executive) Committee of the American Board to the first company of missionaries to Hawaii reveal the idealism and breadth of purpose of the entire Protestant missionary movement, in prose which echoes strongly the rhythms and inflections of the King James Version of the Bible: "Your views are not to be limited to a low or a narrow scale; but you are to open your hearts wide, and set your mark high. You are to aim at nothing short of covering those islands with fruitful fields and pleasant dwellings, and schools and churches; of raising up the whole people to an elevated state of Christian civilization; of bringing, or preparing the means of bringing, thousands and millions of the present and succeeding generations to the mansions of eternal blessedness."

The original decision of the American Board to send missionaries to Hawaii stemmed from reports of sailors and merchants and from the presence in the United States of several Hawaiian youths. One of these, Henry Obookiah, achieved much celebrity because of his conversion to Christianity and his death from typhus fever in 1818 at the age of twenty-six when he was preparing to return to the Islands to convert his people. (In Hawaiian his name was *Opukahaia*, literally, "stomach cut open," given in 1792 to commemorate a Caesarian section of a chiefess in that year.) In 1809, Obookiah came with a ship's captain to New Haven, where Edwin Welles Dwight, then a student but later a devoted minister, found him weeping on the steps of Yale College. Their meeting led to Obookiah's education, along with other Hawaiian youths, at the ABCFM's Foreign Mission School in Cornwall, Connecticut. After Obookiah's death, Dwight published the young native's memoirs in the form of a biographical tract, which went through several editions and aroused much interest in Hawaii as a field for missionary work.

After services in the Park Street Church, the first of eleven regular missionary companies left Boston on October 23, 1819, in the brig *Thaddeus*. The first company consisted of two ordained ministers (the missionaries proper) and five men designated as assistant missionaries (two teachers, a physician, a farmer, and a printer). These seven men and their wives were accompanied by four natives from the mission school at Cornwall.

The American Board insisted that only married men should be sent to convert the heathen. As Rufus Anderson, the board's corresponding secretary in 1832-66, put it: "The experience of the Board favors the marriage of missionaries, as a general rule, and always when they are going to a barbarous people. Wives are a protection among savages, and men can not there long make a tolerable home without them. When well selected in respect to health, education, and piety, wives endure 'hardness' quite as well as their husbands, and sometimes with more faith and patience."

This injunction created a dilemma for many of the missionary candidates, who were as often as not young bachelors at the time of their appointment. Members of the board recommended suitable consorts, and the young men themselves showed considerable ingenuity in acquiring mates. In one case a young doctor called on a likely prospect, and finding that she was away proposed to her sister, who accepted. Many of the missionary wives in the various companies had been married less than five weeks when they boarded ship for the long and dangerous voyage to the Pacific.

The presence of wives had much to do with the ultimate success of the missionaries in Hawaii. For the most part they were earnest and industrious, as dedicated as their young husbands to the gigantic task which faced them. Further, their presence convinced the chiefs and people that the missionaries came with peaceful intentions and went a long way to create an atmosphere of sincerity and good will.

The moment of departure of the first and later companies of missionaries was agonizing. They were venturing into heathen parts little known and about six months removed from their Christian homeland. They contemplated the perils of the long voyage to the Pacific with much the same misgiving as the original Tahitians had probably viewed the canoe trip to Hawaii a thousand years earlier. Once arrived, a tiny minority among "savages," they faced at best hazards and at worst martyrdom. They left in the full expectation of never again seeing their friends, families, or native land.

In these circumstances they naturally dramatized their forthcoming adventure. The mother of a doctor in the third company wrote to his young bride in 1827, "My heart yearns over you with parental fondness. Shall I soon part with you and let you go to far distant Isles of the sea never to behold your face again? Yes, go and teach the poor benighted pagans the knowledge of that Savior whom we hope we love and may long live in His vineyard and be the means of winning many souls to Jesus Christ."

The ships which they took on the 16,000-mile voyage to Hawaii were crowded and small, seldom over 100 feet in length. Invariably the missionaries encountered rough weather in the North Atlantic and suffered the exhausting miseries of seasickness. In addition they often aroused hostility in the ships' crews, who mocked their hymn singing and made their lives unpleasant in a hundred minor ways. In order to terrify their pious passengers, the crews often exaggerated the dangers of storms and told tall, but not wholly improbable, tales of piracy as they entered the South Atlantic.

At Cape Horn, the famous storm-tossed island off the southern tip of South America, the little ships met their gravest real danger. Here they encountered icebergs, sleet, snow, roaring winds, and a strong contrary current. Beating around the Horn can be a terrifying experience, for the weather can change in a flash from dead calm to a gale with the skies leaden and threatening and the seas churning as high as the masthead. Meanwhile, on the decks and in the tiny unheated cabins, passengers and crew alike shivered with numbing cold.

Once around the Horn, the *Thaddeus* and later ships carrying missionaries made steady and quiet progress northwest toward Hawaii. But in these last weeks of the long voyage it was not unusual for tempers to flare high and for antagonisms between the evangelists and the crews to multiply. It was not until March 30, 1820, that the *Thaddeus* anchored off the coast of the island of Hawaii. Hiram Bingham, one of the two ordained ministers and the unofficial head of the first company, wrote with obvious relief, "The long looked for Hawaii appeared in the West. The lofty Mauna Kea lifted its snow crowned summit above the dark and heavy clouds."

The Hawaii which the missionaries and other travelers entered in the 1820's and 1830's was scarcely the verdant and glamorous place which it has since become. Little vegetation covered the towering hills. The lowlands of present Honolulu were parched plains, and the area in back of Waikiki consisted mainly of swampland. In 1832 an American naval officer, however, I was disappointed. Instead of the paradise which Francis Warriner, wrote, "At the first distant glimpse of Oahu, had been floating in my imagination, the island presented a barren and sunburnt appearance." The Reverend Titus Coan recalled his disillusionment on his first sight of Honolulu in 1835. "It was anything but an inviting place. The streets were narrow, irregular, and dirty, the houses mostly small and thatched with grass. . . . Hardly a tree or shrub was seen within the limits of the town." In 1840, George Colvocorosses of the U. S. Exploring Expedition commented sourly, "The plain on which the town stands is almost treeless, while the mountains to the eastward are a mass of naked rock." Henry M. Lyman gave his impression in a single terse complaint: "Dust, heat, and squalor made the Honolulu of that day one of the most uninviting spots that I have ever seen."

The early missionaries, of course, were profoundly shocked at the behavior of the natives, which by the standards of New England was, to say the least, indecorous. On his first day ashore Bingham characterized as "appalling" what he termed the "destitution, degradation, and barbarism, among the almost naked savages." Bingham added, "Some of our number with gushing tears turned away from the spectacle. Others with firmer nerve continued their gaze but were ready to exclaim

'Can these be human beings? . . . Can such beings be civilized? Can they be Christianized? Can we throw ourselves upon these rude shores, and take up our abode, for life, among such a people, for the purpose of training them for heaven?' " The Reverend Charles Stewart of the second company, which arrived in 1823, deplored "the dreadful abominations daily taking place around us, drunkenness and adultery, gambling and theft, deceit, treachery, and death." Others have left vivid accounts of prostitution, incest, and sodomy. Doubtless the missionaries, who expected to find much vice among the heathen, exaggerated their accounts somewhat, and they were perhaps somewhat unjust in judging Polynesians by Puritan standards. On the other hand much unbiased evidence confirms the general accuracy of their descriptions of a primitive race in process of disintegration. Elizabeth Swain Jarves, the wife of a journalist who went to Hawaii in 1837, stigmatized Honolulu as "a most disagreeable, filthy place, where you are subjected to sights, which would make any city lady blush fifty times a day." In desperation the missionaries forbade their children to learn the native language in order, so it was hoped, to keep them from contamination.

In particular the seminudity of the natives appalled the missionaries, much as it delighted mariners of passing ships. Laura Fish Judd, the most eloquent of the missionary wives, described the crowd which she saw on landing in Honolulu in 1828. "One had a shirt minus pantaloons, another had a pair of pantaloons minus a shirt; while a large number were destitute of either. One man looked very grand with an umbrella and shoes, the only foreign articles he could command. . . . They laughed and jabbered, ran on in advance, and turned back to peer into our faces. I laughed and cried too, and hid my face for very shame."

In later years the problem of nudity, once solved, became an amusing recollection. Mark Twain was probably not far from the truth when he wrote in a satiric vein in the 1860's:

"The missionaries provided them with long, loose, calico robes, and that ended the difficulty—for the women would troop through the town, stark naked, with their robes folded under their arms, march to the missionary houses and then proceed to dress! The natives soon manifested a strong proclivity for clothing, but it was shortly apparent that they only wanted it for grandeur. The missionaries imported a quantity of hats, bonnets, and other male and female wearing apparel, instituted a general distribution, and begged the people not to come to church naked, next Sunday, as usual. And they did not; but the national spirit of unselfishness led them to divide up with neighbors who were not at the distribution, and next Sabbath the poor preachers could hardly keep countenance before their vast congregations. In the midst of the reading of a hymn, a brown, stately dame would sweep up the aisle with a world of airs, with nothing in the world on but a stovepipe hat and a pair of cheap gloves."

The early missionaries encountered much physical discomfort. At first they lived in grass houses, which offered scant protection against the dust and rain. Even the first wood-frame houses, built with imported lumber, were scarcely an improvement. Mrs. Judd reported dolefully, "The clapboards are bare and admit quantities of dust. . . . I have emptied quarts of it from my bed cover at night, and it pours in so thickly that in a few minutes it is impossible to distinguish the color of the different articles of furniture."

Provisions were often in short supply. Flour in particular often arrived in deplorable condition after its long journey around Cape Horn. Oliver Emerson, a missionary son, remembered the arrival of a welcome barrel of flour. "On opening it at the head, father found that a thick, hard crust of bilged flour had been formed just within the staves. So he tipped the barrel over on its side and cut it in two with a saw, and in that way easily got at the inner portions of the flour which had not been reached by sea water." The heads of other missionary households used axes to break open the ruined crust.

Upon occasion illness prostrated members of the mission unused to the semitropical climate and exhausted from overwork. Homesickness added a further burden.

A miserable ordeal faced the missionaries on their trips to and from the headquarters in Honolulu, for the seas around the Islands can be extremely rough. Ordinarily these inter-island voyages were made in small schooners crowded with natives and livestock. Occasionally the native helmsmen went casually to sleep while the vessels rocked aimlessly in the waves. Meanwhile natives ate and vomited *poi*, while passengers and livestock wallowed in the muck. Often the women aboard became so weak that they had to be carried ashore. Mrs. Judd commented drily, "If I had ever dreamed of 'yachting by moonlight among the Isles of the Pacific,' one trip has dispelled the illusion forever."

The missionaries had to cope not only with the hardships of their physical surroundings and the unabashed paganism of the natives but also with white-hot hostility from transient sailors and many of the white foreign residents. The first American whaler came to Hawaii in 1819. The discovery of the whaling grounds off Japan in 1820 brought whalers to Hawaii in that year and thereafter as a convenient mid-Pacific place to refit and take on stores. By 1822, about sixty whaling ships touched at Hawaiian ports, mainly Honolulu and Lahaina on Maui, and by 1830 an average of nearly 150 whalers a year, mainly American ships, were coming annually to the Islands, where they commonly stayed two or three months each fall and spring. The presence in the Islands of large numbers of unruly and often vicious crews from these whaling ships caused much disorder and added to the already large difficulties of the missionaries. In addition, American and other vessels of war appeared in the Islands, usually in response to complaints from mariners concerning various grievances including unpaid debts.

From their arrival in the 1820's until well after the middle of the nineteenth century, the missionaries generally evoked rabid opposition from the commercial interests, including the sailors. This furious antagonism between the evangelists and the trading groups was by no means confined to Hawaii. Similar quarrels arose in other parts of the Pacific, and in other underdeveloped areas such as Africa, where the aspirations of the missionaries to uplift and protect the natives ran counter to the debauchery and economic exploitation generally desired by the commercial and seafaring men.

Upon occasion this hostility took the form of wild-eyed violence. In 1826 the crew of the U.S.S. *Dolphin*, the first American warship to visit the Islands, became enraged at the missionary-inspired order banning native women from coming aboard ships in the harbor. They stormed the house of Governor Kalanimoku (nicknamed Billy Pitt) and attacked the staunchly puritan leader, Hiram Bingham. Bingham's own account of the incident reveals not only the rage of the frustrated sailors but his own stubborn courage in the face of danger:

"Being apprised of the riot at the place of assemblage, and hearing the crash of the chief's windows, Mrs. Bingham sent to me and requested me to return home; but fearing my compliance would attract the enemy thither, I preferred to stay on the premises of the chief. Seeing soon a party of sailors directing their steps toward my house, and thinking my wife and child would instantly need my care, without a moment's further hesitation I made speed by another direction and reached my door . . . but to my disappointment I found myself, as well as the rioters, excluded. Mrs. Bingham not expecting me, and seeing the seamen approach, had turned the key against them, and I fell into their hands. . . . Suddenly one of the *Dolphin's* men struck a spiteful blow with a club at my head, which was warded off, partly by the arm of Lydia Namahana, and partly by my umbrella. It was the signal for resistance, for which the natives had waited. They sprang upon the rioters; some they seized, disarmed, and bound, and to some they dealt leveling blows."

The violence did not end with this riot. In 1826, as had also happened the year previous, a furious mob attacked the house of the Reverend William Richards at Lahaina on Maui. In 1827 the crew of the *John Palmer* bombarded the Lahaina mission house with cannon shot.

The American merchant, John Coffin Jones, Jr., of Honolulu, took a particularly vitriolic dislike to the missionaries and in 1826 wrote a diatribe on them which overflowed with hatred. "Trade never will again flourish at these Islands until these missionaries from the Andover mill [Andover Theological Seminary] are recalled. They are continually telling the King and Chiefs that the white people traders are cheating and imposing on them, consequently have depreciated the value of most articles. I believe it is a fact generally acknowledged by all here, that the natives are fifty per cent worse in every vice since the missionaries began their hypocritical labor here; these blood suckers of the community had much better be in their native country gaining their living by the sweat of their brow, than living like lords in this luxurious land, distracting the minds of these children of Nature with the idea that they are to be eternally damned unless they think and act as they do: and that Providence would put a whip in every honest hand to lash such rascals naked through the world."

Clearly, in 1820 the American missionaries faced, not an island paradise, but a rough semitropical frontier, much like other outlying areas in the American West. The natives whom they came to help were drifting rudderlessly in a condition of shock and disintegration. Meanwhile, other white foreigners in the area hotly resented their pious goals and fought them tooth and nail in their determined effort to Christianize Hawaii.

Chapter 5

The Hawaiian Kingdom, 1819-40

THE SINGLE most important fact about the internal history of Hawaii in the reigns of Kamehameha II (1819-24) and Kamehameha III (1825-54), to about 1840, was the gradual domination of the government in these years by the American missionaries. This domination, which coincided with the Christianizing of Hawaii, led to the creation of a state which was theocratic in many respects, and it certainly contributed to save the Hawaiian Kingdom from imperialist seizure by some foreign power.

In Christianizing the Islands, a process which led to control of the Hawaiian government, the missionaries concentrated their attention on the chiefs. Indeed, no other strategy was feasible, for the commoners continued in a generally apathetic condition of subservience to the Hawaiian nobility. Once the main chiefs had been converted, at least the outward and formal Christianization of the masses naturally followed, as had been the case with Christian missionary activity in Europe during the Dark Ages.

What is sometimes overlooked is the small number of American missionaries who brought about this striking religious and political transformation. In the 1820's, for example, fourteen white missionaries (including assistants and wives) arrived with the first company in 1820, followed by an equal number in the second company of 1823. But only sixteen of these twenty-eight white men and women were still in the Islands when the third company of sixteen missionaries arrived in 1828.

Nonetheless, despite their comparatively small numbers, the missionaries had many distinct advantages over most of the other white foreigners in Hawaii. Those who stayed, and most did stay, became permanent residents, in contrast to the great majority of transient mariners, and with permanence came continuity of association, affection, and trust.

In short order the missionaries became expert in the Hawaiian language. They learned to write, speak, and preach in it fluently, and they often served as interpreters. In the 1820's they standardized the Hawaiian alphabet, whereby *r* became *l*

(*Aloha* and *Honolulu* replacing *Aroha* and *Honoruru*) and *t* became *k* (*Waikiki* replacing *Waititi*). In 1822 they produced the first printed work in Hawaiian—an alphabet, speller, and reader—on the mission press. At the same time they began the long and exacting task of translating the Bible into Hawaiian, a cooperative venture. They finished the New Testament in 1832 and the Old Testament in 1839, by which time the entire Bible in Hawaiian was not only translated but printed. By 1842 the two mission presses, at Honolulu and Lahaina, had produced about 100 million pages in the Hawaiian language, not only the Bible but textbooks, tracts, and two newspapers.

Newcomers to the mission quickly learned the Hawaiian language, for without it they could have little effective contact with the native population. Some studied it aboard ship on the long journey to the Islands around Cape Horn, and found to their delight that they were able to converse a little with the natives when they first stepped ashore.

Another decisive factor in the increasing influence of the missionaries was their stature as human beings. Not only were they well educated but they were carefully screened by the American Board, which required letters of recommendation and a searching personal interview before granting an appointment. A typical letter from the board outlined the necessary qualifications of a missionary with characteristic idealism: "He must be a decidedly and actively pious man; so much so as to secure the affections and the confidence of the religious community . . . with his whole heart be devoted to the work of spreading the gospel among the heathen, and willing to spend and be spent in making Christ known among them. He must be a man of energy. . . . He must possess an amiable temper."

Not all the missionaries fully measured up to this counsel of perfection. Their long months at isolated mission posts throughout the Islands, their general intolerance with those who disagreed with them (itself a sign of their strong convictions), and their overwork in often rude surroundings led upon occasion to bickering and petty outbursts. But on the whole they were unselfish, brave, honest, decent, and kindly folk—men and women willing "to spend and be spent" in the service of an ideal. The Hawaiian chiefs often failed to meet the high standards of conduct which the missionaries urged; yet they came in time to trust their missionary friends with a warmth of affection often underrated or ignored by popular novelists and others bent on deriding the entire missionary adventure. When sailors from the *Dolphin* attacked Bingham in 1826, his devoted native followers flew to his defense and dispersed the mob.

The presence of missionary wives aided immeasurably in winning the confidence of the chiefs. They labored as hard as their husbands, and their very presence was a symbol of the good intentions of the mission. In particular they impressed the Hawaiian women with their skill in needlework, which somehow they found time for in addition to teaching, tending the sick, and raising their own large families.

Another element in winning friends among the Hawaiians was the work of the nine physicians among the various missionary companies, such as Dr. Holman in the first, Dr. Blatchely in the second, and Dr. Judd in the third. These men were well-trained according to the not high medical standards of the day; by modern standards they lacked much knowledge and skill. Nonetheless they performed operations (without anaesthesia in the early days), fought epidemics, and established measures of hygiene far in advance of the primitive medical lore of the native population. Many Hawaiians had reason to be profoundly grateful for their medical endeavors.

These forces favorable to the mission took time to become established, and the mission had small beginnings. The missionaries dedicated their first house of worship in August, 1821, on the present site of Kawaiahao Church, across the street from the early mission houses (begun some years later) and facing the present public library in downtown Honolulu. This first church was far from impressive. Many early churches were large grass huts, the walls often eaten away by goats and cattle. In many cases the missionaries simply preached in the outdoors, as indeed they are depicted in old prints.

A significant step forward occurred when Keopuolani, the queen mother, was baptized an hour before her death in September, 1823. But a much greater event occurred with the conversion of Kapiolani, a chiefess of rank. Kapiolani made a courageous and striking profession of her newly acquired Christian faith by descending into the volcano crater of Kilauea in December, 1824, and defying the wrath of the goddess Pele. On the way to the volcano she is reported to have said, "If I am destroyed, then you may all believe in Pele. That fire was kindled by my God. Repent of your sins!" She entered the crater with about 50 attendants. Partway down they paused for songs and prayer, then descended to the bottom, where they encountered the red-hot lava, and returned unharmed.

Kapiolani's conversion to Christianity and dramatic defiance of Pele had a pronounced effect on the native population and certainly enhanced the prestige of the mission. The English poet Tennyson wrote some sentimental verses to celebrate her daring act. Kapiolani died in 1841 after the removal, without anaesthetics, of her entire right breast because of cancer. In this ordeal she showed fortitude comparable to her bravery in the volcano.

Meanwhile tragedy came to the Hawaiian ruling family. In May, 1822, Kamehameha II (Liholiho) received from the king of England a small schooner, the *Prince Regent,* a gift promised many years before by George Vancouver. For a variety of reasons—out of curiosity, to obtain advice, and to seek protection against possible encroachments by Russia or the United States—the young king decided to make a trip to England. The royal party, which left Hawaii on a British whaling ship in November, 1823, included Kamehameha II, his favorite queen Kamamalu, Governor Boki, and several others. En route they stopped at Rio de Janeiro, where Pedro I, the autocratic emperor of the newly independent state of Brazil, received them with elaborate ceremonies. They reached England in May, 1824, and attracted much attention in the public press. At a reception they met such dignitaries as the Duke of Wellington, the hero of Waterloo, but the Hawaiian monarch fell sick of measles before their scheduled meeting with King George IV. In an atmosphere of hopelessness and gloom Queen Kamamalu died on July 8, and the young king died six days later. In September, George IV received Governor Boki and others in the ancient and huge castle at Windsor, overlooking the playing fields of Eton. George IV is reliably reported to have promised England's protection of the Hawaiian Kingdom in case any other state threatened its independence, and to have encouraged the Hawaiians to trust the advice of the American mission. Shortly thereafter the Hawaiian delegation sadly accompanied the royal coffins on the long voyage homeward on board a British frigate commanded by a cousin of Lord Byron, the poet. This tragic episode made a considerable impression in London. Over twenty-five years later a chambermaid in the Adelphi Hotel showed visitors the bed on which Kamehameha II had died and recalled by name some of the Hawaiians in the royal party.

When Kamehameha II left on his ill-fated journey to England, his younger brother Kauikeaouli, a boy of nine, was named heir to the Hawaiian throne. Kaahumanu, the favorite of Kamehameha I, continued as *kuhina nui* (premier) and also assumed the office of regent. This strong-minded and shrewd chiefess had paramount influence in Hawaii until her death in 1832, and did much to bring about the formal conversion of the Islands to Christianity. In close and friendly association with the Binghams, she learned to read and write and recognized quickly the importance of education as a civilizing force. This discovery led to her conversion to Christianity. In time she used her own great political powers to support the objectives of the American mission.

A month after Kamehameha II left for England, Kaahumanu ordered strict observance of the Sabbath. Six months later, in cooperation with a council of chiefs, she issued a code of laws against murder (particularly applicable to the old custom of infanticide), theft, fighting, (one account adds drunkenness here), and breaking the Sabbath. A fifth law decreed that after schools were established, all should learn reading and writing (*palapala*). Other laws followed against gambling and sexual immorality (especially on ships in the harbor). The natives docilely obeyed these new laws, which in their minds replaced the pagan *kapus* abolished in 1819.

The schools ordered by Kaahumanu and others grew rapidly. In 1824 they had some 2,000 pupils. Seven years later there were 1,100 schools and over 50,000 students—about 40 per cent of the total native population. At first mainly adults attended, but after about 1831, when the novelty of *palapala* dimmed, the adult enrollment fell off and a greater proportion of children began to learn their three *R's*. The school buildings themselves, like the early churches, were grass shacks, with adobe seats and boards nailed to poles serving as desks. In one instance the natives converted surfboards into desks. Much improvisation and disappointment resulted. As one of the missionaries reported in 1833, "The fine, large school house built at our station [Honolulu] was blown down last fall, and all the benches, doors, etc., were crushed in the ruins. It was a miserable house, notwithstanding all the praises bestowed on it . . . badly lighted, having no glass windows, the seats and desks of the rudest kind imaginable." One of the earliest tasks of the missionaries was to train native teachers, who alone could cope with the large influx of students. In 1831 a high school was established at Lahaina on Maui, on a plan later adopted by the Hampton Institute of Virginia. In 1839 a school was set up for the offspring of the chiefs, the so-called Chiefs' Children's (or Royal) School.

By this time the missionaries, along with some of the foreign residents, recognized the need for proper schooling for their own children. In the early days it had been customary to send them back to the United States, but this practice created heartbreak and suffering of an acute order. Mrs. Judd reported: "I shall never forget some of these heart-rending parting scenes. Little children, aged only six or seven years, were torn away from their parents, and sent the long voyages around Cape Horn, to seek homes among strangers. They have sometimes fared hard during those long voyages. . . . They have sometimes fallen into the hands of selfish, exacting guardians, and been unkindly dealt with or sadly neglected. . . . On one occasion I accompanied some friends to a ship just starting for America. As the vessel moved from the wharf, there was one affectionate little girl, not more than seven years old, standing on the deck and looking at her father on the shore, the distance between them widening every moment. She stretched out her little arms toward him and shrieked with all her strength, 'Oh, father, dear father, do take me back!' " The result was Punahou School, started in 1841 and opened in 1842, for the children of missionaries and other resident foreigners, the first American school west of the Rocky Mountains.

The course of religion wavered somewhat after Kaahumanu's death in 1832. Although Kamehameha III had unexpectedly consecrated his kingdom to Christianity three years before, the young king was a lukewarm convert. In 1832 he began a debauch which lasted several years, and his example dampened the religious enthusiasm of his bewildered subjects, caught as they were between two worlds, unable to accept their ancient way of life and at the same time unable to understand the complex values of New England Christianity. Many missionaries regretted their earlier optimism and sank into a mood of prolonged despair. The new *kuhina nui* (to 1839) Kinau, the king's half sister, threatened to resign her post, and for a time it appeared that the mission was a failure. But by 1835, Kinau had regained her power, and as Richard Charlton, the British consul, commented, "She is entirely governed by the American Missionaries who through her govern the Islands with unlimited sway." In the years 1837-40 the evangelists had striking success, for in the Great Revival of that period about 20,000 natives joined the church. How thoroughly Hawaii had become Christianized by 1840 is a matter of speculation, for it is impossible to state the extent to which the native converts really understood the faith which they henceforth professed.

In many cases their Christianity was superficial and temporary, but in many others a genuine new piety appeared. At any event, by 1840 Hawaii had officially become a Christian state.

Kamehameha III's debauch, his later alcoholic lapses, and the general native inability to handle strong drink, evoked strong protest and strong action on the part of the American mission. After sporadic attempts to achieve temperance, the government under missionary influence passed liquor laws in 1838 to limit the number of grogshops and to supervise the activities of the remaining ones. Local production and the importation of liquor were prohibited, and a duty was placed on imported wines. These liquor laws, often evaded as they were, raised a howl of protest from foreign traders and mariners.

At the same time the missionaries carried on temperance agitation of the same intense and sentimental variety that was current in the United States. They themselves eschewed not only wine, which they had used sparingly in the first days of the mission, but in many cases tea and coffee as well. In the spring of 1842 the king was persuaded to take a total abstinence pledge (which he did not keep), and a number of chiefs also embraced teetotalism.

In October, 1842, Mrs. Judd reported happily: "Temperance laws are now triumphant, and the nation is a temperance nation, from the king on the throne down to the little children. All are collected into a 'cold-water army.' We have had a grand festival. *Fourteen hundred* children marched in procession with music and banners, dined together, made speeches, and hurrahed in the most approved style. One needs to have lived among such a people, when there was no restraint upon the natural love for stimulants, and to have been a spectator of the excesses when a whole village was drunk. What pencil can portray the loathsome picture? The king adheres to his pledge nobly, and appears to be fully aware that his temporal salvation depends upon it."

Increasingly the missionaries, particularly those at Honolulu, found themselves involved with government problems, for the various rulers depended on them heavily for advice. In 1838 the Reverend William Richards made a hard decision. He resigned from the mission and entered the government as an adviser. He was instantly the subject of much adverse criticism. A Honolulu merchant, Alexander Simpson, later commented in a vein which has become traditional among antimissionary critics, "Thus did individuals, who came out for the avowed purpose of teaching the religion of the meek and lowly Jesus, use their influence which they had acquired for the furtherance of their own ambitious purposes."

Richards was in a difficult position. The American Board had stated clearly in its instructions to the missionaries in Hawaii, "You are to abstain from all interference with the local and political interests of the people. The Kingdom of Christ is not of this world, and it especially behooves a missionary to stand aloof from the private and transient interests of chiefs and rulers." The board was anxious to keep its representatives out of native politics, on principle, and because it feared that Catholic missionaries might counter by organizing imperialist seizures.

On the other hand, involvement with native political affairs was all but unavoidable under the circumstances. Bingham, and later Dr. Judd, assumed the power behind the throne mainly because the native government asked for and needed their help. Further, there has always been a sense in which Christianity demands direct action in the world. In the case of the American Protestant missionaries of the first half of the nineteenth century, the secular aspect of their labors was particularly emphasized. They saw their task as not only saving souls but also engaging in social reforms such as medical and educational improvements. Given this attitude and the circumstances of the day, when the native rulers could not cope with the problems of civilization unaided, it is at least understandable that Richards and others could leave the mission and enter the native government with clear consciences.

Even before Richards joined the government the unofficial missionary advisers found themselves involved in a messy and tangled problem of foreign affairs. In 1827 the first Catholic missionaries had come to Hawaii, and four years later with the connivance of the Protestant mission the government banished them. An unpleasant persecution of natives converted to Catholicism followed, until the more moderate members of the American mission persuaded the chiefs to desist. A Catholic missionary came to the Islands in 1836, where he remained in an uncertain status despite efforts to deport him. In 1837 two Catholic priests, banished in 1831, returned on the *Clementine*, and the government tried to deport them on this ship against the will of the owner. The British consul Charlton demanded damages, because the *Clementine* was of British registry. How deeply Dr. Judd of the mission was involved in the dispute appears from his letter to the board's local business agent asking the help of an American merchant, Peter Brinsmade, in the dispute. Dr. Judd wrote: "Probably the complaint against Charlton should be presented and the papers looked up. If there is no copy of the English of that in the hands of the chiefs, I believe I have one among my papers at Honolulu. Do give Br. Brinsmade a jog and use every effort to keep him awake *now*. He and those with him can and ought to do much."

The affair came to a climax in 1839 with the arrival of the French frigate *Artémise* commanded by Captain C. P. T. Laplace. At this time the French government had assumed a protectorate over all Catholic missionaries in the Pacific and wished also to further French commerce in that area. Laplace had a double complaint, then: the discrimination against Catholic missionaries in Hawaii and the Hawaiian government's ban on the import of French brandy. Laplace threatened war unless the Hawaiian government tolerated Catholicism and paid $20,000 as a surety of good conduct. The Hawaiian government had no choice but to agree. Under the terms of the treaty then negotiated the king agreed that accused Frenchmen should be tried by a jury of foreigners selected by the French consul and that French commodities, especially wine and brandy, should pay no more than 5 per cent duty.

In 1839, the Hawaiian government at the advice of Richards and others in the mission granted a code of laws. A liberal constitution followed in 1840. The king, *kuhina nui*, and the island governors comprised the executive. The king and *kuhina nui* formed with the chiefs the council, or upper house. In addition there was a coequal representative assembly elected by the common people, who for the first time received a measure of political power. The constitution of 1840 also established a supreme court. The missionaries, it is clear, had provided Hawaii not only with Christianity and social benefits but also with a system of government which resembled those of the more advanced states of Occidental civilization.

At the same time the missionaries obeyed the injunction of the American Board to cover the Islands with "fruitful fields and pleasant dwellings and schools and churches," that is, in transplanting New England folkways to Hawaii. Many travelers to the Islands noticed with astonishment the Yankee atmosphere there. In 1835, Francis Warriner, an American naval officer, commented on tea at the Binghams, "The party was so much like one in America, that had I been placed there by accident, or could I have forgotten the circumstances of my visit, I should have fancied myself in New England." Some 30 years later Charles Nordhoff remarked, "The white frame houses with green blinds, the picket-fences whitewashed until they shine, the stone walls, the small barns, the scanty pastures, the little white frame churches scattered about, the narrow 'front yards,' the frequent schoolhouses, usually with but little shade: all are New England, genuine and unadulterated; and you have only to eliminate the palms, the bananas, and other tropical vegetation, to have before you a fine bit of Vermont or the stonier parts of Massachusetts."

Much the same may be said today, for many of the earlier buildings still stand and many of the newer ones follow the New England model. In driving around Oahu, for example, and following a road which has many turns, it is exciting to round a bend and come upon a white frame church which might have been built in Salem, Massachusetts, or Sharon, Connecticut, standing somewhat forlornly in a glade overrun with heavy, tropical vegetation. Around another bend is a stone sugar mill, now falling in ruins. The same weird phenomenon appears in driving along the south shore of Molokai, eastward of Kaunakakai and Kamalo. Except for the trade winds it is unusually quiet. Few people live on Molokai's East End, for the main economic activity centers in the pineapple fields of the western plateau. Along the shore are a few fishponds dating from the days of Kamehameha I and before. The hills leading to the mountains are covered with brambly *kiawe* forests. Yet here and there on the inland (*mauka*) side of the road are perfectly proportioned New England churches, sedate and with clean lines, where small congregations still faithfully listen to the word of Jehovah on the Sabbath. It is strange to see these buildings, empty shells some of them, like the structures of a ghost town, symbols still of a mighty drive and aspiration which for the present has somewhat receded.

New England is still present in the Islands in another, more vital way. At a *kamaaina* party one may experience again what happened to Warriner and Nordhoff so many years ago. The men, many of them educated in New England at prep school and college, wear white shirts and dark suits, as if they were dining in Boston. They wear this same formal, somber clothing at their offices in downtown Honolulu, while the tourists don garish aloha shirts hanging sloppily outside their belts (the *kamaainas*, when they wear aloha shirts in moments of relaxation, almost always tuck them in) and shuffle excitedly along the thoroughfares bordering Waikiki. Not only the conservative clothes reveal the New England origin of many *kamaainas*.

Their faces are clean-chiseled with an unmistakable Yankee look. Again, like the stars of a Hawaiian evening, this phenomenon has to be seen to be appreciated.

It is difficult to make a reasonable judgment about the missionaries. The whole subject is overlaid with prejudice, pro and con, and much ignorance about them also prevails. Although Hawaii is the only place in the world where being a missionary descendant confers the highest social distinction, many of the young descendants in the fourth, fifth, and sixth generations have lost touch with the missionary tradition, and their elders, who as children absorbed much of it directly, are fast disappearing. The times, of course, have changed. The Calvinist ethic of the missionaries seems unduly narrow in a broadening world. Theology has gone out of fashion. The disillusionment which followed World War I turned many people in the "lost generation" against idealism of any sort, so that it became good form to deride everything Victorian, including the missionary movement. This derogatory attitude has persisted. For many people the standard image of the missionary in the Pacific comes from Somerset Maugham's *Rain*. To praise the missionaries is to incur the scorn of professional liberals, but to dismiss them with derision is to do violence to historical truth.

They had an impossible task, for the ancient Hawaiian way of life had been largely destroyed before they reached the Islands. They found a primitive people demoralized and drifting, unable to adjust to the higher civilization that Cook's discovery had forced upon them. But with sincerity and good will, if not always with understanding, the missionaries did the best they could with a problem that, under the circumstances, had no real solution. In the end they built better than they knew, and salvaged a great deal more than might reasonably have been expected. Without the missionaries, and other foreigners sympathetic to their aspirations, Hawaii today might well share the fate of pathetic, strife-torn Cuba.

Two novelists of the nineteenth century, one American and one British, and neither with a built-in pro-missionary bias, sustain this conclusion. In the 1860's Mark Twain stated about the Hawaiian people:

"The missionaries have clothed them, educated them, broken up the tyrannous authority of their chiefs, and given them freedom and the right to enjoy whatever their hands and brains produce with equal laws for all, and punishment for all alike who transgress them. The contrast is so strong—the benefit conferred upon this people by the missionaries is so prominent, so palpable and so unquestionable, that the frankest compliment I can pay them, and the best, is simply to point to the condition of the Sandwich Islands of Captain Cook's time, and their condition today. Their work speaks for itself."

Robert Louis Stevenson stated plainly in 1900:

"Those who have a taste for hearing missions, Protestant or Catholic, decried, must seek their pleasure elsewhere than in my pages. Whether Catholic or Protestant, with all their gross blots, with all their deficiency of candor, of humor, and of common sense, the missionaries are the best and the most useful whites in the Pacific."

Chapter 6

Under the British Flag

IN 1840 THE REVEREND HIRAM BINGHAM left the Islands. After the departure of "King" Bingham, without question the most forceful member of the mission and for many years the uncrowned ruler of Hawaii, the responsibility for the unofficial direction of the government fell increasingly on Dr. Gerrit P. Judd, a physician from Paris Hill (near Utica), New York, who had arrived in 1828 with the third company. In May, 1842, just before Richards and Haalilio left for Europe to negotiate treaties with Britain, France, and the United States to recognize Hawaii's independence, Dr. Judd searched his conscience and joined the Hawaiian government. At first he asked for a temporary discharge from the mission but within a few months he submitted his resignation, in order to devote himself fully to politics. His entrance into the government, although motivated by a sincere desire to aid the Hawaiian people, evoked much bitter protest from his missionary colleagues and from others in the Islands. Before long he became known as King Judd. From the start his duties were broadly stated, and for the next eleven years he was in fact the dictator of the Hawaiian Kingdom.

From the outset of his administration he faced extraordinary problems, mainly those of foreign affairs. At that time the expansion of Europe and America was sending vital social forces into Oceania, and Hawaii acted as a focal point for the rivalry of various powers. Into this semitropical frontier the whale-ships continued to make regular demoralizing voyages. Business establishments of various nationals operated in the Islands in an atmosphere of short-tempered bickering. The American, British, and French traders quarreled hotly. The American Protestant missionaries opposed the French Catholics, and missionaries generally opposed the trading interests. The bewildered Hawaiian chiefs and the listless Hawaiian people had few resources with which either to understand or to control these antagonisms, and protests on the part of various national groups upon occasion led to the appearance of a hostile man-of-war.

Dr. Judd and others had long feared that some foreign power would seize the Hawaiian Kingdom. Their fears redoubled early in August, 1842, when news reached Honolulu that France had taken the Marquesas Islands. Later that month a French warship, commanded by Captain S. Mallet, arrived at Honolulu. Acting under orders, Mallet accused the Hawaiian authorities of having violated the Laplace treaty of 1839. He made a number of overbearing demands, of which one would have given to French Catholic priests in Hawaii the power to appoint several officials in the Hawaiian administration.

Dr. Judd shared a widespread opinion that France intended to seize the Hawaiian Islands. In this, his first diplomatic problem while in full control of the Hawaiian government, he suffered, so he reported, much "anxiety and mental labor." After reflection, he wrote Kamehameha III's reply to Mallet, which promised to respect the Laplace treaty and which explained that a new treaty with France was then in process of negotiation. This soft answer apparently placated Mallet, who left the Islands in September.

But in the swift turn of events a new and much more serious crisis arose shortly thereafter. Late in September the British consul, Richard Charlton, left Hawaii for London with the intention of undermining the projected treaty talks of William Richards. Just before his departure he appointed Alexander Simpson as acting consul during his absence. Simpson was a somewhat irresponsible man with a hasty temper. In company with many others in the commercial colony he despised Dr. Judd. Simpson reported in a diplomatic dispatch, "The king is quite a cipher, and the Governor [Kekuanaoa] of this Island, a man of violent passions, is influenced by Judd, an American of bad character and strong anti-English prejudices." Dr. Judd in turn had reason to abominate Simpson, who was outspoken in his opposition to the Hawaiian government. The two men quarreled furiously, and at one point Simpson challenged Dr. Judd to a duel, but Dr. Judd curtly refused: "I will not fight." In any event, Dr. Judd advised the chiefs not to recognize Simpson's appointment. This petty dispute, typical of the wrangling then common in Honolulu, had profoundly serious consequences. When a Hawaiian court seized Charlton's property during a lawsuit, Simpson complained through diplomatic channels and requested a British naval force to protect the property of British nationals in Hawaii.

On February 10, 1843, in response to Simpson's request, the British frigate *Carysfort* arrived in the port of Honolulu. Its commander was Captain Lord George Paulet, a younger son of the Marquess of Winchester, who later rose to the rank of admiral and was for two years an aide of Queen Victoria. Supporters of the Hawaiian government described him as hotheaded. He doubtless had the maddening condescension of upper-class Victorian officers, and certainly from his point of view he had reason to complain of the obstacles placed in his way by the Hawaiian authorities. A less biased contemporary described him as "a pleasant-looking young man, with a fresh complexion, blue eyes, and short chestnut hair curling all over his head." There is little point in making Paulet the villain of the piece. He was an alert naval officer, not well-informed about the complex politics of the Hawaiian Kingdom, simply trying to do his duty in a difficult situation which he dimly understood. He was under orders from Rear Admiral Richard Thomas, commander of the British Pacific Squadron, to protect British interests in Hawaii and especially to restore Charlton's seized property.

Under the circumstances, he was inclined to trust Simpson implicitly, for Simpson boarded the *Carysfort* immediately after her arrival and gave his own heated version of the case. Simpson advised Paulet not to exchange the usual formal courtesies until the Hawaiian government recognized his appointment as acting consul. Paulet concurred, and refused to receive Dr. Judd officially when Dr. Judd came to call.

A tersely worded correspondence followed. In response to Paulet's demand for an interview, Kamehameha III signed a reply drafted for him, which stated, in part, "We will appoint Dr. Judd, our confidential agent to confer with you, who being a person of integrity and fidelity to our government, and perfectly acquainted with all our affairs, will receive your communications."

Paulet refused to negotiate with Dr. Judd, whom, at Simpson's prompting, he characterized as "the prime mover in the unlawful proceedings of your government against British subjects." Instead Paulet made several demands, including the restoration of Charlton's property, public recognition of Simpson as acting consul, and the settlement of a number of British complaints. Paulet demanded acceptance of these demands by 4 P.M. the next day, or, as he stated ominously, "I shall be obliged to take coercive steps." Paulet then moved the *Carysfort* broadside to Honolulu's fort, ready to fire.

In view of this threat, Dr. Judd and others advised the king to submit, and on the eighteenth of February the king signed a prepared statement that he would comply with Paulet's demands under protest. The letter added that the Hawaiian Kingdom had already sent a diplomatic mission to London to negotiate a general agreement. But this maneuver, which had succeeded with the French Captain Mallet six months before, now failed. Paulet, egged on by Simpson, made additional demands, that the Hawaiian government reverse some decisions made by its courts and pay an indemnity of over $100,000.

At this time the king sank into a mood of utter despair. According to a contemporary report, "the king declared himself a dead man, and expressed his conviction that his ruin was determined. . . . The object was to rob him of his money, and destroy his laws. Money he had not and could not raise it. He could not overturn the decisions of the courts, without destroying the credit of the government, and exposing it to attack on all sides. He would sooner give up all."

Dr. Judd, after some further negotiations, told the king, "They want your islands, and are determined to have them by cession or by conquest. If they take possession by force, you will have no redress; they will keep your islands forever, but if you cede to Lord George Paulet *for the time being*, and refer to Great Britain as umpire, the justice of your cause can be made so clear that you are sure to receive back your sovereignty in due time."

The king hesitated, for a time considered a cession jointly to France and the United States, then finally agreed. Paulet also agreed, for he believed that France intended to seize Hawaii, as just the year before France had seized the Marquesas and Tahiti. A provisional cession of the islands to Great Britain would, so he thought, frustrate this design. Some members of the American mission shared his view of the matter.

The king and chiefs signed the cession papers in an atmosphere of tearful gloom. As Dr. Judd reported, "Deed of cession being ready, the chiefs came in, and it was read. Sorrow and distress marked every countenance. Went to prayer. During prayer, sighs suppressed were often heard. After prayer, not an individual left his knees for a full minute, and I then saw that tears had come to their relief. They sat in silence. The king seized a pen and signed the deed of cession. 'Let it go,' said he."

The formal cession ceremony took place in an equally sorrowful atmosphere. "On Saturday afternoon at three o'clock, on February 25, 1843," Mrs. Judd wrote, "the Hawaiian flag we loved so well, was lowered in the Fort, and an English one run up in its place and saluted by the batteries of the Fort and the guns of the *Carysfort*. English soldiers marched into the Fort and the band played 'God Save the Queen,' and 'Isle of Beauty, fare thee well.' The latter was played by the request of some lady friends of Lord George, and regarded by us as a refined cruelty, which could only emanate from a woman." For the next five months Hawaii was under the British flag.

The provisional British administration functioned through a four-man commission consisting of a British subject, Major Duncan Forbes Mackay, (who resigned early in March), Lieutenant John James Bartholomew Frere of the *Carysfort*, Paulet, and the Hawaiian king or his representative. Kamehameha III asked Dr. Judd to represent him, and Dr. Judd accepted after some hesitation. Paulet's acceptance of Dr. Judd as a commissioner seems odd, but the British naval commander doubtless believed that the commission could not operate effectively unless it included Dr. Judd, or someone else as proficient in the Hawaiian language and as much trusted by the native chiefs.

Certainly the chiefs trusted Dr. Judd. Probably no other foreigner, except possibly Bingham, was so completely trusted by chiefs and commoners alike. In March, 1843, Governor Kekuanaoa of Oahu wrote a report in Hawaiian to Haalilio, then in Europe with Richards, in which he referred to the services of *Kauka* (literally, Doctor) Judd. The report stated, "I and Kauka and our rulers have prayed constantly to God to help us. . . . Kauka has been very strong, at the present time, doing the work of the government, and has been greatly abused."

Kekuanaoa's last statement has ample corroboration. The English residents in Hawaii blamed him for all their grievances, and after the provisional cession many Americans turned against him. At this time his resignation from the mission was still pending, and some of the missionaries loudly protested against his entrance into politics. In typical outbursts Stephen Reynolds, an American merchant, complained that "King Judd rides us down to the dust. . . . The king is nothing—nobody. Judd orders him as you would a boy. . . . Doctor Judd *is* the Cromwell of the world—I mean the Sandwich Island world."

A climax in this stream of vituperation came from the American novelist, Herman Melville, who left Honolulu in August, 1843, after about six months in the Islands. For part of his sojourn in Honolulu Melville worked as a clerk for Isaac Montgomery, a British trader, and this fact may explain in part his hostility to Dr. Judd. In the appendix to *Typee* Melville stated, "High in the favor of the imbecile king at this time was one Dr. Judd, a sanctimonious apothecary-adventurer, who, with other kindred and influential spirits, were animated by an inveterate dislike to England. The ascendancy of a junta of ignorant and designing Methodist [*sic*] elders in the councils of a half-civilized king, ruling with absolute sway over a nation just poised between barbarism and civilization, and exposed by the peculiarities of its relations with foreign states to unusual difficulties, was not precisely calculated to impart a healthy tone to the policy of the government." In later years this passage so infuriated one of Dr. Judd's grandsons that he tore it from his copy of *Typee*.

After the cession both parties to the dispute drew up appeals to the British government. It was agreed that Alexander Simpson should present the British case, and that he should leave Honolulu on a native ship which the commission had appropriated and renamed *Albert* after the young consort of Queen Victoria. At the same time Paulet tried to prevent the Hawaiian government from communicating with London.

Dr. Judd and others decided that it was essential to present the Hawaiian side of the case to the British and American authorities, and hit upon a daring scheme to smuggle dispatches and a Hawaiian envoy out of the Islands. The plan proceeded with secrecy and melodrama. Dr. Judd selected as the envoy James Fowle Baldwin Marshall, an American merchant in his twenty-fifth year, and presented the proposition to him at a secret meeting in a cabin on board the U.S.S. *Boston* while a ball was in progress. Marshall accepted immediately.

Dr. Judd then took elaborate security measures. At night he entered the old royal tomb, a small coral building in front of the royal palace. This tomb, which was near his house, had no windows and a solid door, so that a light inside could not be seen from without. There, using the coffin of Kaahumanu,

Dr. Judd prepared Marshall's papers, with pertinent wording copied from the credentials of John Adams, America's first ambassador to England. A trusted clerk assisted, but as an extra measure of security the envoy's name was for the time being omitted.

A courier in a canoe then went to Lahaina, Maui, to fetch the king. Without delay the king, along with other officials, made a secret trip by night to Oahu, where by torchlight in a coconut grove near Waikiki they endorsed the proceedings and signed the necessary papers. Paulet and Simpson knew nothing of what had happened.

On March 11, 1843, Marshall sailed on the *Albert*, apparently as the agent of Ladd and Co., a firm to which the vessel had been under charter, but actually as the envoy extraordinary and minister plenipotentiary of the Hawaiian Kingdom. With him also sailed Alexander Simpson, the British agent, wholly unaware of the status of his fellow passenger.

On March 13, Dr. Judd sent to William Richards a long account of Marshall's diplomatic mission by the U.S.S. *Boston,* which sailed that day. Dr. Judd wrote, with characteristic conscientiousness, "Should Marshall be lost, or his despatches, you will be somewhat *hema hema* [embarrassed or awkward], and I must try to supply the deficiency, should it occur, by this conveyance. I have sent by the "Boston" the rough draft of my letter to him." About this time, leaders of the Honolulu branch of the Hudson's Bay Company, opened in 1834, sent to the British government a detailed account which generally condemned both Paulet and Simpson.

Dr. Judd left Honolulu early in April to attend the meeting of the Hawaiian legislature at Lahaina on Maui. There he was active in the House of Nobles, where, despite Melville's derision, he offered the native legislators much solace and hope. On his return to Honolulu on May 4 he faced a difficult situation, for during his stay on Maui the other two members of the commission, Paulet and Frere, had broken the terms stated in Paulet's proclamation of the cession. This proclamation had promised that the king, chiefs, and their officials would govern "as regards the native population" and that the commission would limit itself to "all that concerns relations with other powers . . . [except Britain] and the arrangements among foreigners . . . resident on these islands." Paulet had interpreted this stipulation somewhat loosely. The commission had levied an extra import duty of 1 per cent to cover its clerical expenses, and had liberalized the liquor laws. It vetoed a Hawaiian law recently passed concerning auctioneers, which apparently favored the Americans, and decided some disputes which really were within the jurisdiction of the native courts. In addition, it recruited troops and police to be paid by the Hawaiian treasury. Finally, on April 27, it relaxed the laws against fornication by removing, in effect, the missionary-inspired taboo which had prevented native women from going aboard ships. Much open immorality resulted, which infuriated the missionaries. It is clear that Paulet had violated the terms of the proclamation by interfering in the affairs of the kingdom "as regards the native population."

Dr. Judd, who could be furious and formidable upon occasion, had a stormy interview with Paulet on May 8 and protested with particular vigor against the commission's relaxation of the fornication law. He wrote afterwards in his journal, "Many overbearing and insulting expressions were also used, accusing me of being in favor of American interests and opposed to the English. . . . Lord George said this had been an American government but now it was English. I had ruled the nation but could do so no longer." Two days later Dr. Judd wrote a formal protest, which the missionaries refused to print on their press. They had no wish to become involved in this political dispute, and at that time Dr. Judd's resignation from the mission, still pending, was still a sore point. In any case, after another stormy interview with Paulet, Dr. Judd resigned from the commission on May 11. In his letter to Richards, Dr. Judd complained, "The minds of the commissioners have been completely poisoned with prejudice towards the native government, and towards me in particular." He added characteristically, "In presenting my resignation I endeavored to impress upon the commissioners that I acted from principle and not from feeling."

His resignation embarrassed Paulet. Unless there were a representative of the Hawaiian government on the commission, the British government might be charged with responsibility for damages claimed during the cession, and in point of practicality the commission could not rule the Islands effectively without formal liaison with the king. Paulet requested the king to appoint another representative, but the king refused in a letter undoubtedly drafted for him by Dr. Judd. "In case you will consent to restore the laws which you have set aside and firmly maintain the words of the treaty, then Dr. Judd can take his place with you again, but otherwise I am sure I can neither transact business with you or appoint another deputy." Paulet refused to accept the terms of this reply. Late in May he went to Maui to confer with the king, who refused to appoint a new representative to the commission. Clearly the dispute had fallen into stalemate.

During June the wrangling continued. Dr. Judd refused to pay the troops, which the commission had raised, with funds from the Hawaiian treasury, but finally did so on June 20 under formal protest. The commission, that is, Paulet, threatened to remove him from his office in the Hawaiian government. As Dr. Judd noted, "This order brought by Lt. Frere in person in full uniform and with his side arms. I complied and paid the money. Have since learned that it is the intention to turn me out and take possession of the treasury." Shortly thereafter, at Dr. Judd's prompting, the king declared that he was no longer in any way responsible for the commission's acts. In further defiance of Paulet, Dr. Judd took the government records to the royal tomb, where he had drafted Marshall's diplomatic papers. There, in secret, he transacted the business of state.

On July 7, 1843, the arrival of Commodore Lawrence Kearney on the U.S.S. *Constitution* caused a flurry of excitement in Honolulu. Four days later Kearney protested against the cession, and on the fourteenth his ship saluted the Hawaiian flag. Paulet countered by writing the king a furious and threatening letter. At this moment the situation had obviously deteriorated and was fast reaching the breaking point.

The whole affair approached its climax on July 26 with the arrival in Honolulu from Valparaiso of Rear Admiral Richard Thomas, Paulet's commanding officer. Thomas knew from a policy statement from the British foreign office, which he had received after sending Paulet to the Islands, that Britain had no wish to interfere with the internal affairs of the kingdom of Hawaii. Accordingly, Thomas left for Hawaii just as soon as he heard of the seizure, determined to restore Hawaii to independence. His determination, later approved by the British foreign office, squared exactly with the existing policy of the British government, which declared that the seizure had been "entirely unauthorized."

After negotiations with the king and officials, during which he insisted on obtaining firm guarantees of the rights of British subjects in Hawaii, Admiral Thomas restored Hawaii's independence on July 31 by repudiating the provisional cession to Paulet. The restoration took place on a site in Honolulu still called Thomas Square. During the ceremonies the king made a moving speech in which he is said to have used the following words, possibly written or inspired by Dr. Judd: *"Ua mau ke ea o ka aina i ka pono"* (the life of the land is preserved by righteousness). These words have since become the motto of Hawaii.

"The marines," Mrs. Judd wrote, "from the *Dublin, Carysfort,* and other English ships, under their respective officers, were ordered to be on the parade ground on the plain, in full uniform, at eight o'clock, a.m., under Lieutenant Frere. A pavilion was erected for the ladies. Foreign residents of all classes, missionaries, and thousands of natives assembled at an early hour. Admiral Thomas preceded the king in the carriage of the latter. When the king, on horseback, arrived upon the ground, the admiral gave him a salute of twenty-one guns from the field artillery of the squadron. Lord George was not present. At a signal given, the English flag-officer advanced toward the king, surrounded by his guards, bowed his colors most gracefully, while the splendid Hawaiian standard was unfurled, and, as the breeze caught its ample folds, displaying the dove and olive branch in the center, the guns from the *Carysfort* fired first, then the *Dublin,* and the other English ships, followed by two American ships-of-war. Each poured forth a salute of twenty-one guns, which was responded to by the fort and battery of old Punch Bowl. . . . As the cannons ceased, thousands of human voices mingled in one patriotic cheer." A massive and somewhat debauched celebration followed.

This dramatic and romantic episode had a happy sequel. On November 28, 1843, in a joint declaration, England and France recognized Hawaii's independence. The United States abstained, but President Tyler in a previous message (December 30, 1842) to Congress had already recognized Hawaii as an independent state, and in so doing had extended the Monroe Doctrine from the Western hemisphere to the central Pacific.

The entire Paulet seizure is hard to interpret. One of its strange aspects is the reluctance of England, France, or the United States to acquire the Hawaiian Kingdom. Each of these three powers had not yet entered the active and overt age of imperialism which swept over Occidental civilization in the generation after 1870. For the time being each was content for Hawaii and for many other colonial areas to remain free. None of the three powers wanted Hawaii, but at the same time each wanted to prevent the others from acquiring it. There the matter rested.

How close Hawaii came to losing its independence during

the five months of the Paulet seizure is anybody's guess. Admiral Thomas correctly interpreted British policy at the time when he ordered the restoration of Hawaiian independence. On the other hand, had he found the Islands in disorder instead of under the firm control of Dr. Judd, he might well have hesitated, and such hesitation might well have led to a reversal of current British policy. It is at least possible that if Dr. Judd had not been a capable statesman, Hawaii would still be under the British flag instead of being America's fiftieth state.

Chapter 7

The Hawaiian Kingdom, 1842-54

DURING DR. JUDD's administration, which extended from May, 1842, to his dismissal from office in September 1853, the Hawaiian Kingdom faced two major problems. One was to create a stable government, based on suitable institutions and practices and staffed by competent administrators. The other was to maintain Hawaii's status as an independent state despite threats of imperialist seizure, such as the Paulet crisis of 1843. During these years Dr. Judd held various offices: interpreter and recorder and member of the Treasury Board (1842-43), minister of foreign affairs (1843-45), minister of the interior (1845-46), and minister of finance (1846-53). In actual fact he was prime minister of the Hawaiian Kingdom, for the chiefs and the other white men in the government generally acted under his supervision.

The politics of the Hawaiian Kingdom in these formative years were rough and wild, filled with the sound and fury of hot quarrels. Many of the personalities involved were frontier types of the sort now encountered on the television screen when, in the standard Westerns, law and order come to Rotten Gulch. Some were rolling stones of the sort set in motion by the expansion of Europe and by America's westward scramble. They entered Hawaiian politics for a year or so, made policy, left their imprint in various ways, and then departed. Others stayed and with the passing years achieved such prominence that streets were named after them. In any case, they brought vitality to the kingdom, and the various conflicts which resulted were, to say the least, colorful. The records of their activities, well preserved in the Hawaiian archives and in other collections, including those of western Canada, California, Washington, New England, and London, make extraordinarily exciting reading and have a verve and a flavor too often ignored in scientific histories. The hand of custom lay lightly on the Islands, and the opportunities for good or evil were apparently limitless, as were the opportunities for antagonisms and disputes.

One of Dr. Judd's first objectives in coping with this generally unruly situation was to set in order the chaotic finances of the native government. When he took office in May, 1842, the government had no money at all on hand and no official chest for its safekeeping. There was no system of audit, and nobody knew the extent of the national debt, later calculated at $60,000. "The government," so he reported, "kept no accounts, debts were often contracted by irresponsible persons without any provision for their payment, and in many cases where payments had been made, no sufficient vouchers or proof could be found." At once he established regular procedures for payments, set up proper books, arranged for an import duty to provide regular revenue, and acquired an office in Honolulu for the transacting of fiscal business.

By 1846, with Yankee resourcefulness and frugality, he had balanced the kingdom's budget and liquidated the national debt. The next year he reported a surplus. The natives called him *Kauka Okole Kala* (the doctor who sits on the money). When he left office in 1853 his opponents, many of whom had been severely critical of his financial policies, reported that they were "agreeably surprised" to find the treasury accounts in good order. Financial activity of this sort often makes dull reading, but in Hawaii's case it had critical importance. Native governments of the nineteenth century with unsound finances were particularly vulnerable to filibustering expeditions and other forms of imperialist seizures. Dr. Judd's financial labors, which helped to protect Hawaii from such threats, constitute one of his most valuable contributions to the kingdom.

A second major task was to obtain a small number of competent men for the highest government offices. Dr. Judd believed that even the best-trained native Hawaiians, or a *hapa haole* (part white) chief like John Young, son of the adviser to Kamehameha I, were not fully competent to carry on the complex activities of a modern sovereign state. Kamehameha III had insight and considerable capacity, but particularly in the last years of his reign he was often either drunk or apathetic. Dr. Judd grappled with a problem familiar to much-abused colonial administrators. He had not the slightest wish to put the Islands under permanent white control, and he reacted violently against the callous displacement of red Indians then taking place on the American continent. What he proposed, therefore, was to find for the time being a few white men for key offices, operating openly instead of behind the throne as in the two previous decades. In the meantime he hoped that by education and political experience the Hawaiians would gradually learn to govern themselves.

His attitude appears clearly in a speech made by John Young in 1845, undoubtedly inspired by Dr. Judd's political principles. The occasion for the speech arose from the opposition to Dr. Judd led by the native antiquarian, David Malo. Young said in part, "Dr. Judd . . . took the oath of allegiance, and stood in the gap to save us. . . . Did you ever hear of a people destroyed by allegiance? America was overrun, as you have been told, and the red-skins were destroyed. But the white men owed them no allegiance. Do you think that I or Paki can do the work of a white minister? No. The young chiefs will, we hope, be qualified, but now we must have these white men."

Accordingly, Dr. Judd set out to recruit a staff of white foreigners to help him rule Hawaii. Late in February, 1844, he learned of the arrival in Honolulu of John Ricord, a thirty-two-year-old lawyer from western New York. This tall and attractive Yankee epitomized the restless global adventuring so characteristic of the nineteenth century. Before coming to Hawaii he had lived in Louisiana, Texas, Arizona, Florida, and Oregon. When he left Hawaii in 1847 he moved on to Tahiti, Siam, and Liberia, and finally died in Paris in 1861. Dr. Judd sent for Ricord and hired him on the spot, because the government had desperate need for a lawyer and because Dr. Judd wanted to prevent Ricord from offering his legal services to interests opposed to the Hawaiian government. Ricord received formal appointment as attorney-general on March 9.

A year later Dr. Judd arranged for the appointment, as minister of foreign affairs, of a Scottish surgeon, Robert Crichton Wyllie, one of the three or four most important figures in the history of the Hawaiian Kingdom. After service at sea Wyllie made a fortune in South America and went to Hawaii from Mexico with the intention of returning to Scotland by way of China. Instead he stayed in Hawaii, where he served as minister of foreign affairs until his death in 1865. A sensitive and frail bachelor with reddish hair and a slight burr, Wyllie was a conscientious if occasionally garrulous man, who certainly merits a biography, if a biographer can be found to trace his global wanderings and to read his almost illegible handwriting. He is a much neglected figure, whose over-all contribution to Hawaii rivals that of Dr. Judd. Wyllie is remembered today mainly for the street in Honolulu named after him. As a bachelor, he left no descendants in the Islands to perpetuate his memory, whereas Dr. Judd's descendants still living in Hawaii constitute a large and formidable clan.

Along with Wyllie and Ricord, Dr. Judd found a third recruit in William Little Lee, a brilliant and strong-minded lawyer from New York State, who had gone to Honolulu on his way to Oregon toward the end of 1846. Dr. Judd and Ricord persuaded him to enter the government as a judge. Lee retained his judicial post until his death in 1857.

The cabinet in 1846 consisted of Dr. Judd, Ricord, Wyllie, Lee, William Richards (the minister of public instruction), and John Young (the minister of the interior and titular *kuhina nui,* or premier). Because of his long service in Hawaii, his fluency in the Hawaiian language, and his own strong personality, Dr. Judd functioned as prime minister. The journalist James Jackson Jarves had edited the government newspaper, the *Polynesian,* since 1844, and a former missionary, the Reverend Lorrin Andrews, assisted Lee on the bench. By 1851, 48 foreigners were in the service of the Hawaiian government. For the time being, the cabinet worked together in a congenial spirit, but for various related reasons it soon split up in a fury of backbiting and recrimination.

When Ricord took office in March, 1844, Dr. Judd took a step to insure the allegiance of white foreigners, which John Young later mentioned in his speech. Dr. Judd first, and then Ricord, renounced their United States citizenship and became citizens of the kingdom of Hawaii. Other foreigners entering the government service were required by law to become Hawaiian citizens, although British subjects—among them Wyllie, who believed that they could not renounce their British citizenship—took the oath with a reservation.

In order to strengthen further the position of the government, Dr. Judd asked the American missionaries in Hawaii also to become Hawaiian citizens. His request occasioned much opposition and some abuse, but in the end a large number of the missionaries complied.

Dr. Judd's naturalization policy had a further dimension. At his instigation the government passed a law forbidding aliens to acquire fee-simple land. This law, so he hoped, would induce foreigners to become Hawaiian citizens and enlist their support of the government. His wife stated the case clearly. "The principal disputes and difficulties in which the nation had been involved for years have arisen from the complaints of foreigners holding lands . . . and yet claiming the protection and interference of their home government, exercised here through its representative. Now it was thought that if fealty to the rightful sovereignty of the realm was required, in order to hold landed property, it would be necessary to bring all disputes arising therefrom before the Hawaiian courts, to be settled by the only legitimate authorities." Many foreign residents raised a tumult of dissent, but by 1848 some 500 white foreigners had become Hawaiian citizens.

At the same time Dr. Judd wished to sustain the decorum and prestige of the royal Hawaiian government. He tried hard, and ultimately failed, to keep the king sober, and his insistence on temperance became a standing joke in the community. In 1846 a Danish naval officer reported delightedly how the Hawaiian queen spat out a mouthful of tea at a teetotal party given by the Judds. This officer later entertained the king and chiefs on board his ship and wrote, "I was pleased to see that several of the good people had a very good taste of the champagne whenever Mr. Judd turned his back."

Meanwhile, Dr. Judd refurnished the royal palace and introduced the formal diplomatic etiquette of the Congress of Vienna of 1814-15. From time to time the king wore the Windsor uniform recommended to Hawaiian royalty by George IV of England, and Dr. Judd wore a blue coat with gilt insignia along with a white vest and white trousers. At times Dr. Judd's costume also included the hat of a field marshal. Such pomp lent itself easily to satire. An American naval officer commented derisively, "The king, premier [John Young], and Judd had broad red ribbons thrown baldric fashion over breast and shoulders, of such extreme breadth as to give the idea of the wearers having burst their jugular arteries."

Dr. Judd also undertook a reorganization of the government institutions in the three Organic Acts of 1845-47, largely the work of Ricord and Lee. The first act split the executive into five departments: finance, foreign relations, interior, law, and public instruction. Ministers of these departments formed the cabinet, which with the four governors and members named by the king formed the privy council.

The second Organic Act gave further details to regulate the executive and established the Land Commission, which remained in session until 1855 and made over 9,000 title awards. As preliminary steps a special committee consisting of Dr. Judd and three chiefs made the division (*mahele*) of land among the king, chiefs, and common people. This *Great Mahele*, as it was called, removed the feudal tenures and gave to the commoners their properties (*kuleanas*) in fee simple. The work of the Land Commission still forms the basis for all land titles in Hawaii.

The third Organic Act reorganized the judiciary. Begun by Ricord, it was finished by Judge Lee.

Lee also had a major role in drawing up the liberal constitution of 1852. This document formalized the earlier constitution of 1840 and embodied the various political reforms of the three Organic Acts.

All of these constitutional and other changes proceeded against a background of furious personality clashes. The American diplomatic representative, Commissioner George Brown, arrived in Honolulu in October, 1843, and soon embroiled himself in hot-tempered disputes with Dr. Judd and Ricord. He made violent complaints to his government of Dr. Judd's "imbecility" and brought a formal charge of impeachment against Dr. Judd, which ended in acquittal. By the summer of 1845, Brown had made himself so offensive that the king ordered the government not to receive him officially. Brown left Hawaii a year later on a ship which disappeared at sea.

Tense relations also developed with the new British consul-general, William Miller, who arrived in Honolulu early in 1844. The central issue was the settlement of Charlton's land claim, decided in Charlton's favor after protracted bickering. In defending the Hawaiian government Dr. Judd relied heavily on the advice of Ricord, who apparently enjoyed quarreling for the excitement of a good fight. Much friction and recrimination ensued. Miller reported acidly to his government, "Dr. Judd still keeps His Majesty under great restraint, not allowing him to speak scarcely to anybody." This comment led the British foreign secretary, Lord Palmerston, to inquire, "Who is the despotic Dr. Judd?"

In some measure Dr. Judd invited hostility, for upon occasion he could be overbearing to the point of rudeness. In some measure also the turbulence in Hawaii came from the staunch individualism of his opponents and from the generally unsettled climate of the times. Americans in Hawaii tried to overturn the American-controlled government. Wyllie quarreled with his fellow British subject, William Miller, and Miller had a dispute with the Hudson's Bay Company. Americans and Britons alike distrusted the French Catholic missionaries and feared a French imperialist seizure. The recurrent feuds distressed many persons in the Hawaiian government and puzzled diplomatic observers abroad.

In short order quarrels broke out in the Hawaiian government. Ricord left the government service in May, 1847, after an altercation with Dr. Judd. Somewhat ridiculously he professed himself in love with Dr. Judd's eldest daughter, aged only fifteen, and proposed marriage to her. He left Hawaii in August for his further wanderings. About three weeks later Jarves resigned from his post as editor of the *Polynesian,* and blamed his departure on the incivility and general misconduct of Dr. Judd.

In November, 1847, Wyllie broke with Dr. Judd. Wyllie accused him of not rewarding Ricord adequately, of not translating Hawaiian conversations satisfactorily, and of incorrectly drawing up the annual finance report. Wyllie was actually challenging Dr. Judd's headship in the Hawaiian cabinet. Their ensuing feud, which ended in Dr. Judd's dismissal from the government six years later, derived mainly from personal antagonism and ambition. Neither man could understand or respect the other.

In the summer of 1848 Dr. Judd's brother-in-law, Asher B. Bates, went to Honolulu and took office as government attorney. His coming struck a new balance among the effective members of the cabinet. Bates naturally sided with Dr. Judd against Wyllie, who found increasingly an ally in Judge Lee.

A new element of tension entered the already troubled political situation when, in October, 1848, George M. Robertson, a clerk in the ministry of the interior, filed impeachment charges against Dr. Judd, accusing him of embezzlement, lawbreaking, and usurping the duties of the minister of the interior.

Before the trial opened Dr. Judd took direct, and possibly unfortunate, action. He bribed a clerk in the customs office to find out who was attacking him and the government in the opposition newspaper, the *Sandwich Islands News.* The culprit turned out to be Anthony Ten Eyck, the United States commissioner (diplomatic agent) in Hawaii, who had replaced George Brown. This disclosure created a furor and led to Ten Eyck's recall. The impeachment board acquitted Dr. Judd, with Wyllie taking an ominously neutral position. Wyllie later insisted that at one point in the proceedings the king turned against Dr. Judd and urged his conviction. What actually happened may never be known. Probably Wyllie was telling the truth, for at this time the king was drinking heavily and had cause to resent the strait-laced and domineering policies of Dr. Judd.

Real trouble came to the Hawaiian Kingdom in the summer of 1849, precipitated by the French consul, Guillaume Patrice Dillon, a French-born Irishman who thrived upon intrigue. Dillon made several demands, among them equality of privileges for Catholics and Protestants, reduction of the import duty on French brandy, and the use of the French language for all official dealings with Frenchmen in Hawaii. When the Hawaiian government refused, Dillon requested French naval support, as Simpson had requested an English naval force in 1842.

In August, 1849, Rear Admiral Legoarant de Tromelin, commander of the French naval forces in the Pacific, came to Honolulu with two frigates. Negotiations with De Tromelin were futile, even though the Hawaiian government insisted correctly that the disputed questions were already under discussion with the French government. After an ultimatum had expired, De Tromelin sent troops ashore to bully the island kingdom in a way which natives everywhere in the underdeveloped areas of the world came to associate with the worst features of imperialism.

Mrs. Judd reported sadly, "All the guns were thrown from the walls of the fort or spiked. The magazine was opened and the powder poured into the sea. All the old muskets, swords, and bayonets that could be found were broken to pieces, and every article on the premises destroyed, not sparing the old clock on the walls of the governor's house. Two large camphorwood trunks, containing kahili feathers and various articles belonging to Kinau were carried on board the French ships. . . . The ground is covered with broken muskets, cartridge boxes, bayonets, and swords. Every window and door of the governor's house is broken and battered, and the walls are covered with charcoal sketches. Every box, barrel, and calabash is crushed to atoms." Early in September, after further futile talks, the French sailed away with Dillon and with the royal Hawaiian yacht.

At this point Dr. Judd decided to go on a diplomatic mission to the United States, England, and France to obtain from these powers firm assurances of Hawaii's status as an independent nation. He decided to take with him the two princes, then in their teens, Alexander (later Kamehameha IV) and Lot (later Kamehameha V). Apparently he believed that the presence of these two well-schooled Hawaiian youths would impress the American and European diplomats with the civilized progress of the Islands and that at the same time the trip would be a broadening experience for the heirs to the Hawaiian throne. As it happened, his strict control over the boys on the long journey was a factor in their antimissionary attitude in later years.

Dr. Judd took with him secret instructions authorizing him to transfer or sell the sovereignty of Hawaii if need be. These secret instructions equate with the blank sheets of paper, signed by the Hawaiian king, which Richards had taken with him in his diplomatic journey seven years before. In any case, the secret instructions conferred upon Dr. Judd a great responsibility and indicated beyond doubt the full trust placed in him by the Hawaiian government. He left with the princes on September 11 in an atmosphere of tearful anguish.

Back in Honolulu, Wyllie indulged in a spiteful but understandable act of revenge. Although minister of foreign affairs, he had not been consulted about Dr. Judd's diplomatic mission, and he believed that he had more talent as a diplomatist than Dr. Judd. He ignored for the moment that, irrespective of his formal title, Dr. Judd was in fact the head of the Hawaiian government. At any event, in full knowledge that the usefulness of the secret instructions largely depended on their secrecy, Wyllie gave a full account of them to William Miller, the British consul-general, who naturally sent a report about them to London. The net result was that in later negotiations Palmerston knew about, and could therefore discount, the secret instructions that Dr. Judd reserved for an emergency.

In San Francisco, Dr. Judd negotiated with Charles Eames, Ten Eyck's successor as commissioner to Hawaii, a treaty with the United States which formed part of the basis for the final treaty concluded by Jarves several months later. He was glad to leave California, then in the throes of the Gold Rush, and to proceed to New York by way of Panama. After a twelve-day crossing the party reached Liverpool on Christmas eve.

After a month's delay he talked with Palmerston, who promised to use the good offices of the British government to settle the dispute with the French authorities. Dr. Judd and the two princes then traveled to Paris, where he encountered politeness but indifference about effecting a swift settlement. He had several pointless conversations with officials of the French foreign office, and met Louis Napoleon (later Napoleon III), who was impressed with the good manners of the young princes. Throughout Dr. Judd refused to compromise, and the negotiations ended in stalemate. Finally on April 8 he left France for England with a bitter comment, "Have made the acquaintance of many distinguished people, received much courtesy and many compliments, but *justice* in a *grass hut* would suit me better than all this magnificence without it."

During the next month Dr. Judd and the princes stayed in England. Here he met Paulet and Frere, and reminisced about the 1843 seizure. They also had a rather chilly interview with Prince Albert. Dr. Judd obtained from Palmerston a second promise of Britain's good offices in the dispute, and then left with the princes for the United States.

In Washington he had a long interview with the secretary of state, John Middleton Clayton, who stated plainly, "The United States do not want the Islands but will not permit any other nation to have them." Clayton also promised the good offices of the United States in settling the dispute with France. Dr. Judd and the princes had a short audience with President Zachary Taylor, who, as a slave-owning Southerner, undoubtedly regarded the dark-skinned youths with some misgiving.

As they were leaving Washington a conductor mistook Prince Alexander for a Negro and ordered him out of the railway car. This incivil instance of color prejudice, often retold and exaggerated in the retelling, contributed to Alexander's anti-American attitude when he came to the throne four years later.

The party returned to Honolulu on September 9, 1850, after an absence of two days less than a year. The diplomatic mission had not been a success. Dr. Judd had contributed to negotiating a treaty with the United States and had obtained promises of help from both the United States and Great Britain in arranging Hawaii's differences with France. But he had been unable to reach any agreement with France. Whether in the circumstances anyone else could have done better is a question which has no answer. In any case, he decided from his recent experience that Great Britain was an unreliable friend and that the real solution lay in the annexation of Hawaii by the United States.

Shortly after his return Dr. Judd was appalled to find himself under direct attack by Wyllie, who condemned the entire diplomatic mission as a failure. The two men quarreled furiously. Dr. Judd, sensitive and puritanical in his values, was stung to the quick. Henceforth the breach between them was beyond healing.

In December, 1850, France's diplomatic agent, Emile Perrin, arrived in Honolulu. Perrin adopted a bullying attitude and in violation of his instructions presented demands and threatened the monarchy. In a panic the government offered to put Hawaii under the protection of the United States. The American consul, Elisha H. Allen, presented this proposal to the American government, but Daniel Webster opposed the project and nothing was accomplished. Nonetheless France's attitude became more conciliatory, especially after the Hawaiian government concluded a treaty with England in 1851.

Meanwhile in Honolulu fresh feuds erupted. Dr. Judd found himself once again the central figure in a number of acrimonious disputes. Wyllie accused him of governing "on the system of snip, snub, and snarl." Others became more abusive and threatened him with violence. In 1852 real violence occurred when a mob of sailors marched up Nuuanu Valley and made ominous gestures. Dr. Judd stood his ground, but it was obvious that his various opponents waited only for an opportunity to destroy him.

The opportunity came in the spring of 1853, when a smallpox epidemic raged through the Islands and took a frightful toll among the native population. At the height of the crisis a determined clique put pressure on the king to expel Dr. Judd from office. Prince Alexander, the heir to the throne, added his voice to the clamor, and Wyllie certainly did not defend his antagonist of long standing. The king wavered, but finally on the recommendation of Judge Lee decided against Dr. Judd. In September the king dismissed all the cabinet, then reappointed all except Dr. Judd, who was replaced by Elisha H. Allen.

As even his opponents freely admitted, Dr. Judd's services to the Hawaiian Kingdom had been devoted and extensive. Like his pioneer forebears he had broken new ground and created a sovereignty and the instrumentality of administration, and had appointed to high office capable men who shared his love of Hawaii. Unfortunately he was unbending by temperament, and, like Bingham, unable to tolerate opposition. In the end the very men whom he had brought to power united to dislodge him. Wyllie later wrote to him, "It is no flattery to you to say that no history of this kingdom can be true and just that ignores your most valuable services, while, I may say, the universal minister of the later king." Perhaps this statement may serve as his epitaph.

Although out of office Dr. Judd retained his influence with the king and chiefs, and continued to press for the annexation of Hawaii by the United States. Others in Hawaii shared his views, and there were persistent rumors of a filibustering expedition from California to take the Islands by force. Although a native audience hissed Dr. Judd into silence when he proposed annexation, the king ordered Wyllie to begin such a negotiation with the new United States commissioner, David L. Gregg.

On July 4, 1854, a number of American residents in Honolulu made a pro-annexation demonstration in the form of a parade. Mrs. Judd wrote, "A car, decorated with evergreens, in which were seated thirty-two girls of American parentage, dressed in white, wreathed in flowers, each bearing the name of a State on her sash, in large gold letters, was drawn by a power unseen. Next followed 'Young America,' a company of very young men in uniform, with another triumphal chariot." Clearly nationalism, a mainspring of Occidental civilization in the nineteenth century, was at work even in the mid-Pacific.

The annexation proposals called for the admittance of Hawaii to the United States, not as a territory, but as a state, and for an annual pension of $300,000 to be paid by the United States to the king, chiefs, and other dispossessed officials. Although Gregg agreed to these terms, it is possible that they would not have been acceptable to the United States government. In any case, the matter hung fire, largely because Prince Alexander and the British interest in Hawaii opposed annexation.

On December 15, Kamehameha III died, after the longest reign in the history of the Hawaiian Kingdom. With his death all hope of annexation perished. Hawaii retained its independence and did not become part of the United States until 1898.

Chapter 8

The Middle Years of the Kingdom, 1854-74

THE REIGNS of Kamehameha IV (1854-63), Kamehameha V (1863-72), and Lunalilo (1873-74) are sometimes called the middle period of the Hawaiian Kingdom. During this period the American missionaries lost their predominance in Hawaii. Kamehameha IV introduced and sponsored the Church of England, and his successor abrogated the liberal constitution of 1852, which had been framed in accordance with American democratic principles. Both changes evoked dismay and protest from the American missionary interest. Meanwhile the Hawaiian government, largely through the efforts of Wyllie, tried to protect its sovereignty through multinational treaties.

At the death of Kamehameha III the natives followed the ancient custom of mourning. For several days they wailed, and this wild rhythmical noise, eerie and piercing, continued to the beat of hula drums throughout the nights. The funeral procession passed slowly along streets lined with rushes. Kahili bearers wearing red and yellow feather capes accompanied the coffin. Their presence recalled the pomp and dignity of Old Hawaii, but impressive as the ceremony was it reflected a haunting sadness. By then the Hawaiian people were well on their way to disintegration. The days of Old Hawaii, it was clear, would never return.

Alexander Liholiho, who became Kamehameha IV before his twenty-first birthday, was a nephew of the late king. Through his mother, Kinau, he was a grandson of Kamehameha I. An attractive and courteous ruler, he had received a sound education at the Royal School. His trip abroad with his brother Lot under the escort of Dr. Judd in 1849-50 had broadened his outlook and reinforced his aristocratic leanings. During his stay abroad he had come to admire the English government and church. On the other hand the color prejudice which he had encountered in the United States infuriated him. He wrote in his journal, "Here I must state that I am disappointed at the Americans." In a vein of unconcealed irritation he added, "They have no manners, no politeness, not even common civilities, to a stranger." At the same time he had come to resent the puritanical strictness of his missionary teachers and the iron discipline imposed on him by Dr. Judd on the diplomatic journey.

Dr. Judd commented in despair in 1861, "The King, educated by the mission, most of all things dislikes the mission. Having been compelled to be good when a boy, he is determined not to be good as a man. Driven out by morning prayer meeting, monthly concert, Sabbath school, long sermons, and daily exhortations, his heart is hardened to a degree unknown to the heathen. Naturally he chooses associates whose feeling and practices are in union with his own. The love of intoxicating drinks is vastly increasing, the Sabbath disregarded, the marriage vows lightly esteemed, government expenses increased, while the revenue is decreased. The picture is dark; it seems if destruction was near at hand."

The net result was to inculcate in the new king a strong antimissionary attitude. Even before coming to the throne he had opposed annexation of the Islands by the United States and he had used his influence to expel Dr. Judd from the government. As king he continued to be antimissionary, and, although he retained some American advisers, he generally favored Great Britain at the expense of the American interest in Hawaii. In so doing he revived the old tradition of British supremacy in Hawaii which still survives in Beretania Street, the Hawaiian version of Britannia.

At his inauguration in Kawaiahao Church on January 11, 1854, he eulogized his uncle and predecessor, and then stated solemnly, "Today we begin a new era. Let it be one of increased civilization, one of progress, industry, temperance, morality, and all of those virtues which mark a nation's progress. The importance of unity is that which I wish to impress upon your minds. Let us be one and we shall not fail." This eloquent speech impressed the huge audience assembled to witness the colorful inauguration ceremonies. Its note of optimism was encouraging. But later events add a flavor of irony to these brave words, for Kamehameha IV soon became the central figure in a series of tragic disasters.

The most pressing early problems of the reign were diplomatic. Kamehameha IV and his advisers decided that the best way to forestall annexation of Hawaii by the United States was to negotiate a reciprocity treaty with the United States whereby each nation admitted the products of the other duty-free. Such a treaty, it was believed, would satisfy the American pressure groups in Hawaii and elsewhere that were urging the annexation of the Islands. At the same time members of the Hawaiian government, especially Wyllie, hoped to get a treaty with foreign powers—France, Great Britain, and the United States, and possibly also with Russia—to guarantee Hawaii's independence.

Judge William L. Lee of the Hawaiian government, who was about to visit the United States on personal business, received the assignment, along with full instructions and credentials, to negotiate both diplomatic projects. Lee reached Washington in July, 1855, and called on President Franklin Pierce, who stated clearly the current American policy about Hawaii: "The United States did not desire to annex the Islands, but they would not allow them to pass into other hands." Pierce added, "I incline to the opinion that the wisest policy for both countries is that of independence, and a free interchange of products."

The President and cabinet then approved a reciprocity treaty with Hawaii, which Lee and the American secretary of state, William L. Marcy, signed on July 20. The treaty was not all-embracing and limited the Hawaiian commodities entering the United States duty-free to unrefined sugar, molasses, coffee, livestock, and a few other items. The Hawaiian government ratified it in September, but it was not approved by the United States Senate. The Louisiana sugar interest opposed it, and the opinion was also expressed that the treaty might lead to the illegal import of sugar from China, the Philippines, and elsewhere by way of Hawaii.

Lee attempted but failed to get a three-way treaty among France, Great Britain, and the United States to guarantee Hawaii's independence. But he managed to obtain from these powers assurances that they would protect Hawaii from a forcible seizure.

While this complex diplomacy was under way, in Honolulu the king was preparing to take a bride. The young woman selected was known as Emma Rooke, a granddaughter of John Young, Kamehameha I's adviser, and a great-granddaughter of Kamehameha I's younger brother. She had been adopted by Dr. Thomas Charles Byde Rooke, a British physician who came to Hawaii in 1829. Under his influence she became thoroughly pro-British in attitude. A kindly and strong-minded woman, Queen Emma had much weight in public affairs.

The royal wedding took place in Kawaiahao Church, sometimes called Honolulu's Westminster Abbey, on June 19, 1856. In his excitement Kamehameha IV forgot the ring. Chief Justice Allen relieved the situation by taking off his own ring and handing it to the king. The Reverend Richard Armstrong officiated. Significantly, he used the wedding service of the Anglican Church. Shortly thereafter the British agent in Hawaii expressed the pious hope that henceforth the king would behave with greater propriety—a statement with ominous overtones. For the time being propriety apparently prevailed, but it was not to last.

On May 20, 1858, Queen Emma gave birth to a son, christened Albert Edward Kauikeaouli Leiopapa a Kamehameha ("the beloved child of a long line of chiefs, a sign in the heavens"). The infant also received the title of His Royal Highness the Prince of Hawaii (*Ka Haku o Hawaii*). At a public ceremony Kamehameha IV made an eloquent and romantic speech to the troops which reflected his own exalted feelings. "The expressions of loyalty you have just uttered are very welcome to me. There is no tie between a head of a government and his troops like that of mutual good wishes and a common object. Such exists between us, and may it never cease to exist. So long as it does we have nothing to fear of one another, but everything to hope." A number of descriptions exist of the love and tenderness of "Aleck" and "Emma" for one another and for "Baby."

A year after the birth of the little prince tragedy shattered the idyllic domesticity of the royal couple. On September 11, 1859, when the royal family was on a visit to Maui, Kamehameha IV shot his secretary, an American named Henry A. Neilson, with a pistol. The king had heard reports of Neilson's misconduct in which the queen's name was mentioned. For several days the king turned over these malicious reports in his mind, in the meantime drinking heavily. The shooting occurred on the evening of the eleventh. Although severely wounded in the chest, Neilson recovered for the time being, but he died two and one-half years later.

This act of violence drove Kamehameha IV to excruciating remorse. He satisfied himself that the reports about Neilson were only gossip, and he faced the terrible fact that he had assaulted an innocent man. His associates feared that he would commit suicide, and they had difficulty in persuading him not to abdicate. Wyllie paraphrased Shakespeare and urged, "Let Richard be himself again," and in the end the king took this sane advice.

The Neilson tragedy had extended consequences, for in the months to follow Kamehameha IV turned seriously to religion.

Encouraged by Queen Emma and by Wyllie he revived an old project to establish an Anglican church in Hawaii. At the same time he wanted to find an Anglican tutor for his young son.

In December, 1859, on the king's orders, Wyllie informed the Hawaiian consul-general in London of the wish of the king and queen for an Episcopal church in the Islands. The king offered a site for the church building and offered also to pay part of the minister's salary. Wyllie, who took delight in making a simple subject appear complicated, added, "The king himself, taking all the interest in the education, morals, and religion of his people which becomes him as a sovereign, believes that an Episcopal church here besides supplying a want long felt by many British and American families, would operate beneficially in narrowing the existing broad antagonism of the Calvinistic and Catholic creeds, and thereby promote that brotherly feeling between the clergy of both that so well becomes the followers of the same Lord." Prediction is a tricky business. As it happened, the coming of the Anglicans provoked rather than quieted theological disputes.

In the course of the negotiations the project was broadened to include the establishment of a complete Anglican missionary organization, with a bishop and two clergymen. Among the supporters of this enlarged project was Bishop Samuel Wilberforce, the son of the celebrated anti-slavery agitator and the opponent of Charles Darwin's evolutionary theory.

On October 11, 1862, Bishop Thomas Nettleship Staley arrived in Honolulu to take up his duties as head of the new diocese of Hawaii. He came at a most inopportune moment, and found the Hawaiian royal family in the depths of sorrow. Just two weeks before his arrival the little Prince of Hawaii died, having been baptized by another clergyman.

The settlement of the Anglican church in the Islands aroused furious opposition on the part of the American missionaries. The king took their hostility rather lightly and commented, "I am sorry to hear that Judd Corwin and Co. [Dr. Judd and the Congregational minister, Eli S. Corwin] are so inimical to the establishment of Episcopacy here. I wonder if they really are in earnest in objecting to peoples getting in to heaven by any way they please?" Nonetheless, some of the American missionaries attacked the "popery" of the new church. This charge, which revived prejudices as old as the Protestant Reformation, appeared plausible since the new church became known as the Hawaiian Reformed Catholic Church. Others believed sincerely that the coming of the Anglicans was a prelude to a British imperialist seizure of the Islands.

Active and former American missionaries and their families naturally resented the newcomers who threatened the supremacy of the American mission in Hawaii. Dr. Judd complained bitterly a few years later: "Kamehameha IV by introducing a bishop, clergy, schoolmasters and sisters of charity from England, prepared the way for an union of church and state and the general diffusion among the wealthier classes [of] certain high toned monarchial principles in opposition to those of the American missionaries. . . . The labors of the American missionaries are ignored and the men to whom the king, the chiefs and the people owe their education and their independence are set aside and forgotten."

The year after the arrival of the Anglicans the status of the American missionaries changed. The American Board of Commissioners for Foreign Missions in 1863 all but severed its connection with the American mission in Hawaii, which henceforth operated under the direction of the Hawaiian Evangelical Association (the Hawaiian Board), founded in 1854. The withdrawal of the American Board was tacit recognition that Hawaii had been Christianized and no longer needed a foreign mission.

About this time also another rival to the American missionaries appeared. Mormons had entered Hawaii in 1846 and had established a mission four years later, but in 1858 the whites among them had been called back to Utah. In 1861, Walter Murray Gibson, a clever and unscrupulous man who later took a prominent part in politics, came to Hawaii to reorganize the Mormon congregation. Within a few years this reckless and doubledealing adventurer had defrauded his congregation and taken a long step toward establishing himself financially in the Islands.

In the last years of the reign of Kamehameha IV, Wyllie labored earnestly, and at times somewhat ridiculously, to strengthen Hawaii's diplomatic position. In 1857 he negotiated a compromise treaty with France, ratified by both states in the following year, which ended the major troubles of the Hawaiian Kingdom with that nation. In 1860 he commissioned Sir John Bowring, a distinguished Oriental linguist who had served as governor of Hong Kong, to try to get a formal joint guarantee of Hawaii's independence by the European powers. The two men labored conscientiously. Bowring negotiated treaties for

Hawaii with Belgium, Italy, the Netherlands, Spain, and Switzerland. The whole affair has something of the flavor of Gilbert and Sullivan. But the grand object of this diplomacy was not achieved.

Wyllie's eager and energetic imagination received a fresh stimulus in 1860, when the first Japanese diplomatic mission to the United States stopped off in Honolulu. A spate of formal documents then issued from the Hawaiian Foreign Office with the avowed object of establishing diplomatic relations with that newly opened Oriental kingdom. In due course the Japanese authorities politely turned down Wyllie's overtures, and Hawaii's first treaty with Japan was not signed until 1871. But in the course of the proceedings the Laird of Rosebank, as Wyllie jocularly styled himself, came up with a proposal which makes *Alice in Wonderland* read like a scholarly article. It is possible that Wyllie had lost his sense of humor, or that he was merely indulging it. In either case, he proposed as Hawaii's envoy to patriarchal Japan Lady Franklin, the widow of the explorer, who happened then to be in Honolulu. Wyllie justified his weird plan on the precedent of the Peace of Cambrai of 1529, sometimes called the Ladies' Peace, which had been negotiated by Louise of Savoy on behalf of her son, King Francis I of France, and Margaret of Austria on behalf of her nephew, Charles V, the Holy Roman Emperor. Fortunately Kamehameha IV had the common sense to veto this scatterbrained scheme.

One of Kamehameha IV's more enduring acts was the foundation in 1859 of Queen's Hospital, named after his beloved wife. The next year construction work was begun on the site of the present hospital near Punchbowl. Kamehameha IV took an active interest in this worthwhile project and personally solicited funds for it. The hospital was originally intended to benefit needy Hawaiians.

Kamehameha IV died prematurely at the age of twenty-nine on November 30, 1863. In the months preceding his death he had been engaged in translating the Anglican prayer book into Hawaiian.

At the time of his death no formal provision had been made for the royal succession. The Privy Council then met with the *kuhina nui* (Princess Victoria Kamamalu) and proclaimed Prince Lot, the late king's elder brother, as King Kamehameha V. The new king had received a good education and had traveled abroad with his brother and Dr. Judd during the diplomatic mission of 1849-50. He was energetic and capable, although somewhat reserved, and had served creditably as minister of the interior. He shared his brother's antimissionary feelings and continued his pro-British policy. A portly and positive bachelor, he showed his distaste for the puritanism of the American mission by reviving ancient Hawaiian practices, among them the *hula*. In addition, and in further repudiation of American principles, he revived the despotism of the ancient Hawaiian kings. He was a grandson of Kamehameha I (the Great), whom he resembled in physique and disposition.

Of the chief figures in the new administration three were British, two were American, and one was French. The British ministers were Wyllie, at that time a venerable and much respected figure, along with George M. Robertson and Charles G. Hopkins (shortly thereafter replaced by a Scottish physician, Dr. Ferdinand W. Hutchison). The Americans were the jurists Elisha H. Allen and Charles C. Harris, a capable yet overbearing man mercilessly pilloried by Mark Twain. At Wyllie's suggestion the king appointed as minister of finance a French diplomatist, Charles de Varigny, then serving as acting French consul in Honolulu. Varigny, who later wrote a picturesque book about Hawaii, became foreign minister on Wyllie's death in 1865.

From the first Kamehameha V refused to take the oath to uphold the liberal constitution of 1852. He was afraid that too much liberalism in Hawaii might lead to a republic and that a republic might lead to annexation of the Islands by the United States.

In May, 1864, Kamehameha V summoned a convention to revise the constitution, which met in July. This arbitrary proceeding evoked much protest, but the king persevered and toured the Islands making speeches on behalf of his project. The constitutional convention, which met in historic Kawaiahao Church, split over the issue of requiring property qualifications and a literacy test for voters. Dr. Judd, who was one of the twenty-six elected delegates, was particularly vocal in support of democratic principles. It soon became apparent that a deadlock had been reached. With characteristic bluntness, Kamehameha V cut the Gordian knot. He dissolved the convention on August 13, abrogated the liberal constitution of 1852, and said simply, "I will give you a constitution."

The new constitution of 1864 abolished the office of *kuhina nui*, restricted the powers of the Privy Council, and established a single-chamber legislature for nobles and representatives. Property qualifications and literacy tests (for those born after

1840) were required of both representatives and voters. Dr. Judd predicted darkly that anarchy and even bloodshed might follow, but the new constitution actually stabilized the royal authority and endured for twenty-three years.

In 1865, the year after the new constitution was established, Kamehameha V made a characteristic gesture and an often quoted remark which indicate clearly the benevolent quality of his despotism. In that year a bill came before the legislature to repeal the penalties for selling or giving liquor to natives. Kamehameha V himself enjoyed liquor, but he also understood the Hawaiian weakness for strong drink. He announced his opposition to the bill by saying, "I will never sign the death warrant of my people." Consequently the bill was voted down on its second reading.

Also in 1865, Kamehameha V signed a bill to cope with leprosy, which had appeared in Hawaii some years before. Later that year the Board of Health established a leper colony on a small peninsula on Molokai's north coast, isolated from the rest of that island, and from the world, by a towering *pali*.

During his reign Kamehameha V made two major efforts to obtain a reciprocity treaty with the United States. In the spring of 1864 Chief Justice Elisha H. Allen left for Washington to negotiate this and other treaties. He talked with President Lincoln, William H. Seward, the secretary of state, and a number of other officials. Seward's final answer was disappointing: "The present temporary state of civil war renders such a negotiation inconvenient and inexpedient." But Seward added encouragingly that he was willing to resume discussion of the matter at a later date.

In 1867 the Hawaiian government tried again. In May of that year the American minister to Hawaii, General Edward M. McCook, met with the Hawaiian envoy, Charles C. Harris, in San Francisco. After discussion the two men signed a reciprocity treaty, which the Hawaiian government ratified four months later. But this treaty shared the same fate as the one negotiated by Judge Lee twelve years previously. It was defeated in the United States Senate in 1870. Many circumstances led to its defeat. Some opponents of the treaty argued that it would confer no real benefits on the United States. Expansionists saw in it an obstacle to the eventual annexation of Hawaii by the United States.

Kamehameha V died on his forty-second birthday on December 11, 1872, and once again the succession remained uncertain. In the weeks to follow several candidates appeared, among them the High Chiefess Bernice Pauahi (Mrs. Charles R. Bishop), Princess Ruth Keelikolani, Prince David Kalakaua, and Prince William Charles Lunalilo, grandson of a half-brother of Kamehameha I. On his deathbed Kamehameha V named as his successor Bernice Pauahi, to whom he had been betrothed in his youth. This remarkable and charming woman, a descendant of Kamehameha I, had married instead the banker and statesman in the Hawaiian government, Charles Reed Bishop. Out of the extensive private lands of the Kamehameha family which she inherited (the so-called Bishop estate) she founded in her will the Kamehameha schools for children of Hawaiian ancestry, and her husband later founded the world famous Bernice Pauahi Bishop Museum of Polynesian Ethnology (familiarly called the Bishop Museum) to perpetuate her memory. Bernice Pauahi declined Kamehameha V's offer of the throne, reportedly with the words, "Oh, no, do not think of me. There are others." She then suggested Princess Ruth, and Queen Emma, the widow of Kamehameha IV. This situation is a compound of various layers of meaning and emotion, for the dying king had fallen in love with Queen Emma, had proposed marriage to her, and had been refused. In addition Queen Emma reported that he had offered to name her as his successor and that this offer also she had refused.

It is impossible to take seriously the candidacy of Princess Ruth, one of the richest and fattest women in the kingdom. Her Gargantuan frame and coarse features, as depicted in various old prints, leave an impression of overwhelming and immovable mass. She could neither speak nor understand English. Her accession to the throne undoubtedly would have led to political madness.

The two serious candidates were Kalakaua, who indeed later became king of Hawaii, and Lunalilo. Kalakaua conducted a loud and rollicking campaign. He addressed the people in the style of Old Hawaii: "O my people! My countrymen of old! Arise! This is the voice! Ho! all ye tribes! Ho! my own ancient people." His platform began with his support of Kamehameha I's Law of the Splintered Paddle and continued with the repeal of personal taxes, the expulsion of foreigners from the government, and amendment of the constitution of 1864.

At a plebiscite on January 1, 1873, the people of Hawaii voted overwhelmingly for Lunalilo, and a week later the legislature confirmed his choice unanimously, with one of the nobles, the brother-in-law of Kalakaua, abstaining. Lunalilo is consequently known as the People's King.

Lunalilo (literally, Out of Sight Above) was indeed popular. Prince Bill, as he was familiarly called before he came to the throne, was a frail, sensitive, and well-read monarch, unfortunately afflicted with tuberculosis and alcoholism. Lady Franklin admired his good looks and good manners, and Mark Twain was captivated with his charm. "Prince William is a man of fine, large build . . . affable, gentlemanly, open, frank, manly; is as independent as a lord and has the spirit and will of the old Conqueror himself. He is intelligent, shrewd, sensible; is a man of first-rate abilities in fact. I like the man." But others, among them Alfred Castle, soon complained of his "drunken, rowdy ways."

The cabinet ministers consisted of a Scot, Robert Stirling, and three Americans, Charles R. Bishop, Edwin O. Hall, a former secular member of the American mission, and Albert Francis Judd, a younger son of Dr. G. P. Judd, recently returned to the Islands after graduating from Yale and taking a law degree at Harvard. Charles Hastings Judd, another of Dr. Judd's sons, became adjutant-general of Hawaii's armed forces.

Lunalilo's government reopened negotiations with the United States for a reciprocity treaty and proposed granting Pearl Harbor, then called the Pearl River Lagoon, to the United States as a port and coaling base. But this proposal found little support in the American government and many Hawaiians opposed it. Toward the end of the year the negotiation lapsed.

In September, 1873, an incident occurred which might have had serious consequences. The Household Troops, about sixty in number, mutinied because they resented the discipline of their Hungarian drillmaster and of Adjutant Judd. A half dozen or so of the troops, who had been sent to the guard house for deserting their sentry posts, broke out and seized the palace dining room. In the scuffle which followed Adjutant Judd was knocked down and kicked. The Honolulu Rifles, a volunteer organization, came to the rescue, but it was incompletely manned, some of its members being, as they said, too busy to report for duty. At one point it was decided to break the mutiny by shutting off the water in the palace, then held by the mutineers. When the plumber arrived, the rebellious troops swarmed out and returned with buckets and tubs of water in order to prepare themselves for a siege. A few mutineers calmly flagged passing cabs and left the area. The situation portended revolution, but none came. Shortly thereafter the king ended the mutiny by promising an amnesty. After the disturbance ended, the king abolished the Household Troops except for the band.

Lunalilo, called *lokomaikai* (merciful or gracious) by his compatriots, died on February 3, 1874, after reigning just over a year. In his will he established Lunalilo Home on Oahu, a charitable institution for aged and infirm persons of Hawaiian descent. Lunalilo's tomb in Kawaiahao churchyard bears the simple inscription *Ka Moi,* The King.

Chapter 9

The Last Years of the Kingdom, 1874-93

THE MOST important event in the last twenty years of the Hawaiian Kingdom was the signing of a reciprocity treaty with the United States in the reign of Kalakaua (1874-91), Hawaii's last king. But political instability and corruption marred his reign, as they did the reign of his sister and successor, Queen Liliuokalani, Hawaii's last royal ruler. In 1893 a revolution broke out which put an end to the Hawaiian monarchy and established a republic.

At Lunalilo's death the succession was once again in dispute. Kalakaua, whom Lunalilo had defeated in the previous year, immediately declared his candidacy. The next day Queen Emma, the widow of Kamehameha IV, announced hers. Queen Emma had visited England in the years 1865-66, where she met Queen Victoria and the poet laureate, Tennyson. Her dignity and cultivation impressed the English, as did her piety, which the Archbishop of Canterbury characterized as "almost saintly." Although many Americans in Hawaii suspected unjustly that her trip was part of a plot leading to a British seizure of Hawaii, she naturally had the support of the not inconsiderable British interest in the Islands. In addition she had the enthusiastic backing of a large segment of the native population.

The legislature met in the courthouse to settle the issue on February 12, 1874, and elected Kalakaua as king by a vote of thirty-nine to six. When the result was announced, supporters of Queen Emma staged a full-scale riot. Lorrin Thurston reported vividly, "The people in the yard received this news with an angry shout, which speedily became a roar of angry execration, as though a stick had been twisted in a giant beehive." After assaulting the committee of three who emerged to announce the election, Thurston's account continues, the mob broke into the courthouse. "That place was gutted. Some members of the legislature were mobbed because they had voted for Kalakaua and pandemonium ensued. A rain of books, chairs, tables and other furniture poured from the doors and windows of the court house, upstairs and downstairs."

American and British marines, summoned at the king's request, landed from ships in the harbor and restored order by nightfall. As a precautionary measure, Kalakaua's inauguration on the thirteenth took place, not in Kawaiahao Church, as was traditional, but with small ceremony at Kinau Hale (Kinau's house) near the palace. The riot dismayed the respectable foreign residents, in that it revealed the fundamental political weakness of the monarchy. Alfred Castle commented sadly, "When shall we have a government that is not afraid of its own shadow?" This inauspicious beginning was an ominous portent of further disorders to follow.

Kalakaua could be extremely gracious and merry. Indeed, he is known traditionally as Hawaii's Merry Monarch. Robert Louis Stevenson called him "a very fine, intelligent fellow," and Henry Adams admired his knowledge. He could drink enormous quantities of liquor without showing it, possibly because, as it was said, he fortified himself first with milk and poi. He understood thoroughly and well the temper of his people, and both as a writer and speaker he was invariably effective. His charm had much to do with the successful negotiation of the reciprocity treaty with the United States. On the other hand, as the record of his reign abundantly demonstrates, he was lacking in that degree of judgment and purpose which distinguishes a statesman from a politician.

In June, 1874, the king received a petition from almost all the merchants and planters of the kingdom urging the immediate negotiation of a reciprocity treaty with the United States and predicting "serious disaster" if such a treaty was not obtained. After authorization from the legislature and with the concurrence of the cabinet and privy council the king appointed Chief Justice Allen as the Hawaiian envoy for the negotiation, with Henry A. P. Carter of Honolulu's Brewer and Company as his assistant.

In October the two envoys left for the United States, and on November 17 the king followed on board the U.S.S. *Benicia.* His party included the American minister to Hawaii, Henry A.

Peirce, and Governor John O. Dominis, who had married Liliuokalani in 1862. Liliuokalani remained behind as regent.

The arrival of the royal party in San Francisco created a huge sensation. A newspaper reported, "It isn't every day that a king comes to San Francisco." Kalakaua was in fact the first reigning monarch to visit the United States. (Louis Napoleon had gone to New York some years before his accession as Napoleon III, and in 1876 Pedro II of Brazil took a trip to the United States.)

In Washington, President Ulysses S. Grant received Kalakaua with full honors. On Christmas day he gave a gala reception. He was to speak before Congress, but because he had caught a bad cold he merely attended while his speech was read for him. Kalakaua later visited New York and New England. He returned to Hawaii in February, 1875. The good will which he generated for Hawaii certainly facilitated the reciprocity negotiations.

The Louisiana sugar interest and New Englanders trading in West Indian sugar opposed the treaty. But Senator George Sewell Boutwell of Massachusetts and others argued that if the treaty did not pass, Hawaii's business and sovereignty might be transferred to another power. Boutwell stated eloquently, "If we reject this treaty we transfer these islands either to France or Great Britain, and we diminish our markets, we diminish our political power, we limit the influence of our institutions, we circumscribe American ideas, we retard the progress of American civilization." His remarks contained a hard core of truth. In 1873, Hawaii sent over one-third of its sugar to Australia, British Columbia, and New Zealand, and Hawaiian sugar planters were already discussing the possibility of a reciprocity treaty with these areas.

The United States insisted on adding a clause (Article IV) to the treaty, by which the Hawaiian king agreed that "so long as this treaty shall remain in force, he will not lease or otherwise dispose of or create any lien upon any port, harbor, or other territory in his dominion, or grant any special privilege or rights of use therein, to any other power, state, or government, nor make any treaty by which any other nation shall obtain the same privileges, relative to the admission of any articles free of duty, hereby secured to the United States." Without this clause, with its oblique reference to Pearl Harbor and its promise of the exclusive right of reciprocity to the United States, the treaty probably could not have been concluded.

The treaty was signed in January, 1875. Ratification and

enabling acts on the part of both Hawaii and the United States followed. It went into effect on September 9, 1876. The reciprocity treaty removed the possibility of a Hawaiian alignment with Britain or France and put Hawaii firmly within the political and economic orbit of the United States. It also put Hawaii's economy on a sound basis. Without it, as William R. Castle, Jr. has commented, "Hawaii would have dwindled into the usual nerveless, helpless tropical colony, waiting to be swallowed by the first strong nation which considered it worthwhile to run the risk of possible complications with other powers."

When the treaty was renewed in 1887 it contained an amendment which granted to the United States the "exclusive right to enter the harbor of Pearl River . . . and to establish and to maintain there a coaling and repair station for the use of vessels of the United States." But the United States did not make use of this important right until after Hawaii's annexation in 1898. Secretary of State Thomas Bayard commented in 1887, "We have no navy to put in it in the first place and . . . our merchant shipping did not need it."

In domestic politics Kalakaua began well. His own attractive personality insured him support among the native population, especially as universal suffrage, proposed by Lunalilo, had been re-enacted in 1874. His first cabinet contained honest and able men: William Lothian Green, the former British acting consul-general, as minister of foreign affairs; Hermann A. Widemann, a naturalized German, as minister of the interior; Alfred S. Hartwell, a former New Englander, as attorney-general; and a chief, Paul Nahaolelua, as minister of finance.

Unfortunately, in 1876 Kalakaua dismissed this cabinet and appointed another, as was his right constitutionally. Although the replacements were capable men, the sudden overthrow of the cabinet emphasized the instability already latent in the monarchy and in time led to gross abuses.

In 1878, Claus Spreckels, a sugar magnate from the West Coast, persuaded the king (by means of a loan) to dismiss the cabinet, because its members had refused to grant him water rights on Maui. The new cabinet granted the rights.

A new crisis arose two years later. Kalakaua tried to put through a bill to sell liquor to the Hawaiians and to license the sale of opium in the kingdom. Both failed, but he managed to obtain for Celso Caesar Moreno, an Italian opportunist, a subsidy for a steamship line between Hawaii and China. In August the king dismissed his cabinet and appointed Moreno as prime minister.

Instantly hot protests arose, from the citizenry and foreign embassies alike. Two days later an assembly in the old church at Kaumakapili resolved that Moreno's appointment, "inconsistent with the principles of the constitutional monarchy as handed down by the Kamehamehas and Lunalilo, is therein hostile to the permanence of Hawaiian independence, the perpetuity of the Hawaiian race, and the security of life, liberty, and property in the Hawaiian Islands." A committee of thirteen presented the protest to the king, who revoked Moreno's appointment. Shortly thereafter Moreno left Hawaii for Italy with Robert W. Wilcox, later prominent as a revolutionary, and two other *hapa-haole* boys, ostensibly to educate them abroad at public expense, but really, as was commonly said, to have the Hawaiian government pay his own expenses on the journey.

Kalakaua then grandiosely decided to take a trip around the world. The royal party left Honolulu in January, 1881, for San Francisco and there took a steamer for Japan. In Yokohama the emperor of Japan lavishly entertained Kalakaua and presented him with the Star and Broad Scarlet Cordon of the Order of the Rising Sun. Kalakaua in his turn presented the emperor with the Grand Cross of the Order of Kamehameha. The rest of the journey was equally delightful, a prolonged orgy of pomp and magnanimity. Kalakaua passed in state through Hong Kong, Singapore, and Rangoon. He was the guest of the maharaja of Jahore and of the viceroy of India. In Italy he encountered his former prime minister Moreno and learned that Moreno had been passing off the youths in his charge as Kalakaua's natural sons. His itinerary was indeed full. He had an audience with Pope Leo XIII and visited Queen Victoria at Windsor. He passed through Belgium, met Kaiser Wilhelm I of Germany, and went also to Austria, France, Spain, and Portugal. In the United States he visited New York, Washington, Philadelphia, and Chicago before proceeding westward to San Francisco for the boat home. He reached Honolulu in October, the first king to circumnavigate the globe.

On his journey, of which his aide William Armstrong has left a colorful account, Kalakaua enjoyed himself immensely. In Austria he bought a battery of field guns, and in England he ordered two jeweled crowns, one for himself and one for his queen, reported to have cost $10,000 apiece. No one who understands the Hawaiian temperament will dismiss these purchases, and the journey itself, as a vulgar display. It was simply a long, spontaneous outburst of good spirits on Kalakaua's part, proof positive that he richly deserves his nickname, the Merry Monarch.

Back in Honolulu he arranged for a magnificent coronation ceremony on February 12, 1883, the ninth anniversary of his election as king. The coronation took place in a pavilion erected in front of the new royal palace. With his own hands Kalakaua placed the royal crown on his head, then put the smaller crown on the head of his consort Queen Kapiolani.

The palace itself reflected the king's love of magnificence. Much of the interior was built with rare Hawaiian woods. Pale blue silk adorned the chambers, and the furniture was made of ebony and gold. The throne room (incidentally the only throne room now in the United States) had rose-colored satin drapes and delicate crystal chandeliers. Art historians may someday take note of this Polynesian baroque.

The king's personal life was equally colorful and gay. Many anecdotes exist of his drinking bouts, amours, and gambling sessions. An often-repeated story has it that he won a large poker pot from Spreckels, the sugar baron, who held four aces, by insisting that four kings, plus his own royal person, made five kings, which bettered Spreckels' hand.

After his return from his trip around the world, the king's good-humored dalliance crossed the line and became political irresponsibility. The years from 1882 to 1887 were a time of mirth and joviality. They also witnessed extravagance and corruption reminiscent of the court of Louis XVI of France or of New York in the era of Boss Tweed.

A rare and slick rascal, Walter Murray Gibson (called Kipikona by the Hawaiians), insinuated himself into the royal favor and during these five years dominated the Hawaiian Kingdom. Gibson's career has the unbelievable quality of a cheap adventure story. Much of his early life is unknowable, for the main account of it is his own, and Gibson was not noted for telling the truth. He spoke of his birth at sea enroute from Europe to America, of his adventures among the Indian tribes, and of vague exploits in Mexico and in the California Gold Rush of 1849. In the 1850's he became involved in a filibuster in the Dutch East Indies, for which he was jailed; but he escaped, possibly with the connivance of the Dutch who wished to get him out of the area. He first attracted attention in Hawaii when he defrauded the Mormons on Lanai in the early 1860's. Thereafter he moved to Honolulu and entered politics.

It is impossible to determine how much of the corruption and unwisdom in the political affairs of the monarchy resulted from Gibson's scheming nature and how much resulted from the irresponsible attitude of the king. In point of sober fact, the king must take full blame for the mess which ensued, for no king in his right mind would have tolerated such an unscrupulous prime minister.

The scandals were large and juicy. Spreckels received 24,000 acres of crown land on Maui for only $10,000. The legislature of 1882 appropriated $10,000 for a Board of Genealogy and $30,000 for coronation expenses. The legislature of 1886 gave the government the right to sell a monopoly on the opium traffic in Hawaii for $30,000. In time the national debt soared to well over $2,000,000. Other abuses included the sale of government offices, repeal of the liquor laws, illegal land leases, and even the sale of exemptions to lepers so that they might avoid being sent to the settlement at Kalaupapa. All of this graft proceeded in a poisoned political atmosphere. Gibson did not hesitate to foment racial antagonisms to win support among the natives against responsible white foreigners who wished to reform the administration. One of his favorite slogans was "Hawaii for the Hawaiians," which, freely translated, meant "Hawaii for Gibson."

The kingdom's foreign policy was equally reckless. In 1887, Kalakaua made a treaty with the government of Samoa to form a confederation. At this time Kalakaua dreamed of uniting all Polynesia into an empire, with himself as the Colossus of the Pacific. To make a naval display he refitted a small steamer and renamed it the *Kaimiloa*. The crew consisted mainly of Hawaiian youths released from the House of Correction. The voyage of the *Kaimiloa* to Samoa was a shambles compounded of theft, drunkenness, and mutiny. Robert Louis Stevenson described it as "a scene of disaster and dilapidation."

The conclusion is inescapable that, left to their own resources, the Hawaiians were incapable of maintaining a respectable government in contact with the civilized world. It is in this perspective that the honest, if somewhat narrow, labors of the missionaries in the earlier days of the kingdom achieve true proportions. In view of the excesses of Kalakaua and Gibson, the labors of former missionaries like William Richards and Dr. Judd, and of non-missionary foreigners like Wyllie and Elisha H. Allen, deserve more credit than they have usually received.

The climax in Kalakaua's political saturnalia came in 1887, when it became known that he was personally involved in large-scale bribery connected with the sale of opium. Members of the recently organized reform organization, the Hawaiian League, decided that immediate action was required. One of its leaders,

Lorrin A. Thurston, complained of the "aggressions, extravagances, and debaucheries" of the administration. A protest meeting at the armory on Beretania Street on June 30 passed resolutions asking the king to dismiss the cabinet and undertake specific reforms.

Kalakaua complied. Gibson left the kingdom and died of tuberculosis in San Francisco early the next year. The "Bayonet Constitution" which resulted from this bloodless revolution restricted the power of the king. He could no longer dismiss his ministers without the consent of the legislature, and the cabinet had to ratify each of his official acts. In addition, a two-thirds vote of the legislature could override a royal veto, and the nobles, previously appointed by the king, were henceforth to be elected by voters with a comparatively high property qualification. This last provision added to the political weight of the wealthier foreigners, who controlled the noble elections. Clearly the forces of liberalism and reform had triumphed.

A reform ministry took office. Its leaders were William L. Green, Godfrey Brown, Clarence W. Ashford, and Thurston. Ashford and Thurston, a missionary descendant who later had an extremely prominent part in Hawaiian politics, were the most vigorous members of the new administration.

At this time much resentment arose. The king felt humiliated at the reduction of his powers, and many natives shared this feeling. The old tradition of despotic authority, coupled with Gibson's slogan of "Hawaii for Hawaiians," created an atmosphere unfavorable to liberal reform. In addition, many natives resented the Pearl Harbor amendment which was part of the reciprocity treaty with the United States as finally renewed late in 1887. To make matters even more difficult, disagreement checked the effectiveness of the cabinet.

The rising tension reached its climax on July 30, 1889, when Robert W. Wilcox, who had studied with Moreno in Italy, led about 150 revolutionaries in an attack on the palace. Fortunately the king was absent. After a day of desultory fighting the cabinet suppressed the revolt with the loss of only seven rebels killed. A native jury later acquitted Wilcox of treason after he testified that he had acted with the king's approval.

In the next year Kalakaua's health failed. In November he made a trip to San Francisco, for a change in climate. There he died on January 20, 1891, in his suite in the Palace Hotel.

Queen Liliuokalani, Kalakaua's sister and the last monarch of the Hawaiian Kingdom, was fifty-two years old when she ascended the throne. A woman of dignity and will, she had received a good education at the Royal School. She had served as regent during Kalakaua's trips overseas, and she had attended Queen Victoria's first Jubilee of 1887 accompanied by Queen Kapiolani. She generally shared her brother's authoritarian views, believed in "Hawaii for the Hawaiians," and resented both the Bayonet Constitution of 1887 and the Pearl Harbor amendment in the renewed reciprocity treaty, which she criticized simply in the firm words, "It should not have been done."

When she came to the throne, the kingdom throbbed with the political discontents left over from the previous reign. In addition, Hawaii faced economic disaster. The McKinley Tariff of 1890 had in effect abrogated the reciprocity treaty by putting raw sugar on the list of items admitted duty-free into the United States and by giving a bounty of two cents a pound on sugar produced in the United States. The net result was to precipitate a severe economic depression in Hawaii and to strengthen sentiment in favor of annexation to the United States. Negotiations with the American government failed to ease this economic pinch.

In the 1892 session of the legislature there was a three-way battle for political supremacy among the Reform Party, the queen's National Reform Party, and the so-called Liberal Party, an opportunist group led by Wilcox. Meanwhile a secret organization, the Annexation Club, in which Thurston had a prominent role, was formed to take measures for an eventual political union with the United States.

On January 12, 1893, the National Reform and Liberal interests combined to expel the reform cabinet. Two days later it became known that the queen planned to issue a new authoritarian constitution like that of 1864, but the cabinet refused to endorse this measure. That afternoon a Committee of Safety, controlled by members of the Annexation Club, was organized at Thurston's house on Judd Street. The committee decided that the time had come to overthrow the monarchy and open annexation negotiations.

On the sixteenth the committee held a mass meeting at the armory. The meeting condemned the queen's conduct and empowered the committee to "further devise such ways and means as might be necessary to secure the permanent maintenance of law and order and the protection of life, liberty and property in Hawaii." That same afternoon the American minister to

Hawaii, John L. Stevens, who favored annexation, arranged for troops to land from the U.S.S. *Boston,* ostensibly to protect American life and property.

The following afternoon, January 17, 1893, the committee seized the government office building and read a proclamation establishing a provisional government under Judge Sanford B. Dole "until terms of union with the United States of America have been negotiated and agreed upon."

On the advice of friends, Queen Liliuokalani yielded, as she stated, "to the superior force of the United States of America . . . until such time as the Government of the United States shall, upon the facts being presented to it, undo the action of its representative and reinstate me in the authority which I claim as the constitutional sovereign of the Hawaiian Islands."

That evening armed volunteers gathered at the revolutionary headquarters in the government building. They sang "Solomon Levi," "The Battle Hymn of the Republic," and then rose to sing "My Country 'Tis of Thee." After the first stanza an orderly shouted, "Stop your damn noise. The queen has surrendered. Orders are to keep quiet." The revolution, and the Hawaiian monarchy, had come to an end.

Queen Liliuokalani, who reigned less than two years, survived until 1917. Her most memorable contribution to Hawaii occurred in 1878, long before she began her short reign. After a visit to friends on windward Oahu, at the foot of Waimanalo Pali, she paused while an officer in the party made an extended farewell to his sweetheart. On the way up the pali road she began to hum a song of farewell. By the time the members of the party arrived at Honolulu they were singing "Aloha Oe."

Chapter 10

Economic and Social Development, to 1900

DURING THE 98 YEARS of the united Hawaiian monarchy (1795-1893), the two main economic factors were the decline of the native population and the rise of sugar as Hawaii's biggest source of wealth. The first led to the recruiting of foreign laborers, which resulted in Hawaii's present polyglot population. The second led to close economic ties with and eventual annexation by the United States. Throughout, and despite both opposition and misrepresentation, the missionaries and their descendants had a major part in developing the economic resources of the Islands and in setting the social tone of community life there.

In the early days of the kingdom, Hawaii became a popular port of call to provision transient merchantmen. For a time American and other ships in the Northwest fur trade stopped at the Islands on their way westward to China, and starting about 1810 the Islands enjoyed a boom in the export of sandalwood to the Orient. But by about 1830 both of these sources of revenue had dwindled. Russian imperialists and agents of the Hudson's Bay Company drove American merchant adventurers from much of the Pacific Northwest. About the same time the valuable sandalwood forests had been thoroughly despoiled.

The arrival of the first whaleship in Hawaiian waters in 1819 brought both wealth and social chaos to the Islanders. By 1830 an average of 150 whalers a year touched Hawaiian ports, mainly Honolulu and Lahaina, but also Hilo and Kawaihae on the Big Island and Koloa on Kauai. In the years 1843-60 the average rose to well over 400. It reached its peak in 1846 when the American whale fleet as a whole had 736 ships, its greatest number, and when a total of 596 whalers entered Hawaiian ports. As many as 549 whalers came to Hawaii as late as 1859. Until the outbreak of the American Civil War in 1861, whaling was Hawaii's greatest source of wealth, so much so that Wyllie believed that without it "the Sandwich Islands would relapse into their primitive insignificance." But the native population paid a high price in disease and debauchery for the whaling revenue. Riots of serious proportions were not uncommon among the whaling crews. The continuing demand for firewood on the part of the whalers deforested many areas and created a serious problem of soil erosion. In addition, Hawaiian youths delighted in the zest of whaling or going to sea in other ships. In the late 1840's about a fifth of Hawaii's young *kanakas* were away at sea, a circumstance which certainly contributed to the decline of the native population.

Aside from sugar, which later became king of the Islands' economy, a number of diversified crops were tried with varying success. The ancient Hawaiians had raised sweet potatoes and taro, along with dogs, chickens, and swine, and these traditional staples continued. Early visitors to Hawaii introduced cattle, sheep, and goats (called *kaos* by natives, who mistook them for cows), as well as a number of vegetables and fruits.

A period of experimentation followed when, by often costly trials, farmers learned which produce was best suited to Hawaii's climate, labor supply, and market.

In 1825, John Wilkinson, an English agricultural expert and former West Indian planter, arrived in Honolulu on the same ship which carried home the remains of Kamehameha II and his queen. Wilkinson brought with him coffee trees from Rio de Janeiro, which were planted, along with sugar cane, in Manoa Valley, inland from Waikiki. The British consul general, Richard Charlton, also planted coffee there, with plants from Manila. In the late 1820's missionaries on the Kona coast of Hawaii began to grow coffee. Kona coffee later became one of Hawaii's most prized products. In 1842 coffee was grown successfully at Hanalei on Kauai. By 1848 the various plantations in the Islands were exporting almost thirty tons of coffee a year, in addition to coffee sold locally to residents and mariners. Ten years later a blight ruined the coffee production on Kauai, but it continued in Kona.

About 1840 serious efforts were made, especially on Maui, to raise white potatoes. The experiment prospered and reached boom proportions during the California Gold Rush of 1849, when potatoes, among other Hawaiian commodities, found a ready market at high prices on the West Coast. But in the years immediately following the boom collapsed and American producers captured the California market.

In the 1850's wheat-growing was attempted on Maui, and somewhat later on Hawaii. At one time the Islands had three flour mills; but misfortunes and uncertainties hampered this enterprise, and it did not succeed.

In the years 1836-45 an attempt was made to produce silk on Kauai. Two agriculturists planted thousands of mulberry slips, the standard food of silkworms, and imported machinery and silkworm eggs. Some silk was produced, but drought, heavy winds, and pests ruined the mulberry plants, and by 1845 the project was abandoned in favor of sugar. About the same time attempts were made, with limited success, to raise cotton and spin cotton cloth.

Between 1851 and 1884 Hawaii exported much *pulu*, a soft fiber of the tree fern, used as stuffing for pillows and mattresses. But this industry collapsed when it became known that *pulu* dust injured the lungs.

In the late 1850's planters made unsuccessful experiments with Oriental rice. But in the 1860's rice seed from South Carolina flourished. A boom followed, with rice being planted in abandoned taro patches. In some places farmers removed the taro and replaced it with rice. Despite fluctuations, rice became for many years Hawaii's second most valuable crop, after sugar, for export and for local consumption by Hawaii's growing Oriental population.

From time to time Hawaiian records mention pineapples, later to become a major crop in the Islands. But their cultivation in the mid-nineteenth century was haphazard and the fruit itself was mediocre.

Cattle brought to the Islands by Vancouver and others multiplied rapidly. Wyllie estimated their number in 1846 as 35,000 and twenty years later they numbered about 100,000, including about 40,000 running wild. Ranching for beef, tallow, and hides for the local and South American market became a profitable business. Sometime before 1830, Mexican or Spanish cowboys, called by the Hawaiians *paniolos* (from *Español*), came to the Islands to round up these wild and semiwild beasts. They brought with them the lasso and the deep saddle still used in the Islands, and they taught the natives how to drive cattle. In all probability they also introduced to Hawaii the traditional and exciting way of loading cattle aboard ship by swimming them through the waves, which reportedly originated in the Gulf of California. The Hawaiians adored ranching. It provided excitement flavored with real danger, for wild cattle can be, to say the least, threatening. Anyone who has galloped down a steep and rocky slope covered with thorny *kiawe* trees, bending low in the saddle with his right arm crooked forward to protect his face from the slashing *kiawe* thorns, felt the sticky heat of the windless gulches, and listened to the cattle braying and the lilting shouts of the cowhands in hot pursuit, will recognize a cattle drive for what it was and is—a grueling but rewarding sport. Even the occasional drenching in a shower is only a temporary annoyance, for the rain is warm and the wet clothes soon dry in the sunshine which follows. It is odd to contemplate that a large part of Hawaii, which evokes an image of palm trees, beaches, and blue surf, is actually given over to ranching. Here in the Crossroads of the Pacific one may follow the herd through dust clouds to the branding corral and encounter scenes and incidents typical of other states in the American West. As late as 1856, cattlemen in the Islands claimed correctly that ranching was at that time a greater source of wealth than sugar.

In the late 1850's enterprising merchants in Honolulu exploited the trade in guano (bird droppings used as fertilizer) found on desolate and waterless sandspit islands near the equator. Some profits were made from this dreary and exhausting trade. But the coming of the American Civil War cut off the Southern market. Shortly thereafter, for this and other reasons, the guano trade came to an end.

With the passing years, Hawaii's economy shared the general rising trend characteristic of the nineteenth century, with revenue from provisioning the whaleships, and from ranching, sugar, rice, coffee, *pulu,* and a few other commodities. In the years 1844-60, the value of Hawaii's exports increased almost fivefold, from $169,641, to $807,459.

In the 1830's the American missionaries had turned actively to the secular goal in their instructions to cover Hawaii with "fruitful fields and pleasant dwellings." At their annual meeting in 1838 they decided that they should "devote a portion of their time to instructing the natives into the best method of cultivating their lands, and of raising flocks and herds." In the next year they decided to earn part of their expenses by investing in and operating plantations and sugar mills. A number of missionaries, among them Bingham, Dr. Judd, and Richard Armstrong, participated in these ventures and tried, with varying and often disappointing results, to teach the Hawaiians how to farm their lands with profit.

In the summer of 1850 the Royal Hawaiian Agricultural Society was established to promote farming in the Islands. For the first five or six years of its existence the society was active and useful, with meetings, exhibits, and published reports. A number of prominent foreigners, among them Judge Lee, its first president, directed its activities. But in time the organization languished.

The California Gold Rush of 1849 brought a measure of unstable prosperity to the Islands. Natives and foreigners alike flocked from Hawaii to the gold fields. Prices soared. Some of the forty-niners even sent their laundry from the West Coast to Honolulu, and came themselves for a warm winter in the Islands. As Mrs. Judd reported, "Multitudes from California poured in upon us for food and shelter, from their own inclement regions. . . . All the hotels, boardinghouses, and untenanted buildings became full. Food grew scarce. Prices ran up exorbitantly high, and still the tide of immigration poured in. Flour was thirty dollars per barrel! . . . Spring came, the rain ceased, and the tide of humanity set back to the *El Dorado,* leaving the evil of high prices and increased wages for all kinds of labor."

Newspaper reports reflected skyrocketing optimism, and a boom began in potatoes and other commodities. But a sharp decline soon followed, and many planters and speculators went bankrupt. Mrs. Judd wrote sadly, "In August, 1851, it was stated, on good authority, that Hawaiian produce to the amount of four hundred thousand dollars could be furnished at short notice; but unfortunately the market was overstocked, and there were no purchasers or ships to take it to California. Irish potatoes rotted in the ground, and onions and other vegetables scarcely paid the expense of digging."

About 1860 the Pacific whaling industry declined because of a number of circumstances. Increasingly the old whaling grounds became fished out and the remaining whales were to be found mainly in remoter areas, among them the Arctic seas. The drilling of America's first successful oil well in Pennsylvania in 1859 made it possible, in the years to follow, for petroleum products to offer overwhelming competition to whale oil as an illuminant. Costs of outfitting and refitting whaleships rose. The American Civil War cut the Pacific whale fleet in half, and of those that stayed in Pacific waters some fifty were lost to Confederate cruisers, especially the *Alabama* and *Shenandoah*. After the war, over thirty whaleships were caught in the Arctic ice and had to be abandoned in 1871, and a dozen more were similarly lost in 1876.

The decline of the whaling industry caused much temporary economic distress in Hawaii. John S. Emerson reported, "All our means to help out our family support are suddenly cut off, as the whaling fleet has left the Islands. Beef which sold for $18 or $25 per head two years ago cannot now be sold for $10; within a few days Mr. Chamberlain has sold his whole herd of good cattle at $3.50 per head, and he threw in the calves."

The net result was to strike a blow at diversified farming in Hawaii. After 1860 farmers in the Islands turned increasingly to the large-scale production of sugar. The development of the sugar industry made Hawaii prosperous, but the decline in diversified agriculture had some unfortunate economic effects which still beset Hawaii's economy.

At the time of Cook's discovery in 1778, sugar grew naturally and plentifully in the Islands up to elevations of 3,500 feet, presumably brought to Hawaii on the "long voyages." Originally there were five varieties of native sugar, the most common being a white cane like the Tahitian.

The earliest sugar-making is said to have occurred in 1802, when a Chinese from a sandalwood ship produced some on

Lanai. The Spanish settler, Francisco de Paula Marin, who took a keen interest in agriculture, produced some molasses in 1817. Hawaii's first sizeable sugar plantation was that of John Wilkinson, who, in partnership with Governor Boki, planted many acres of cane in Manoa Valley in 1825. But Wilkinson's untimely death in the following year, coupled with a shortage of equipment, capital, and labor, led to the abandonment of this enterprise. About this time several foreign residents began to raise cane for the manufacture of rum, but the missionary interest stoutly opposed the project, and Kaahumanu ordered the fields destroyed.

Hawaii's first large-scale sugar plantation was established by the American firm of Ladd and Company at Koloa, Kauai, in 1835. Native labor was recruited at twelve and one-half cents a day, plus fish and *poi*. Local chiefs, angry that the plantation attracted their retainers, forbade the natives to work there and forbade also the sale of food to the plantation manager. The equipment was far from adequate. For lack of draft animals at one time as many as forty natives were hitched to a plow. After a year the manager complained, "I have had more annoyance from the chiefs and difficulties with the natives than I had thought it possible for a white man to bear." But the owners persevered. When it was reported in 1838 that they had produced two and one-half tons of sugar from a single acre, a higher yield than was usual in the West Indies, there was much enthusiastic praise of their success. Unfortunately Ladd and Company had a series of financial misfortunes. But under Dr. Robert W. Wood, who took possession of the Koloa Plantation in 1848, the enterprise moved swiftly forward.

Production of sugar in Hawaii increased rapidly. Exports rose from 4 tons in 1836 to 150 in 1845 and 722 in 1860. These exports were in addition to sugar sold locally, and they do not include substantial quantities of molasses exported, which amounted to 109,000 gallons in 1860.

The American Civil War, which gradually isolated Southern sugar from the world market, stimulated the already vigorous sugar industry in Hawaii. Exports of Hawaiian sugar increased over tenfold in the years 1860-65, from 722 to 7,659 tons. In the years to follow, despite a temporary recession, the sugar exports increased still further, and passed the 10,000-ton mark in 1871.

A number of technical improvements contributed heavily to the development of sugar in Hawaii, which had to compete with sugar grown in the Philippines and other areas where labor costs were much lower. A new deep plow and a centrifugal machine to separate sugar from molasses appeared in the early 1850's. Steam power to run the mills, extensive fertilization, and the vacuum pan to boil down sugar appeared in the 1860's. Hawaii's first extensive irrigation ditch for a sugar plantation was dug in 1856 at Lihue, Kauai, under the direction of William H. Rice. This ditch was ten miles long, and by means of a tunnel brought mountain water to the fields. About 1854 a better variety of cane was imported from Tahiti. It was called Lahaina cane after the port through which it first entered the Islands. One of its descendants, the celebrated H-109, produced fifteen tons of sugar per acre.

The sugar industry developed in an atmosphere of excitement and general efficiency. After about 1860 a change for the better took place in the caliber of many of Hawaii's white planters. Before that time the majority were traders turned planter, with little technical agricultural skill. They were, besides, bitterly hostile as a rule to the American mission and dissatisfied with the Hawaiian government in which former missionaries had a large influence. After about 1860 the main planters, with the notable exception of Spreckels, were either *kamaainas* or men who had lived for many years in the islands. Some were sons of missionaries, such as Samuel T. Alexander and Henry P. Baldwin. Others were foreigners of various nationalities who had settled in Hawaii, among them James Campbell of Ireland, Vlademar Knudsen of Norway, Paul Isenberg of Germany, and James Makee of the United States. These men were thoroughly familiar with Hawaii's problems, and, in contrast to their counterparts in the first half of the nineteenth century, tended to be generally more cordial to both the government and the missionary interest.

At this point it may be stated with emphasis that the new resident planters included both missionary descendants and other white foreigners. The old canard that the missionaries came to Hawaii to convert the heathen and ended by stealing, or buying at absurdly low prices, the best land of the natives is just that—a canard. Detailed and accurate scholarship has proved that the original missionaries received very little land from the natives, and some of what they received was in the form of payment for services to the government. Many died poor. One of them was offered, and refused, Manoa Valley in back of Waikiki. The similarity of the names of the original missionaries and a number of later wealthy families is sometimes merely a coincidence. The *Bishop* of the Bishop Estate was Charles R. Bishop, a banker, not the Reverend Artemas Bishop of the American mission. In other cases, the missionary descendants, born in Hawaii and ambitious to get ahead, merely took normal advantage of their headstart and through initiative and hard work became leaders in the second and later generations in developing the economy of the Islands, their original home. But old legends die hard, and this one is still repeated by professional liberals who have not taken the trouble to inform themselves about what really happened.

Hawaii's sugar industry had three major needs, a market, capital, and an efficient supply of labor. The reciprocity treaty with the United States, which went into effect in 1876, created a good market, and this market in time attracted the needed capital to Hawaii. The labor problem was far more serious.

Throughout the nineteenth century the native population continued to decline, from about 85,000 in 1850 to about 40,000 in 1890. Before the large influx of foreign laborers, the total population of the Islands fell to its lowest point probably in 1875 or 1876, when it stood at only about 55,000. Obviously a severe labor shortage was in the making. Wyllie commented gloomily in 1863, "Unless we get more population, we are a doomed nation."

Meanwhile, there were many complaints that the surviving natives were indolent and improvident. It is possible to overstate this situation, and the "laziness" of the natives has been somewhat exaggerated. In times of need, or in employments like ranching and seafaring which he enjoyed, the Hawaiian could and did work as hard as any other man. But he was certainly not suited to the discipline of the plantation. In 1846, Wyllie observed, "In the whole Islands you nowhere see natives at hard labor or regular labor, except for short intervals for the Kings and Landlords and at their own caprice. . . . It may safely be reported that the whole labor of the entire ablebodied population does not amount to four hours per day during the year." Probably that was a fair statement. In large part the unwillingness of the Hawaiian to work hard resulted from shock and loss of morale as he came into contact with the higher civilization of the white foreigners.

Upon occasion the Hawaiian became expert in avoiding work. There is much truth in the satiric statement of George W. Bates written in the 1850's: "No beast of prey watches his victim with a closer scrutiny than the kanaka watches his employer. In his presence he makes every effort to appear active and useful; but the very minute he disappears it is a signal for a general cessation of work, and one keeps a 'look-out' while the group indulges in every variety of gossip. On the reappearance of their master, the sentinel gives the alarm, and every man is found to be at work as though he meant never again to lay down his tools."

Responsible people in the Islands gave much thought to the labor problem. Judge Lee believed that the Islands could support five million people, but added, "There is one agent, however, that we require, who holds the key of success—the great brawny-armed, huge-fisted giant called *labor*." In 1850 the legislature forbade natives to emigrate without royal permission and legalized contract labor with a period of service of up to five years for natives and ten for foreigners. Under the terms of this act the Royal Hawaiian Agricultural Society arranged for the importation of some 300 Chinese coolies in the years 1851-52, to serve for five years at three dollars a month, plus food, shelter, and clothing. Including transport and maintenance, they cost the planters about nine dollars a month.

In 1855, Kamehameha IV decided that the coolies were unduly troublesome, as indeed some of them were, and advocated instead better medical care to check the decline in the Hawaiian population (a recommendation which led to the founding of Queen's Hospital) and the importation of natives from Polynesia. Some South Sea Islanders came to Hawaii as a consequence, including a few from Pitcairn Island, but they proved unsatisfactory.

In 1864 the Hawaiian government created the Bureau of Immigration to supervise the recruiting of foreign labor and to promote immigration in general. By the end of 1865, 1,306 Chinese coolies had come to Hawaii under contract. In 1868 the Hawaiian consul in Japan recruited 148 Japanese workers. One of the purposes of Kalakaua's trip around the world in 1881 was to investigate sources of foreign labor.

By 1890, Hawaii's labor problem was well on its way to solution. In the years 1877-90, about 55,000 laborers came to Hawaii. The 1890 census reported a total population of 90,000, including 15,000 Chinese, 12,000 Japanese, and 9,000 Portuguese.

With imported labor the Hawaiian sugar industry took giant steps forward, assisted technically by the Honolulu Iron Works, founded in 1853, and in matters requiring cooperation by the Planters' Labor and Supply Company, founded in 1882. Extensive irrigation projects materialized. In 1876-78, S. T. Alexander and H. P. Baldwin built the Hamakua ditch, which brought water from Mount Haleakala seventeen miles to the parched Haiku, Paia, and Grove Ranch plantations of central Maui. The ditch had a capacity of forty million gallons a day, and by a pipeline crossed gorges up to 450 feet deep. When the laborers refused to descend one gorge on ropes, Baldwin, who had lost an arm, led the way down, gripping the rope with one arm, and the men, humiliated by this daring act, followed. In later years other, even larger, ditches were built. Hawaii's sugar exports increased twelvefold in the years 1871-91, to 137,000 tons. So great was this rise in production that planters in the United States suspected (falsely) that the Hawaiian Kingdom was exporting as its own product sugar actually grown in other countries.

Other phases of Hawaii's economy also developed. After fitful and unsuccessful beginnings in the 1850's, regular inter-island steamship service was organized in 1860, with the 400-ton steamer *Kilauea*, operated at first by the Hawaiian Steam Navigation Company and later by the government. By 1890 the Inter-Island Steam Navigation Company and the Wilder Steamship Company (which merged in 1905) had fourteen steamers in service. Regular steamship service was established with San Francisco in 1867 and with Australia in 1870. Land transport also improved. A horse trail down the *pali* was built in 1845, and, after widening, was first used by a one-horse express wagon in 1861. But roads as a whole developed slowly on Oahu and elsewhere in the Islands. In 1888 work was started on a streetcar line, drawn by mules, in Honolulu. That same year the Oahu Railway and Land Company received a franchise to lay tracks between Honolulu and Ewa. At one time it was contemplated to build a railroad all around Oahu. On March 23, 1888, Princess Kaiulani turned a master switch and for the first time lit the streets of Honolulu with electricity. About this time Honolulu developed an extensive telephone system.

Throughout the nineteenth century Hawaii, and in particular Honolulu, acquired the amenities of life gradually and with deserved pride on the part of foreign residents who remembered well the rough conditions of the "old days." Much the same sort of phenomenon is part of the local history of other western American communities. By mid-century the natives generally wore conventional clothing, with women wearing the loose Mother Hubbard gown (*holoku*) common to Polynesia, although fish and vegetable peddlers among the men still appeared wearing only the loincloth (*malo*). The first newspaper in English printed west of the Rocky Mountains was the *Sandwich Island Gazette* (1836), and the first quarterly review published in the Pacific Ocean area, the *Hawaiian Spectator*, was published in the years 1838-39 on the mission press. In 1850, Honolulu residents organized an Atheneum Society with lectures and a library, and a circulating library followed three years later. Piano and singing lessons became available, along with concerts and theatrical performances by local or transient artists. In 1870 the government organized the Royal Hawaiian Band, for many years directed by Captain Henry Berger, a German, the composer of Hawaii's anthem, *Hawaii Ponoi*, who came to Honolulu in 1872. In 1871-72 the government built the Hawaiian Hotel (later called the Royal Hawaiian Hotel, but not to be confused with the present hotel of that name) at the corner of Hotel and Richards Streets in downtown Honolulu. Here was the first bid for the tourist trade.

In many respects social life in the Islands was like that of the antebellum South. Mrs. Judd captured exactly the spirit of Honolulu society in the early 1860's: "For amusements we have school festivals and examinations, agricultural exhibitions, ladies' fancy fairs, moonlight rides on horseback, sea bathing at the fashionable water-place, Waikiki, balls and parties for those who wish them, and two sewing societies." She added, in words which would delight the present-day Hawaii Visitors Bureau, "It may be said, with some qualification, that our sun always shines, our trees are always green, our trade-winds always blow, our atmosphere is always pure."

Chapter 11

The Provisional Government, Republic, and Annexation, 1893-1900

THE OVERTHROW of the Hawaiian monarchy and the dethroning of Queen Liliuokalani provoked a fierce controversy both in Hawaii and in the United States. The strange story of the long delay before the American annexation of Hawaii reveals the conflict of powerful forces in the last years of the nineteenth century. On the one hand, supporters of nationalism favored the queen and Hawaii for the Hawaiians. But supporters of that extension of nationalism known as imperialism or "manifest destiny" urged the United States to take the Islands. Other forces emerged. Advocates of democracy opposed restoring the monarchy in Hawaii. American sugar interests opposed annexation for economic reasons. At the same time other well-meaning Americans opposed annexation because of Hawaii's large Oriental population. In so doing they were evoking fear of the "Yellow Peril" with its roots in the medieval conquest of Jenghiz Khan. Political and personal conflicts on various levels complicated the issues and created further turbulence. Simple ignorance and irresponsible journalism distorted the whole affair and helped to create a false impression of Hawaii. On this and later occasions Hawaii suffered largely because people in high places were badly informed. The whole truth about these stormy years may never be known, for the heat generated by the conflicting issues still overlies all but the simplest accounts of what happened.

On January 19, 1893, two days after the Provisional Government was proclaimed, five commissioners of the new administration left Honolulu for Washington to negotiate the annexation of Hawaii by the United States. They were Charles L. Carter, William R. Castle, Joseph Marsden, Lorrin A. Thurston, and William C. Wilder. They reached San Francisco on January 28 and arrived in Washington on February 3. Secretary of State John W. Foster received them warmly, and eleven days later the annexation treaty was signed. On February 15, President Benjamin Harrison submitted it to the Senate with a message requesting immediate action. Haste was necessary for Harrison had been defeated by Grover Cleveland in the election of 1892 and his term of office would expire on March 4.

The treaty provided for the annexation of Hawaii as "an integral part" of the United States, which would assume Hawaii's debt, pay an annuity of $20,000 to Queen Liliuokalani, and grant outright the sum of $150,000 to Princess Kaiulani, the heiress-presumptive to the throne. The Hawaiian government would cede to the United States all government buildings and property. Further importation of Chinese labor to Hawaii was to be forbidden. Within a year all revenue and customs regulations of the United States would be in force.

Meanwhile in Honolulu events moved swiftly. On February 1, the American diplomatic representative, John L. Stevens, proclaimed Hawaii a protectorate of the United States. American flags appeared on the government buildings, the U.S.S.

Boston fired a salute, and American troops took regular stations ashore. Stevens was an enthusiastic annexationist. He wrote that day to Secretary of State Foster, "The Hawaiian pear is now fully ripe, and this is the golden hour for the United States to pluck it." He added that if annexation were delayed "these people, by their necessities, might be forced towards becoming a British colony." Several considerations influenced Stevens' decision. Among them were a demand by the Japanese consul in Hawaii for suffrage for the Japanese in the Islands and a rumor that Queen Liliuokalani might give them the vote in return for their political allegiance.

The pending treaty precipitated America's first great debate on imperialism. Much of the press which was expansionist and in favor of a big navy, urged Hawaii's annexation. The New York *Press* stated, "We must plant the stars and stripes in Honolulu." The New York *Independent* declared, "The ripe apple falls into our hands, and we would be very foolish if we should throw it away." The Washington *Star,* in reference to a rumor that Queen Liliuokalani had sought British assistance, asked dramatically, "Shall we take Hawaii and thereby prosper and magnify ourselves, or shall we let England take it, and thereby enfeeble and humiliate us?" On February 5 the New York *Tribune* asserted, "The popular verdict is clear, unequivocal and practically unanimous. Hawaii is welcome." Many specific annexationist arguments appeared—that it was the duty of the white race to colonize Hawaii, a typical imperialist theme, and that Hawaii's annexation was essential to America's national defense and expanding economy. A somewhat misleading annexationist jingle in questionable taste became popular, "Liliuokalani, give us your little brown hannie."

Part of the press, however, was outspoken in opposing annexation. The New York *Evening Post* criticized the haste with which the annexation treaty had been drawn in the last weeks of Harrison's administration and suggested that this "snap-annexation" gave "a sort of sunset glow" to the short remaining time of his presidential term. The Chicago *Herald* charged that annexation was a plot on the part of Hawaii's sugar interest, and added that because America was already predominant in Hawaii political union was unnecessary. The *Nation* reprinted a patronizing statement of the New York *Evening Post,* which advised the planters of Hawaii to continue "sending us your sugar and other tropical products, and sitting under your own fig-trees, in the full assurance that none will dare make you afraid."

t Cleveland took office on March 4, 1893. A thornorable and conscientious man, he was in principle o imperialism. As he later stated, "I regarded, and still regard, the proposed annexation of these islands as . . . a perversion of our national mission. The mission of our nation is to build up and make a greater country out of what we have, instead of annexing islands." His secretary of state, Walter Quintin Gresham, advised withdrawing the annexation treaty. Gresham disliked dealing with Hawaii's Provisional Government, composed, as he stated "of a lot of adventurers." On March 9, five days after he took office, Cleveland recalled the treaty from the Senate. Two days later he appointed James Henderson Blount of Georgia, a former congressman and former chairman of the House Foreign Affairs Committee, to investigate with "paramount" authority the circumstances of the Hawaiian revolution. Cleveland's motive, as he later stated, was to discover the truth and to vindicate America's "national honor, conscience, and love of justice." "Paramount" Blount, as he soon was called, arrived in Honolulu on March 29.

Meanwhile, Princess Kaiulani went to Washington from England, where she was in school. Her guardian, Theophilus Harris Davies, an Englishman long prominent in Hawaiian sugar, accompanied her on her trip. He was opposed to annexation and issued an appeal in her name to restore the monarchy. This appeal stated sentimentally, "Unbidden I stand upon your shores today, where I thought so soon to receive a royal welcome . . . strong in the strength of seventy million people, who in this free land will hear my cry, and will refuse to let their flag cover dishonor to mine." This attractive and charming young woman made a particularly favorable impression on Mrs. Cleveland. Princess Kaiulani died in 1899 at the early age of twenty-four.

In Honolulu, Blount conferred with Sanford Dole and on the first of April ordered the United States flag lowered from the Government Building. The ceremony took place at eleven o'clock in the morning. At that time many other American flags were displayed in Honolulu and many residents wore buttons and badges of red, white, and blue. The San Francisco *Chronicle* reported, "A trim bandsman in white stepped forward, glanced at the clock and raised the bugle to his lips. There was a long, ringing note or two, and then the flag, emblem of all Hawaii's new-born hopes, fell from its place. All over the throng came perfect silence. One heard the rustle of palm leaves in the wind."

This cruel event evoked loud protest in the United States.

A statement in the New York *Commercial Advertiser* reflected the dismay, and also the prejudices, of a large segment of the American people. "In ordering Old Glory pulled down at Honolulu, President Cleveland turned back the hands on the dial of civilization. . . . The dream of an American republic at the crossroads of the Pacific . . . has been shattered by Grover Cleveland, the Buffalo liliputian! He has ordered his man Blount, a Southern reactionary, to allow the gathering fabric of a stable government at Honolulu and of nobler things to fall to pieces. He has declared . . . that the Hawaiian Islands shall be tossed a prize into the arena of international strife, for which the Japanese, the English, and heaven knows who else may scramble and quarrel."

Blount conducted an inquiry and concluded that the revolution could not have succeeded without the collusion of the American minister, John L. Stevens, who had ordered the landing of American troops. He also concluded that a majority of the natives favored the restoration of the monarchy.

Blount, whose home was in Macon, Georgia, left Honolulu on August 8. The Hawaiian Band, led by Henry Berger, appropriately saluted him by playing "Marching Through Georgia."

In Washington, President Cleveland decided, on the basis of Blount's report, that the United States should restore Queen Liliuokalani to the throne. Although American public opinion was divided on the issue, the Atlanta *Constitution* reported scornfully, "The Democratic party has not been in the habit of restoring monarchies anywhere, and as Mr. Gresham is not a Democrat he may have made a mistake in this matter."

Cleveland appointed a new American minister to Hawaii, Albert Sydney Willis, of Kentucky. His instructions were to present himself to the Provisional Government and then tell the queen that President Cleveland wished to restore her to power if she would show clemency to her opponents. If she agreed, Willis was to request the Provisional Government to abdicate in her favor. If either refused he was to refer the matter to the State Department for further instructions.

In his first interview with Queen Liliuokalani on November 13, Willis found that she was unwilling to grant an amnesty. She stated, "There are certain laws of my government by which I shall abide. My decisions would be as the law directs, that such persons should be beheaded and their property confiscated." Willis persevered, and just before Christmas received from her written assurance that she would grant an amnesty and assume the obligations of the Provisional Government. Willis on December 20 called on Dole and the cabinet and demanded that the Provisional Government surrender its powers to Queen Liliuokalani. In a long and clear reply, dated December 23, Dole refused, saying, "I am instructed to inform you, Mr. Minister, that the Provisional Government of the Hawaiian Islands respectfully and unhesitatingly declines to entertain the proposition of the President of the United States that it should surrender its authority to the ex-Queen."

The situation, as Cleveland realized, had reached an impasse. The Provisional Government, in office for almost a year, had a strong hold on the Islands. Further, American public opinion would not tolerate the use of military force against fellow Americans in Hawaii in order to restore a Polynesian queen. Tension remained high in Hawaii until it was learned that Cleveland had referred the whole matter to the American Congress on December 18.

A noisy debate followed, with much colorful and strident editorializing in the newspapers. The net result of the verbiage and clamor was that both the Senate and the House voted for non-interference of the United States in Hawaiian affairs.

The members of the Provisional Government, realizing that they had failed in their cherished objective of making Hawaii part of the United States, decided to establish a republic and to wait patiently for annexation at some future date. On March 15, 1894, an act was passed to call a constitutional convention.

This body met on May 30 and considered a constitution drafted mainly by Dole and Thurston. The new constitution was approved on July 3 and became effective the day following.

The constitution named Dole as president of the Republic of Hawaii with a term of office of six years. Dole took office on July 4 in an impressive ceremony. Chief Justice Albert Francis Judd administered the oath of office, a large Hawaiian flag flew, and the band played "Hawaii Ponoi." The executive power was vested in the president and a four-man cabinet appointed by him. Members of the two-house legislature had to be literate, in either English or Hawaiian, and had to take an oath of loyalty to the republic. Property qualifications were established, higher for members of the senate than for members of the house of representatives, and also for those voting for senators. The object of the constitution-makers was to exclude from politics Orientals and other recently arrived contract laborers, and to keep control of the state in the hands of people favorable to annexation. The conservative nature of this policy was indicated by Dole in his inaugural address when he expressed the hope that "freedom shall never come to mean license in the vocabulary of the Republic."

Early in 1895 the republic survived a minor revolution. Supporters of Liliuokalani, including Robert W. Wilcox and Samuel Nolwein, conspired to overthrow the government. The rebels landed their guns from the schooner *Wahlberg*, which had arrived from San Francisco some time before, at Kahala, east of Diamond Head, then a dusty and thinly settled area. On the evening of January 6 they began to move along the shore toward Honolulu. A sharp skirmish with government supporters followed, in which a distinguished and well beloved partisan of the republic, Charles L. Carter, was killed.

In the next few days some fighting continued, with a field gun firing at Diamond Head assisted by a second gun mounted on a tug at sea. Within two weeks the revolution had been completely crushed. Some 200 persons were arrested, including the queen, who formally renounced the throne. A military court tried the prisoners for treason and lesser crimes. Three death sentences were made, but the condemned persons later received reprieves. By the end of 1895 all persons imprisoned because of involvement in the revolt were released. Queen Liliuokalani received a conditional pardon on September 7. Its success in putting down the revolt and its clemency in dealing with the insurgents put the republic in a position of political and moral strength in the Islands.

About this time increasing prosperity came to Hawaii. The Wilson-Gorman tariff of 1894 abolished the sugar-bounty system and in effect restored the Reciprocity Treaty. With tariff preference restored, Hawaiian sugar boomed. As before, contract laborers streamed to the Islands, in particular from Japan. By 1896, Japanese laborers in Hawaii numbered 24,407, nearly a quarter of Hawaii's population. This situation caused much concern among the Hawaiian authorities, and attempts were made to find other sources of labor. Italians, American Negroes, and Armenians were considered.

In 1896-97 friction arose between the Japanese government and the Republic of Hawaii. In 1896 the Hawaiian legislature passed (but Dole later vetoed) a bill which put an almost prohibitive tariff on Japanese *sake*, a drink popular with the Japanese contract laborers. In March, 1897, Hawaiian immigration officials refused to admit 1,175 Japanese laborers because of fraudulent practices on the part of the Japanese emigration companies. The Japanese government, in a confident mood because of its victory (1894-95) over China, protested sharply and in May, 1897, sent a warship, the *Naniwa,* to Honolulu. Wild rumors spread that this vessel would cooperate with the Japanese laborers ashore to attack the Islands.

In Washington the Hawaiian authorities had long agitated for annexation, and the Hawaiian legislature had passed a resolution in favor of annexation the year before. The diplomatic crisis with Japan sharpened the annexation issue, for there was talk that Japan might take over the Islands. The Republican administration of President William McKinley was sympathetic to annexation. McKinley stated, "We need Hawaii just as much and a good deal more than we did California. It is manifest destiny." On June 16 an annexation treaty, drafted by the former American secretary of state, John W. Foster, was signed and sent to the Senate with a supporting message from McKinley and the present secretary of state, John Sherman. The Hawaiian government acted promptly. The treaty passed the Hawaiian senate and was signed by President Dole on September 10.

In the meantime the Japanese government protested sharply that the treaty upset the *status quo* in the Pacific, jeopardized the treaty rights of Japanese subjects in Hawaii, and made more difficult the settlement of Japan's pending diplomatic differences with the Hawaiian government. But by December the Japanese government withdrew its protest, and in due course settled its differences with the Hawaiian government on receiving an indemnity of $75,000 in July, 1898.

The real problem lay with the United States Senate, where the American sugar interests revived all the old familiar arguments against admitting Hawaii to the United States. Claus Spreckels, now prominent in the American sugar trust, agitated powerfully against annexation. It soon appeared that Democrats in the Senate would block the treaty, for a two-thirds vote was needed for ratification. Richard Olney, secretary of state under Cleveland, reported that the whole annexation scheme was "in the soup." Reports from the Hawaiian press stated that it was "dead as a door nail." The *Nation* characterized it as "dead beyond the hope of resurrection."

To further the cause of annexation President and Mrs. Dole made a trip to Washington. They left on January 7, 1898, and returned on March 4. In Washington, President McKinley entertained them at a state dinner in their honor. They met congressmen and other officials and in general made an excellent impression. The New York *Outlook,* which was lukewarm toward annexation, commented significantly, "It is unique in the history of the United States that a ruler should come from another nation offering to lay down his own office in order that his country may become an integral part of the nation."

Proponents of annexation decided to force the issue through by a joint resolution, which needed only a simple majority in both houses of Congress, a method used in the annexation of Texas in 1845. On March 16 a resolution in favor of annexation was introduced in the Senate, and on May 4 a similar resolution was introduced in the House.

The outbreak of the Spanish-American War on April 25 following the sinking of the *Maine* on February 15 created a furore of expansionist sentiment and certainly influenced American public opinion in favor of annexing Hawaii, especially as it underscored Hawaii's strategic usefulness in the Pacific. American troops on their way to the Philippines found a warm welcome in Hawaii. They attended a huge picnic, some of them chanting, "We want pie." They rode free on Honolulu's street cars, wrote thousands of letters home on the stationery of the Hawaiian government, and mailed them home postage free. The newly formed Red Cross organization in Hawaii offered its services to troops in transit.

Expansionists like Alfred T. Mahan, the distinguished exponent of the importance of sea power, revived the old argument that the Hawaiian Islands were America's first line of defense in the Pacific. In the House of Representatives, Henry R. Gibson urged fervently, "Manifest Destiny says, 'Take them in.' The American people say, 'Take them.' Obedient to the voice of the people, I shall cast my vote to take them in."

The House resolved in favor of annexation on June 15, 1898, by a large majority, 209 to 91. On July 6 the Senate passed the joint resolution by 42 to 21. President McKinley signed it on July 7, saying, "Annexation is not change; it is consummation." At long last Hawaii was part of the United States of America.

The next day Cleveland commented sourly, "Hawaii is ours. As I look back upon the first steps in this miserable business, I am ashamed of the whole affair." He added with a note of resignation, "However, I know of nobody who can stand it better than I. That's one way of looking at it—and perhaps as comfortable, and as good a way as any other."

When the news about annexation reached Hawaii on July 13,

it was received, so the American Minister Harold M. Sewall reported, "with unbounded enthusiasm." Shouting crowds thronged the streets. Factory whistles blew, fire bells sounded, and firecrackers added their sharp clatter to the celebration. At the Government Building cannon fired a 100-gun salute. The band played American tunes. At one point Henry Berger handed his baton to Dr. John S. McGrew, long an ardent advocate of annexation, and indeed known as the Father of Annexation, who conducted the band in "The Star-Spangled Banner." That night there was a great bonfire at the foot of Punchbowl.

The formal transfer of sovereignty took place on August 12, 1898, a date which many *kamaainas* still fondly remember. Some of the older ones proudly recall standing in the crowd and watching the ceremonies with damp eyes.

President Dole received from Minister Sewall a certified copy of the joint resolution, and then formally ceded the sovereignty of the Republic of Hawaii to the United States. The Hawaiian Band played "Hawaii Ponoi," and the Hawaiian flag was lowered. At noon the band of the U.S.S. *Philadelphia* played "The Star-Spangled Banner," and the American flag was raised, the same flag which Blount had lowered five years before, given to Dole by an American naval officer for safekeeping at that time. Chief Justice Judd then administered the oath of office to Dole and the cabinet.

For the next two years the republic's government administered the Islands until the detailed process of annexation was completed. The American Congress had not yet decided on the form of government for Hawaii as part of the United States. There were other problems. Hawaii's diplomatic agents abroad, for example, had to be recalled. It was not until April 30, 1900, that President McKinley approved the act establishing the Territory of Hawaii.

Chapter 12

The United States Territory of Hawaii, 1900-41

THE ANNEXATION RESOLUTION of 1898, called the Newlands Resolution after its sponsor, Senator F. G. Newlands of Nevada, stated in part, "Until Congress shall provide for the government of such islands, all the civil, judicial, and military powers exercised by the officers of the existing government in said islands shall be vested in such person or persons and shall be exercised in such manner as the President of the United States shall direct." For almost two years President Dole and his associates continued to govern Hawaii, and during this interim period the government functioned so well that few people in Hawaii had reason to notice the formal cession of sovereignty to the United States.

The Newlands Resolution also stated, "The President shall appoint five commissioners, at least two of whom shall be residents of the Hawaiian Islands, who shall, as soon as reasonably practicable, recommend to Congress such legislation concerning the Hawaiian Islands as they shall deem necessary or proper." Accordingly President McKinley appointed three congressmen, Senator Shelby M. Cullom of Illinois, Senator John T. Morgan of Alabama, and Representative R. R. Hitt. The Hawaiian residents appointed by McKinley were President Dole and Judge Walter F. Frear, who later became Hawaii's third territorial governor.

The five commissioners met in Hawaii and conducted hearings. In December, 1898, they presented their report to Congress, including a proposed constitution for the Territory of Hawaii. For a number of reasons Congress was slow to act, and the bill making Hawaii an incorporated Territory of the United States was not signed by McKinley until April 30, 1900. This Organic Act went into effect on June 14, 1900. At that time the United States had four other territories, Alaska, Arizona, New Mexico and Oklahoma. Many people, in particular President Dole, assumed that territorial status for Hawaii would inevitably result in statehood at some future date.

Hawaii's new constitution provided for a governor and a secretary appointed by the President of the United States, with the secretary serving in the capacity of lieutenant-governor. The governor appointed the department heads of his administration. The President appointed the judges in the territorial supreme, circuit, and federal district courts, and the chief justice of Hawaii's supreme court appointed the other magistrates. There was a bicameral legislature, a senate with fifteen members and a house of representatives with thirty members. The United States Congress had the right to review territorial legislation, much as the British Privy Council had had the right to review the legislation of the American colonies before the Revolution. Voting was by universal manhood suffrage, with citizens of the republic becoming citizens of the United States.

The proposed constitution contained a property qualification for voters which might have eased the political difficulties of the early 1900's, but the Congress removed this provision.

President McKinley wisely appointed Dole as Hawaii's first territorial governor. Dole was inaugurated with appropriate ceremonies at the capitol on June 14, 1900.

At this time and for the next two decades Hawaiians and part-Hawaiians dominated the electorate, since Hawaii's alien Oriental population was not eligible for citizenship. Although Republican and Democratic parties had been formed, a Home Rule party controlled the first legislature and sent the former rebel, Robert W. Wilcox, as Hawaii's voteless delegate to Congress. But as it happened Wilcox made a mediocre impression in Washington. Congressmen interested in Hawaiian affairs consulted instead the local representative of the Honolulu Merchants' Association and Chamber of Commerce.

Meanwhile the Home Rule party revived the slogan of Walter Murray Gibson, "Hawaii for the Hawaiians." In general the party proved itself lacking in responsibility, and abuses reminiscent of King Kalakaua's reign began to reappear. The legislature, which was in session 129 days, argued pointlessly over matters such as jail delivery and the poll tax, and spent so much time discussing a tax on female dogs that it has become known as the "Lady Dog Legislature."

Of more serious consequence was its refusal to vote the necessary taxes and its joint resolution to the President of the United States charging Dole with incompetence and voting a lack of confidence in him. Dole naturally expressed his displeasure with such conduct.

The charges and counter-charges set off a fiery debate in the American press. President Theodore Roosevelt (McKinley having been assassinated in September, 1901), requested Dole to come to Washington to report on Hawaii's troubled political situation. Dole complied, and spent an evening with the President discussing Hawaiian affairs in a friendly and informal atmosphere. Roosevelt later made an official statement expressing his confidence in Dole's administration, and Dole returned triumphantly to the islands in June, 1902.

The whole affair discredited the Home Rule party. In the election held in the fall of 1902 the Republicans obtained a substantial majority in the legislature, which they retained until 1946. The Home Rule party declined and later disappeared. Wilcox was defeated as delegate by Prince Jonah Kuhio Kalanianaole, a nephew of Queen Liliuokalani and a chief in his own right. Prince Kuhio, known familiarly as "Prince Cupid," continued to serve as delegate until his death in 1922. Many *kamaainas* recall fondly the Hawaiian hospitality extended to them in Washington by the prince and his charming consort, Elizabeth.

In due course the new Territory of Hawaii took steps to create a system of local government. The first legislature in 1901 passed a badly conceived bill to establish county governments, but Dole blocked it with a pocket veto. The absence of a formal scheme of local administration drew pointed criticism from the United States Senate. A county government bill passed in 1903 was declared unconstitutional, and county governments were not finally set up until two years later. In the years to follow much friction arose between the central government and the various local administrations. These problems and tensions were by no means confined to Hawaii. Other territories of the United States as well as newly admitted states had comparable administrative difficulties in the years of their formative period.

In 1903, on the death of Judge Morris M. Estee, presiding officer of the Federal District Court in Hawaii, Dole resigned as governor of the territory. He succeeded Estee in the Federal District Court until 1916, when he ended a long and distinguished career of public service to Hawaii. Sanford Dole died in 1926. Many people in the Islands still recall his handsome face and long beard, and speak with respect of his tact and integrity.

The secretary of the territory, George R. Carter, succeeded Dole and became Hawaii's second territorial governor. He served in 1903-7. One of his major tasks, inherited from his predecessor, was to guide the inexperienced legislators and in so doing to help the young territory establish a sound administration. In this difficult assignment he was extremely successful.

Hawaii's third territorial governor was Walter F. Frear (1907-13) formerly chief justice of Hawaii's Supreme Court. His administration was prudent. He was particularly interested in homesteading and in public works.

During Hawaii's first decade as a part of the United States, the army established itself firmly in the Islands. On August 16, 1898, four days after the formal cession of sovereignty, the first garrison of United States troops landed in Oahu. These troops, and others who followed on the next day, consisted of the First New York Volunteer Infantry and the Third Battalion, Second U.S. Volunteer Engineers, mobilized for service in the war against Spain. They established temporary quarters called

Camp McKinley near Kapiolani Park in back of Waikiki, close to the site of Honolulu's present zoo. Troops of the regular army later relieved them. Camp McKinley, never meant to be a permanent garrison, was occupied for several years until such time as regular military posts could be built.

The territory's first permanent garrison was Fort Shafter (named after a celebrated American hero of the Spanish-American War), on the Kahuiki Military Reservation west of Honolulu and near Pearl Harbor. Some of its buildings were occupied in 1907, but for years thereafter Honolulu residents complained about the rude and jerry-built appearance of many of the shacks serving as barracks.

Before the outbreak of World War I, the United States Army in Hawaii had developed a plan for the military defense of Honolulu Harbor and Pearl Harbor with a series of forts. In addition to Fort Shafter, the army's headquarters, the army in time established Fort Armstrong at the entrance to Honolulu Harbor on Kaakaukukui Reef; Fort De Russy at Waikiki; Fort Ruger on Diamond Head; and Forts Kamehameha and Weaver near Pearl Harbor. In 1909, Schofield Barracks, named after an ardent American annexationist, General John McAllister Schofield, and located on the Leilehua Plateau in the middle of Oahu, was first occupied. Eventually Schofield Barracks became the biggest garrison in the United States. Its location, freshened by the trade winds, is moderately cool and pleasant.

The United States had had the right to use Pearl Harbor since 1887, but this right was not exercised until after annexation. This large, fan-shaped, and landlocked harbor is certainly the best in the Pacific and one of the best in the world. The natives called it *Wai Momi* (Pearl River), because it contained vast beds of pearl oysters, and for many years residents of Oahu had used it as a yachting basin. Establishing a naval base there presented two main problems—dredging the narrow channel at its entrance and constructing docks and other installations. In 1900 the United States Congress first appropriated funds to improve Pearl Harbor, and in 1908 Congress approved it as a naval base.

The channel-dredging was completed in 1911, and on December 14 of that year the U.S.S. *California* entered the harbor, the first large ship to make use of this famous base. Appropriate ceremonies, including music from the Hawaiian Band under Berger, along with numerous whistle salutes, marked this auspicious occasion.

Meanwhile work was well under way on roads, docks, and industrial installations. In addition the base acquired an administration building, a coaling station, a floating crane, a powder magazine, and quarters for its enlisted and commissioned personnel. In 1909 work was started on a huge drydock, over 800 feet long and 100 feet wide. Natives shook their heads and muttered that no good would come of this installation located over the home of the shark queen. As it happened, their forebodings were substantiated. In February, 1913, after four years' work, the unfinished structure collapsed. Engineers blamed the disaster on hydraulic pressure, but the Hawaiians had another, simpler explanation. Nonetheless, work was resumed, and the drydock was completed in 1919.

In 1917 the army established an aviation center at Fort Kamehameha and a field on Ford Island in Pearl Harbor (later turned over to the navy). Others followed, among them Wheeler Field near Schofield Barracks and Hickham Field near Pearl Harbor.

Hawaii's fourth territorial governor, and its first Democrat in that high office, was Lucius E. Pinkham, the former president of the Board of Health, appointed by Woodrow Wilson. His term of office extended from November, 1913, to June, 1918. Naturally problems arising from the World War occupied much of his attention, but he also took a keen interest in draining the swamps in back of Waikiki and in establishing a community center in Honolulu—projects actually executed by his successors.

World War I, unlike World War II, had little direct impact on the Pacific. Japan entered the war in 1914 on the Allied side, and in this era of comparatively slow travel the Islands seemed remote indeed from the European battlefields. A Honolulu doctor, who volunteered his services to the American Ambulance Corps and worked, along with his wife, in France between July, 1915, and October, 1916, reported somewhat sadly on his journey homeward, "If the realization of what the war meant was feeble in New York, it faded away as one went West, until on the Pacific coast we found that the war was almost an unusual topic of conversation."

Before the entrance of the United States into the war in 1917, residents of Hawaii made a substantial contribution in such organizations as the War Relief Committee, formed in 1914, and in the Red Cross. Meanwhile, patriotic leaders took steps to strengthen the National Guard of Hawaii. A dramatic incident occurred in 1916, when several German ships which had taken refuge in Honolulu Harbor were found to have been sabotaged by their crews.

After the United States entered the war the National Guard entered federal service and relieved regular army troops stationed in the Islands. Almost 10,000 residents of Hawaii served in the armed forces, mainly at home but some overseas. The war brought to Hawaii the familiar liberty loans, home gardens, and meatless days. Red Cross volunteers in white uniforms and caps made surgical dressings in the throne room of Iolani Palace. The war also disrupted travel to and from the mainland, and the tourist trade almost disappeared. Other changes occurred. The old Royal Hawaiian Hotel in downtown Honolulu became the Army and Navy YMCA. An incident with important economic consequences took place when a new firm, American Factors, Ltd., took over the assets of the German sugar firm of Hackfeld and Company.

During the war, on November 11, 1917, Queen Liliuokalani died at the age of seventy-nine in her spacious home, Washington Place, later to become the official residence of the governors of Hawaii. During her last years she had spent much time on the mainland, vainly trying to obtain damages from the United States government. Nonetheless, she died in comfortable circumstances with a pension from the Territory of Hawaii. She died without bitterness, having long since become reconciled to both Lorrin Thurston and Sanford Dole. As a token of their enduring respect and devotion, Hawaiian women came to Washington Place daily before her death to present her with flower *leis*.

Charles J. McCarthy, Hawaii's fifth territorial governor and second Democrat in that post, served in the years 1918-21. He completed many improvements recommended by Governor Pinkham, and took a strong stand in favor of statehood for the Islands. His successor, Wallace R. Farrington, a Republican appointed by President Warren Harding and re-appointed by President Calvin Coolidge, served in the years 1921-29. His tenure of office fell in the era of postwar prosperity and would-be normalcy. The times were quiet, and the achievements steady but unspectacular, as they were for the most part in the rest of the United States. With the war won, and the world apparently safe for democracy, improvement and expansion but not radical change seemed to be the order of the day. Farrington busied himself with administrative and fiscal reform, which certainly strengthened the territorial government. The threat of carpetbagging seemed remote and home rule seemed assured when Congress passed in 1921 legislation requiring important territorial and federal officeholders, except the secretary, to have resided in Hawaii for three years prior to taking office. Public and private construction proceeded on a large scale. The women's Outdoor Circle campaigned successfully to prohibit billboard advertising in 1927, then undertook an ambitious program to beautify the roads with trees and shrubs.

In the early 1920's there was much agitation, warmly supported by Prince Kuhio among others, to encourage homesteading on the part of the Hawaiians and part-Hawaiians, many of whom lived precariously in substandard city districts. In response to this agitation Congress passed in 1921 the Hawaiian Homes Commission Act. Much energy and treasure went into the noble project of returning the natives to the land, and ended by producing only meager results. The inescapable fact of the matter seems to be that the Hawaiians are not suited to farming; and that small-scale and diversified farming was not suitable for Hawaii in that stage of its development. Hawaiian homesteaders on Molokai, for example, survived mainly because of a mutually advantageous agreement with pineapple companies who produced and then bought fruit raised on homestead land. At least—and to sum up a complex and bewildering subject—homesteading in Hawaii has not so far been a success.

Governor Lawrence M. Judd, a grandson of Dr. G. P. Judd, took office in July, 1929, as an appointee of President Herbert Hoover. During his administration, in particular after 1931, the navy undertook an extensive project to enlarge and improve the base at Pearl Harbor, since maneuvers in the 1920's had demonstrated that only a few battleships could be accommodated there. In time, and with ominous overtones of future disaster, facilities at Pearl Harbor were enlarged to the point that it could contain the entire Pacific fleet. Navy and Marine air stations were also established at Kaneohe, on the windward side of Oahu, and at Barber's Point to the east of Pearl Harbor.

In the fall of 1929 with the stock market crash in Wall Street the Great Depression began and smashed to splinters the normalcy era. Hawaii shared with the rest of the United States the blighting effect of the lean years which followed. Governor Judd had the difficult and distasteful task of supervising retrenchment in the territory's budget. Meanwhile, as elsewhere in America, unemployment reached critical proportions.

Other events followed which, taken together, made Governor

Judd's administration one of the most troubled since the formation of the territory. In 1931 the Massie case convulsed the Islands and the nation. A group of ruffians raped the wife of a young naval officer in Honolulu. At the trial the evidence was so inconclusive that the jury could reach no verdict. Before a second trial was begun, the naval officer, his mother-in-law, and two sailors killed one of the defendants. At their trial they were convicted of manslaughter and sentenced to imprisonment for ten years. Governor Judd then commuted this sentence to one hour.

Much controversy existed in Hawaii about the case, as was only natural under the circumstances. But the controversy was far less important than the publicity which accompanied it. In short, the Massie case became a catastrophe for Hawaii.

Journalists and sensation seekers combined to keep it boldly in the headlines in the American press. There was much wild talk about Hawaiian "savages" and the "unwritten law." The impression prevailed that Hawaii was a place where it was unsafe for a woman to venture in public unescorted. In the excitement it was conveniently overlooked that rape and lynching were by no means confined to the Hawaiian Islands. Defenders of Hawaii found it hard to make themselves heard and believed, for at that time the Islands were little known on the mainland.

In any case the United States Senate requested Seth W. Richardson, an assistant United States attorney general, to investigate. Richardson found nothing to justify the lurid and irresponsible rumors prevalent about Hawaii, but his report cited some defects in law enforcement in the Islands. A crime commission appointed by Governor Judd in 1930, before the Massie case occurred, had already made a similar investigation, and corrective measures were already in progress.

Richardson recommended some legal reforms for Hawaii. He also recommended repeal of the requirement that appointed officials of the territory be residents. A bill embodying this recommendation was introduced in Congress in April, 1932. The Navy demanded a commission form of government which resulted in a bill to put Hawaii largely under joint Army-Navy control. Neither bill became law. In 1933, Franklin D. Roosevelt asked Congress for authority to appoint a non-resident as governor of Hawaii, but a bill to that effect, introduced in the House of Representatives, was not passed.

To Islanders these proceedings were a serious threat to home rule. Islanders made a stout defense of their position and passed legislation in 1931, 1932, and 1933 reforming parts of the law and its means of enforcement. The whole affair contained a full measure of bitterness, and some *kamaainas* believed that the Navy had tried to smear Hawaii in order to justify the misconduct of a naval officer.

In the years 1934-42, Joseph B. Poindexter, a former federal judge, served as Hawaii's eighth territorial governor. He was the third Democrat appointed to that post. Much of his first term, to 1938, was concerned with the depression. In this period the New Deal established its various agencies for economic relief and recovery, which operated in Hawaii much as they did in other parts of the United States. Much useful, and some useless, work was accomplished, since these agencies tended to be more concerned with stimulating the flow of money in the community than in effecting long-range economic improvements. In Hawaii, as elsewhere, this policy, which seemed wasteful to many, was the subject of much debate.

Just as Hawaii was starting to recover, the United States Congress struck a blow at Hawaii's economy with the Jones-Costigan Sugar Control Act, which clearly discriminated against Hawaiian sugar. This measure, which went into effect on June 8, 1934, attempted to prevent overproduction, but mainland sugar interests managed to get fixed quotas, while Hawaii was put with United States possessions and foreign countries, with its quota determined by the secretary of agriculture. The act provided that if the quota were further reduced, the reductions would take place in the foreign and overseas areas. Other provisions of the act were equally discriminatory.

The secretary of agriculture, Henry A. Wallace, an ardent New Dealer, set Hawaii's sugar quota about 8 per cent below its normal production level of recent years. This situation caused much elation among mainland sugar producers, but it made the Americans in Hawaii fighting mad. The Jones-Costigan Act, in effect, declared that residents of the territory were second-class citizens, to be treated on the same level as foreigners. The act, by way of understatement, did not contribute to Mr. Roosevelt's popularity in Hawaii.

Hawaii's sugar producers instituted a suit in the supreme court of the District of Columbia, on the ground that the Jones-Costigan Act denied them their constitutional rights as Americans. Justice Jennings Bailey dismissed the suit. He admitted that Hawaii was an "integral part" of the United States, but he insisted that Congress had full power to legislate for Hawaii and was entitled to discriminate against it. The argument was, to say the least, peculiar, for "integral part" and "discriminate" make strange bedfellows.

The sugar producers declared their intention of appealing Bailey's decision, but a compromise was reached with the Secretary of Agriculture, who raised Hawaii's quota. Nonetheless, some *kamaainas* were disappointed that the sugar interest did not carry the fight to the United States Supreme Court in order to clarify Hawaii's status in the nation.

About this time many Americans in Hawaii became seriously concerned with their constitutional position as residents of a territory. In the recent past they had been subjected to the threat of carpetbagging, the smear in the press as the result of the Massie case, and economic discrimination in the Jones-Costigan Act. They were tired of being treated as second-class citizens, and resolved that the only real solution to their difficulties lay in becoming a full-fledged state.

Chapter 13

The Melting Pot

THE SIMPLE FACTS about Hawaii's polyglot population in 1900-1940 are presented in the following table.

POPULATION OF HAWAII, 1900-1940

(By Numbers)

	1900	1910	1920	1930	1940
Japanese	61,115	79,675	109,274	139,631	157,905
Caucasian	26,252	39,158	49,140	73,702	103,791
Hawaiian and Part-Hawaiian	38,254	38,547	41,750	50,860	64,310
Filipino	—	2,361	21,031	63,052	52,569
Chinese	25,762	21,674	23,507	27,179	28,774
Puerto Rican	—	4,890	5,602	6,671	8,296
Korean	—	4,533	4,950	6,461	6,851
Other	2,618	1,071	658	780	834
Total	154,001	191,909	255,912	368,336	423,330

(By Percentages)

Japanese	39.7	41.5	42.7	37.9	37.3
Caucasian	17.1	20.4	19.3	20.0	24.5
Hawaiian and Part-Hawaiian	24.8	20.1	16.3	13.7	15.2
Filipino	—	1.2	8.2	17.1	12.4
Chinese	16.7	11.3	9.2	7.4	6.8
Puerto Rican	—	2.5	2.2	1.8	2.0
Korean	—	2.4	1.9	1.8	1.6
Other	1.7	.6	.2	.3	.2
Total	100.0	100.0	100.0	100.0	100.0

Hawaii's continuing need for labor and the continuing inability of the native Hawaiians to adjust to plantation discipline led to the recruiting of various racial groups. This recruiting, in turn, led to Hawaii's present racially mixed population. Here it is well to pause briefly and remember that an almost identical phenomenon was occurring simultaneously on the mainland, which has become a melting pot of ethnic and racial groups taken from all parts of Europe and from some parts of Africa and Asia. White Americans as a whole are an ethnic mixture. The present-day population of Hawaii is an ethnic and, in an increasing degree, a racial mixture. Much nonsense, of course, attaches to the word *race,* as a still alive echo of imperialism, Kipling, and Hitler's Germany. Old wives' tales abound to the effect that one "race" is superior to another, as if skin pigmentation and other minor differences were critical determinants. They are not, as every anthropologist knows. Other superstitions state that a mixed breed brings out the worst characteristics in each of the parent stocks. (Breeders of race horses, registered dogs, and prize cattle would indeed be surprised if that myth were correct. They would immediately go out of business.) The fact of the matter seems to be that "race" is a comparatively minor factor, if a significant factor at all, in determining the way of life of a people.

Hawaii's present population is a compound of seven main groups, Hawaiian (themselves a "racial" compound), Caucasian, Japanese, Filipino, Chinese, Puerto Rican, and Korean, with a tiny sprinkling of many others. Naval intelligence officials in World War I censored mail in 52 languages and dialects. Some members of these groups have intermarried, and some have not. What seems to be basic here is not "race" but ethnic conditioning which leads to a broad sharing and mutual enrichment by way of borrowing part of the other fellow's customs and traditions. On the mainland (never refer to it as "The States" to a resident of Hawaii) this amalgam has happened too. The English presented the United States with its language, law, and tradition of constitutional government. But, as every student of American history well knows, other peoples have added their own ethnic ways to this English core. In Hawaii one finds a combination of *haoles*, "Portugees", *Pakes* (Chinese), Buddha-heads (Japanese), *Kanakas*, Manongs (Filipinos), and *Borinkis* (Puerto Ricans). In each case there has been a blending of diverse elements. What "racial" complexities differentiate Hawaii's blend from that of the mainland seem to be, in this light, of little basic importance.

Recruitment of Chinese contract labor began in 1851. The value of the original coolies seemed questionable. They were hard to handle, especially in view of the language barrier and in view of the fact that there was no Chinese consul in Hawaii at that time to mediate differences. Many Hawaiian residents raised strong objections to their presence. Nonetheless, by 1890 about 25,000 Chinese came to Hawaii, about a third from California. Of this total about 15,000 were still in the Islands to be counted in the 1890 census. Annexation in 1898 legally ended further emigration of the Chinese to Hawaii. They numbered 25,000 in 1900 and 28,000 in 1940, but by that time many had married outside their race and their offspring appeared in the official figures as part-Hawaiian.

The Chinese in general functioned well as plantation laborers. They cut sugar cane industriously with razor-sharp knives, and after work bathed one another in the nude with a hose in front of their small cottages, unconcerned with the impression which this spectacle created on passers-by. But as soon as their labor contracts expired many drifted to the towns, particularly Honolulu. There in a laxly supervised municipal administration they settled down in living conditions which, by American standards, were, to say the least, appalling. Vice, gambling, opium, and occasional bloody fights (the notion that the Chinese are "serene" is one that dies hard) added an overtone of zest to their squalor. But for most, of course, even this existence was a long step up in the world, as the slums of New York's lower East Side were incomparably better than the ghettos of Warsaw or the back streets of Rome and Paris. In Honolulu many opened little stores or other businesses.

Many of their children passed through Hawaii's school system to become clerks, accountants, salesmen and white-collar workers in general, and many of their grandchildren became highly respected professional men. A distinctive feature of the Chinese in Hawaii is their complex system of business syndicates (*huis*), which are extensive and extremely efficient.

Others, having left the plantations, became market gardeners. Some *kamaainas* still remember the Chinese vegetable peddlers, dog-trotting through the streets with their produce in two round open baskets, one at either end of a pole balanced precariously over one shoulder. From these they sold produce such as lettuce, eggplant, lotus roots, and strawberries. They wore pigtails and shouted at one another in a high-pitched singsong. *Haole* boys living in lower Nuuanu Valley, now men well past middle age, remember with sly laughter how they tormented these industrious *Pake* peddlers, overthrowing their baskets and pulling their pigtails. But this was only occasional rowdyish sport, unlike the vicious persecution endured by the patient and long-suffering Chinese in California.

In December, 1899, and for the next few months the Chinese community suffered a disaster which proved to be a disguised blessing. Bubonic plague broke out in Honolulu. Many *haole* and other residents camped out in the still desolate land on the eastern end of Oahu, while Board of Health and other inspectors investigated the plague in the Chinatown slums. They decided to burn the infected buildings. On January 20, 1900, one such fire raged beyond control and ended in destroying some 38 acres of disease-ridden shacks and tenements. Four to six thousand Chinese, Hawaiians, and Japanese lost their homes, and found shelter in Kawaiahao Church and other public buildings until temporary quarters could be erected for them north of the city. The plague and fire were calamitous, but the net result was to obliterate a frightful slum and in the long run vastly to improve living conditions for Chinese and other residents of downtown Honolulu.

Hawaii's Bureau of Immigration began in 1878 to import Portuguese, along with a few Spanish, from the Madeira and other islands where the climate generally resembled that of Hawaii. There were about 9,000 Portuguese in Hawaii in 1890 and about double that number 10 years later. The territory's Board of Immigration, established in 1905, imported 12,000 more Portuguese and Spanish in the years 1906-13.

These sturdy and hard-working peasants were admirable laborers, but they were costly to import. They adapted themselves well to the Islands, where they soon took deep root, and many intermarried with the natives. Those who remember old Manuel Joao of Molokai, and have watched him deftly balance a heavy timber over his shoulder at an age when most men use a cane, can testify to the hardy and stoical quality of this ethnic group. Toward the end of his life Manuel was honored after fifty years' service to the Molokai Ranch, and his industry there certainly set a high example for his many descendants. Although technically Caucasians, the Portuguese were not considered to be *haoles* proper, and for many years the census and other bureaus listed them separately in the statistical tables. Some of the older *kamaainas* still refer to the "Portugees" as a separate "race."

The Portuguese have contributed much to the customs and patois of the present-day Islanders. The novelist Armine von Tempski of Maui has recalled with pleasure in her colorful memoirs how the Portuguese at Christmas made yellow loaves of bread three feet in diameter containing whole hard-boiled eggs, while the Japanese made *mochi,* a variety of rice cake, and the Hawaiians feasted on *poi,* sweet potatoes, fat heifers, turkeys, and wild *puaas* (hogs).

The Portuguese also brought with them something which *malihinis* regard as traditionally Hawaiian. A modified smaller version of the Portuguese guitar has become known, in the Islands and elsewhere, as the ukulele, or more simply as the uke. In Hawaiian, ukulele means literally "flea" or "jumping insect," traditionally a reference to the swift movements of the hand of the *ukulele* player. It is a forerunner of the electronic guitar customarily associated with "Hawaiian" music.

The first Japanese contract laborers came to Hawaii in 1868, but there were difficulties in their recruitment, and the Japanese government did not sanction further emigration to Hawaii until 1884, three years after King Kalakaua's visit to Japan. The second batch of Japanese contract laborers arrived in Hawaii in 1885. By 1908 some 180,000 Japanese had come to Hawaii, but of these 126,000 left the Islands, some for the mainland but mostly to return to Japan. They numbered about 12,000 in the census of 1890 and 61,000 in 1900. At that time and for the next 40 years or so they represented about two-fifths of Hawaii's population.

The so-called Gentleman's Agreement of 1907-8, a series of diplomatic notes exchanged between Theodore Roosevelt's administration and Japan, ended the coming of further Japanese laborers to Hawaii. But until the Immigration Act of 1924, which totally prohibited the entrance of Japanese into the United States, a number of "picture brides" came to Hawaii.

Like the Chinese, the Japanese soon left the plantations and settled down as laborers and domestic servants, or took other jobs in the towns and cities, while some turned to chicken-raising and market-gardening. Among the Japanese, the *Issei* (first generation) stayed mainly among themselves and rarely married outside their own group. They preserved their old ways and traditions by sending their children to the Japanese-language schools. But the *Nisei* (second generation), American-born and thoroughly Americanized in their way of life, frequently married outsiders, as did the *Sansei* (third generation).

Visitors to Hawaii until recent years remember well the Japanese servants in the homes of the well-to-do *haoles*. The *Issei* among them, gentle and immaculate and cheerful, worked hard and happily, aware that they were much better off than in Japan. They wore colorful cotton kimonos and *zoris* (open sandals), and shuffled about quietly at their daily tasks. Their speech was broken, but their hearts were gay. They bowed respectfully at their employers, hissed greetings, and showed affection with full smiles and sparkling eyes. Still today a few such are left, wrinkled now and bent with age, loyal and sober, and without resentment that the United States in its wisdom denied them (until 1952) the chance of becoming citizens of their adopted land. Outside, the *Issei* yard "boy" goes dutifully about his familiar tasks, bandy-legged in faded cotton denims, speaking a broken pidgin and showing his content in an often toothless grin.

The *Nisei*, American-born and United States citizens, are usually longer limbed and tall, the result of good nourishment in childhood. Some still follow some of the old ways, but the majority are ambitious to get on in the world. In Hawaii, as elsewhere in the United States, it is increasingly difficult to find domestic servants once the remaining ones have died or departed, and in their desire to rise the *Nisei* and later generations are following a familiar American pattern.

Among the Japanese themselves there is a curious division. Japanese from Japan proper have, in varying degrees, an ingrained contempt for Japanese from Okinawa. This snobbish exclusiveness is far stronger among the *Issei* than among their descendants.

As the Japanese immigration stopped with the Gentleman's Agreement of 1907-8, planters turned to Filipinos, a few of whom had been brought to Hawaii in 1906. In the years from

1907 until 1931, when the importation of labor ceased temporarily, almost 125,000 Filipinos came to Hawaii. Of these many stayed; there were 21,000 in 1920 and 52,000 in 1940.

Some Filipinos made a trip back to their homeland to bring brides to Hawaii, for, in contrast to the Japanese, the practice of sending for "picture brides" was not well established among them. Some who resisted gambling or were lucky at it, and others from ordinary thrift, returned home and invested their money in a small plantation of their own. For still others among the Filipinos, Hawaii has provided a strange but comfortable place of self-enforced exile, where in monastic austerity and seclusion they have lived out their lives on lonely plantations. There are instances, for example on Libby's Maunaloa pineapple plantation on Molokai, where absentee Filipino husbands have not seen their wives and children for over 40 years.

Ordinarily this impulsive and sensitive group is close to the bottom of the hierarchy of Hawaii's mixed population. It is a common saying in the Islands that when a Japanese and a Filipino have an automobile accident, the Filipino is always wrong.

It is an unforgettable experience to have worked with these slight but wiry brown-faced men in the plantation fields. Many of the laborers, universally called Bull (pronounced Bool), had pock-marked skins and coarse features, but others had clean-cut and handsome faces, possibly with a trace of Spanish in their ancestry, as indeed some of the older men had a smattering of Spanish in their speech. Although they occasionally got drunk, gambled, and staged cruel cockfights, in the fields they were ordinarily tractable and lighthearted. One rule, easily learned, kept perfect order among them during working hours: never reprimand a Filipino in a tone of voice loud enough to be overheard by his fellow workers.

The planters also introduced comparatively small numbers of Puerto Ricans and Koreans, who totaled 8,200 and 6,800 respectively, in 1940. The Koreans generally proved to be reliable and industrious, but the Puerto Ricans were much less satisfactory as field workers.

Attempts have been made with little success to attract white colonists from the mainland and to recruit laborers from other groups. Early in the twentieth century, for example, the Board of Immigration brought over 2,000 Russians to Hawaii, but of these only a few remained.

The characteristics of Hawaii's mixed immigrant population

resemble generally those of other American communities. The original immigrants faced an almost insurmountable language barrier and tended to cling strongly to their distinctive customs and traditions. They generally had low status in the community, as indeed most of them had been underprivileged in their homelands. But low as their social position and living standards were in the Islands, their adopted country offered them much more, materially and in other ways, than they had had in their original homes. Universally they were content.

Their children, American-born and consequently citizens, learned English with varying degrees of correctness and fluency in the schools. There also they learned the traditions and values of the American way of life. In some instances the churches and, more importantly, organizations such as the Boy Scouts and Girl Scouts contributed to the Americanization process. This American-born second generation often lacked self-confidence and because of imperfect education found it hard to compete with the *haoles* in higher social, cultural, and economic brackets. The third generation has begun to give the *haoles* much more effective competition.

With the passage of time the older group-exclusiveness has begun to break down with increasing rapidity. In the years just before the outbreak of World War II, about one-third of the marriages in Hawaii crossed racial lines. As in Indonesia and parts of Asia, there was more intermarriage in the urban than in the rural areas.

As the melting pot progressed, an incredibly rich and varied body of pidgin English arose. Pidgin of the old-fashioned variety is rare today in Honolulu, but it persists among older immigrants and is common in many of the outlying rural areas. Some of it, fortunately, has been recorded, and some *kamaainas* and others interested in Hawaiiana have extensive and fascinating collections of these records. Anyone who has heard the record of Little Red Riding Hood in pidgin English, and who understands enough of the patois to make sense of it, has had a warm and rich experience.

Some of the pidgin, for example that of the Chinese, has counterparts elsewhere, especially as it reproduces the familiar Chinese transposition of the letters *r* and *l*. In this speech *very* became *velly*, and *friend* became *flen*.

Other varieties of pidgin are even more colorful, especially as it proceeds with a singsong swing, as if it were a variety of poetic chant. Common English phrases include "too much" (very), "more better" (pronounced maw betuh, and the whole phrase meaning "better"), "planty" (plenty), and "da kine" (the kind), which is a catchall phrase meaning "that way."

Practitioners of pidgin often begin with a loud "Eh!" then proceed swiftly and to the point. "Eh, thees [this] wan [one] too much no good. Ees [is] *pilau* [smelly]. Maw betuh [more better] you tek [take] that wan."

A particularly succinct specimen of clear pidgin was once spoken by a Japanese yard boy on Molokai. "Chicken *kaukau* [food] *pau* [done], me *kaukau pau*, me go *hanahana* [work]." What he was saying was, "After I have fed the chickens and had my own meal, I will go to work."

Although pidgin naturally picked up many familiar Hawaiian words, contrary to the usual impression *kaukau* was not one of them. The Hawaiian words for *eat* are *ai* and *paina*, and the Hawaiian word for *food* is *mea ai* (literally, eat-material). *Kaukau* is one of the few Chinese derivatives commonly used in Hawaii not only in pidgin but in the ordinary speech of the most cultivated Islanders. There seems to be little question that *kaukau* is Cantonese in origin, related to *chow-chow, chow mein* (noodle-food), or just plain *chow*.

The late Senator George P. Cooke used to tell with gusto the story of what a little Portuguese boy shouted when he saw his first elephant in a circus parade. "Hay, Hosay, kahm see da gret beeg ruba bool wit a tail in front like-a behin'!"

Senator Cooke has also recorded the reaction of a cowboy on seeing his first airplane, as related by James Munro, then assistant manager of the Molokai Ranch. "Eh, you know the trough at Kakaako gulch, well I fix the float and tap and I hear rh-rh-rh, and I think Mister Jim come in his E.M.F. [every morning fix] auto so I hurry my job but I hear rh-rh-rh. So I climb my horse and ride up the ridge. I no see Jim but hear rh-rh-rh. I look up and see airplane. By golly, he *pololei* [level] go, he no do like this [moving outstretched arms up and down], no, he *pololei* go." The foreman asked, "Sure no go like this?" [moving arms up and down like a bird in flight]. "No, he *pololei* go." Foreman: "Funny how he can." Ranger: "By and by he see a cloud above Mauna Loa [with gestures]. You think he go underneath? No he go straight inside cloud, *puka* [go through] 'nother side."

How much English the older plantation hands understand is problematical. Edward Norbeck, in his study of a Hawaiian plantation community, has repeated the comment of a supervisor that they understand English "when they want to." Norbeck also has reported a typical interchange of words between a field supervisor and a *luna* (foreman). "Git?" "Git!" All of this is a brilliant abbreviation for "Do you have any [slips, fruit, etc.]?" "Yes, I do." The negative response to the question would be simply, "No git."

The variety of foods for these various racial and ethnic groups is as rich as the pidgin. In any major supermarket (locally pronounced, soo-pah-mah-kit), *malihinis* are invariably amazed, not only at the profusion of fruit (at generally low prices by mainland standards) but also at the long rows of cans and jars of exotic foods. These foods include Chinese cabbage, bamboo shoots, and bean sprouts, along with seaweed and other Japanese condiments such as *sushi* (cold rice cakes), *udon* (noodles), and *daikon* (pickled radishes). In addition there are many Filipino specialties, prominent among them canned seafood. The same store, of course, sells *poi* (sometimes fresh but usually canned), *poha* (gooseberry) jam, Kona coffee, macadamia nuts, and rice in twenty-five-pound sacks.

Over the years stereotypes have accumulated as the various racial and ethnic groups have formed opinions about one another. A typical *haole* opinion would have it that the Japanese are clean, clannish, and better at memory work than in creative thinking; that the Chinese are industrious and make exceptionally good businessmen; that Filipinos are emotionally unstable; that Koreans have hot tempers; and that the Hawaiians are lovable but inclined to be lazy.

Sociologists who have studied the melting pot have uncovered a maze of other inter-group attitudes. Some antagonisms have appeared, as there are racial and ethnic antagonisms in other parts of the United States. But in general Hawaii's race relationships have been harmonious, and mutual tolerance has reached a remarkably high level. As early as 1861, Laura Fish Judd commented, "The little Hawaiian kingdom is certainly an anomaly among earthly governments. Antagonistic races dwell together on the same footing, under the same laws, justly and equally administered, and in comparative harmony. Distinction of color does not mar social intercourse, nor as yet create jealous animosities, thanks to the self-denying pioneers for this felicitous starting-point."

There is nothing "inevitable" about this situation. Other American communities have upon occasion lapsed into racial persecutions. To take only one example among the many which might be cited, the white inhabitants of California mistreated the Chinese there in the last quarter of the nineteenth century to the point that the phrase, "he doesn't have a Chinaman's chance," is still used to describe a hopeless case.

Hawaii's record of racial tolerance is far from perfect, but it is a record of which Hawaii can be justly proud. A special subcommittee of the United States House of Representatives, which visited Hawaii in 1958, reported, "If the races on the mainland, races stemming back ethnically to other lands, were to mix as successfully as they already have in Hawaii, our democracy would be advanced by a century."

Chapter 14

Economic and Social Development, 1900-40

IN THE YEARS 1900-1940 it became clear that diversified farming was not well-suited to Hawaii's economy. Coffee continued to be grown but acreage devoted to it declined from 6,451 in 1899 to 5,553 in 1936. Acreage devoted to rice declined even more sharply in these years, from 9,130 to 1,276. On Oahu most of the rice fields later reverted to taro or were planted with sugar cane, in part because of competition from machine-produced rice in California.

At one time honey was a flourishing Hawaiian export. The American Sugar Company on Molokai established one of the largest apiaries in the world to produce pure floral honey in over 2,000 hives from the pale yellow blossoms of the algarroba trees. Until World War I Germany was the main market for Molokai honey, which soon thereafter found other markets, California in particular. Starting in 1920 a blend of Molokai and California honey was widely distributed on the West Coast. But in 1933 the California Assembly passed a bill forbidding the mixing of California and "foreign" honey—a measure which, as interpreted, closed the California market to honey produced in the Islands. This act, incidentally, further increased the resentment of Islanders at being indirectly classified as second-class citizens of the United States. Thereafter honey production declined in the Islands, and what was left of the industry suffered a major blow with the spread of American foul brood (a bacterial disease affecting the larvae of bees) in the late 1930's. The misadventures connected with honey production are typical of similar difficulties experienced with other diversified farming ventures.

Other small-scale agricultural projects either failed or found only limited success. These included bananas, cotton, rubber, sisal, tea, and tobacco. In many cases farmers in Hawaii could not compete with other areas of the world where labor costs were immeasurably lower. Arable land in the Islands amounts to only about 300,000 acres, and it has proved difficult to raise both cash and subsistence crops on this comparatively small area. Lack of water and high inter-island shipping costs also have been major factors in discouraging diversified farming.

In the years 1900-1940 sugar remained the king of Hawaii's crops. Acreage devoted to sugar increased from about 127,000 acres in 1900 to 235,000 acres thirty-five years later. Production of sugar rose from 153,000 tons in 1895 to 602,000 tons in 1915, and passed the one million-ton mark in 1932.

In large measure the over-all increase in sugar production and the increased production per acre have resulted from the resourcefulness and imagination of the sugar planters themselves. Facing the competition of foreign producers with much lower labor costs, the Hawaiian sugar planters resorted to scientific and mechanical methods to lower production costs and increase the yield per acre. The result was scientific farming rarely equaled elsewhere in the world.

In 1895 the various plantations cooperated to form the Hawaiian Sugar Planters' Association, known familiarly as the HSPA, which established its experiment station on a scientific basis not only to breed new varieties of cane and to develop the technology of cane production but also to combat various insect pests and blights. Much valuable experimental work was done with fertilizers and irrigation, with sprays against weeds and pests, and with mulch paper laid on the ground between the rows of cane to control the weeds.

Many mechanical devices were developed to harvest and transport the cane to the mill. Here the Honolulu Iron Works had a major role. Modern plantations produced up to 100 tons of cane per acre, which in turn produced up to about 14 tons of sugar. Once harvested, this cane must reach the mill within about twenty-four hours, or else much of the juice will ferment or drain away. Under such circumstances technological efficiency in harvesting, transport, and milling are mandatory.

The HSPA fought and won a dramatic battle against insect pests. At the turn of the century the sugar cane leaf hopper appeared and soon threatened the entire sugar crop. Scientists sent to Australia found a parasite of the leaf hopper, which checked the blight. Other scientists searched as far afield as Fiji and Formosa for other parasites. About the same time an entomologist in the service of the HSPA found in New Guinea a parasitic fly to feed upon the sugar cane borer. When beetles threatened the cane just before the outbreak of World War I, the HSPA imported wasps from the Philippines which preyed on the beetle grubs. In 1932, as a further measure of protection, large toads were imported from Puerto Rico which devour all manner of insects, even scorpions. In addition, a strict plant quarantine was instituted in 1903.

Obviously sugar production requires much capital. It takes two years to grow cane. Meanwhile the fields must be irrigated, fertilized, sprayed, and weeded. The machinery for these operations, as well as for harvesting, is complex and expensive. In the late 1930's the HSPA had almost 100 employees and an annual budget of half a million dollars. In sum, a plantation is much like an outdoor industry, or as Carey McWilliams described it in 1939, a "factory in the field."

Sugar, Hawaii's biggest cash crop in the years 1900-1940 and after, has had its ups and downs. The price of raw sugar fell to just over two cents a pound in 1913 but skyrocketed to over twenty-three cents a pound in 1920. In the latter period the sugar planters indeed prospered, but a slump followed in 1923. Under the circumstances it is easy to understand the indignation and near-panic when the Jones-Costigan Sugar Control Act of 1934 reduced Hawaii's sugar quota. The New Deal's Henry A. Wallace was, in the eyes of *kamaainas,* threatening Hawaii's main economic lifeline.

From small beginnings in the nineteenth century, pineapples became Hawaii's second most valuable cash crop in the years 1900-1940. Pineapples grow well on land unsuited to sugar cane—in dry coastal areas and at elevations up to 2,000 feet. Unlike sugar, pineapples require no irrigation. Consequently they can be grown in areas which formerly were uncultivated, or which supported only a few cattle, without infringing on already productive cane fields.

A few pineapples of inferior quality had been grown in Hawaii in the nineteenth century, but the first satisfactory variety of this popular fruit was the Smooth Cayenne, introduced from Jamaica in 1886 by Captain John Kidwell, an Englishman from Devonshire. In the 1890's mainly unsuccessful attempts were made to can the fruit, which often spoiled if shipped fresh (even though unripe) to the West Coast. At this time the pineapple industry was in its earliest infancy. In 1899 only seventy-nine acres were devoted to raising pineapples. Over four times as much land was then devoted to bananas.

The major early promoter of Hawaii's pineapple industry was James Drummond Dole, a cousin of Sanford Dole. James Dole came to Hawaii in 1899, and soon became interested in the pineapple industry. He began with sixty acres at Wahiawa, near Pearl Harbor. In 1901 he organized the Hawaiian Pineapple Company with an initial capitalization of $20,000. His first crop, in 1903, yielded 1,893 cases of canned fruit.

Dole wisely realized that the key to the pineapple industry was efficient canning, for some of the first cans of pineapples had an unfortunate tendency to explode. Much study and experiment solved this initial difficulty. In 1906, Dole built a canning factory in Honolulu's Iwilei district which has become the world's largest fruit cannery. This factory, with its large, high water tank shaped like a pineapple, is a standard visiting attraction for tourists.

The pineapple industry grew rapidly. In 1922 the Hawaiian Pineapple Company bought almost the entire island of Lanai from members of the Baldwin family for pineapple cultivation. Lanai is sometimes called the Isle of Pines because of the pines and pineapples planted there. This is Hawaii's second privately owned major island, the other being Niihau, owned by the Robinson family. In 1931 the pack of the Hawaiian Pineapple Company reached almost five million cases, but the company encountered financial difficulties during the depression, when it became affiliated with Hawaii's sugar factors, known familiarly as the Big Five. Dole died in 1958 with the assurance that he had made a substantial contribution to Hawaii's economy.

In Hawaii the pineapple industry as a whole prospered. Plantations were established on Maui, Kauai, Oahu, and Lanai, and to a much lesser extent on the Big Island. In 1923, Libby, McNeill and Libby and in 1927 the California Packing Corporation (Del Monte) leased extensive acreage for pineapple growing on Molokai. Acreage devoted to pineapples rose from 3,900 to about 79,000 in the years 1909-29. Valuable byproducts include vinegar and pineapple bran.

Like sugar, pineapples require extensive capitalization and mechanization. Instead of seeds, shoots (called suckers or slips) from the parent plant are used as propagating material. These shoots, planted through mulch paper to control weeds, produce fruit-bearing plants three to four feet high in fifteen to twenty months after planting. Ordinarily the first, or plant, crop matures fully in July and August, and yields up to forty tons or more per acre. Later crops are called ratoons, and it has been usual to harvest two to four of these ratoon crops before disking the field preparatory to replanting.

In the process of cultivation, airplanes and tank trucks supply fertilizers and insect sprays, and the total operation requires a large fleet of trucks and mechanical devices. Harvesting is a rush job, with supervisory personnel in communication with the plantation headquarters and with one another by radio telephone. The fruit, which is picked ripe, ordinarily reaches the cannery in Honolulu within twenty-four hours. Such speed is essential, for the picked fruit quickly spoils. There are also canneries on Maui and Kauai. Inter-island transport of the fruit to the cannery is by barge. People who have ridden the tug which—burdened as it is by the dead weight of the barge— bobs about merrily in the waves, will recall it as a harrowing experience, probably comparable to inter-island travel in the missionary days. Only the hardiest can resist seasickness on such an occasion.

Once in the cannery the fruit is swiftly processed as hundreds of glove-wearing female employees direct its passage through complicated machines. One of these, the Ginaca machine invented in 1913, shells and cores the fruit in a single operation. Other machines produce pineapple juice and crushed fruit.

In cooperation and in the development of scientific farming, the pineapple planters followed the example of the sugar magnates. In 1914 the HSPA undertook research on various pests and blights afflicting pineapples, and a later cooperative venture led to the formation of the Pineapple Research Institute. Technicians studied varieties of pineapples in Central America and extended their research as far as Fiji and Africa. The late Thornton Lyman, a genial *kamaaina* of Molokai, had a rich store of anecdotes about his African adventure. Specific improvements were the iron-sulfate spray, first used in 1916, and an oil spray to fight the mealy bug, which, as it caused wilt, threatened the crop in the 1920's. Mulch paper to control weeds was first used in 1924.

Unlike the sugar growers, who found a ready market for a staple commodity, the pineapple planters had to undertake a large and sustained advertising campaign to educate the public to eat pineapples, previously considered a luxury item. Associations of Hawaiian pineapple growers in 1908 and later spent substantial sums on advertising and thereby created a market for their product. Here Dole showed his genius as a promoter. In 1902 he called on the United States secretary of agriculture, James Wilson, to complain that a law of long standing which prohibited the introduction of snakes to Hawaii had by mischance not been added to the territorial statutes. A reporter, who later interviewed Dole, headlined his account of Dole as the "Saint Patrick of Hawaii," and in so doing provided the pineapple industry with much welcome publicity. Twenty-five years later Dole offered two prizes, one of $25,000 and one of $10,000 for the winners of a transpacific air race from California to the Islands. This "Dole Derby," taken in connection with other continuing publicity, kept Hawaii's pineapples before the public and insured the continuance of a ready market for this valuable crop.

A much criticized feature of Hawaii's economy before 1940 had been the rise of the so-called Big Five. These were not, as is sometimes supposed, five families. They were five business firms, which, operating as agents, controlled over 95 per cent of the sugar production in the Islands. In 1931, American Factors, Ltd., the successor of the German firm of Hackfeld and Company, represented twelve plantations which produced 31.3 per cent of Hawaii's sugar. The others were C. Brewer and Company, Ltd., with twelve plantations and 22.5 per cent; Alexander and Baldwin, with six plantations and 20.6 per cent; Castle and Cooke, Ltd., with four plantations and 13.7 per cent; and Theo. H. Davies and Company, Ltd., a firm of British origin, with six plantations and 7.5 per cent. Four other firms represented the four remaining plantations with under 4.4 per cent of the sugar crop.

Through its profits from the prospering sugar industry the Big Five extended its operations into other areas of Hawaii's economy. By means of stock ownership, service contracts, land leases, and holding companies, bolstered by interlocking directorates and intermarriages among the families of its owners, the Big Five developed highly monopolistic tendencies. It controlled part of the pineapple industry in addition to sugar, and dominated Hawaii's public utilities, main banks and insurance companies, and public transit system, as well as wholesale and retail merchandising for the plantations. It controlled, too, Hawaii's inter-island navigation, as well as the Matson Steamship Company, which had a near-monopoly on freight and passenger service to and from the Islands. In addition, the Big Five had extensive interests in Hawaii's hotel and entertainment industry, including motion picture theaters and radio.

It has been estimated that some eighty corporation directors all but dominated the economic life of the Islands. In the first four decades of the twentieth century the power of the Big Five increased, because with its enormous resources it could ride out any depression, and in such times could and did buy out firms in or near bankruptcy. In the 1930's the Big Five met some competition when S. H. Kress and Company established a big dime store in Honolulu, and in 1940 Sears, Roebuck and Company opened a big and attractive retail outlet there. These inroads caused leaders of the Big Five some concern, but at that time they remained securely in control of the major part of Island economy. In addition, the small number of families affiliated with the Big Five generally controlled territorial politics through the Republican party and set the tone of the upper bracket of social life.

Hawaii's Big Five was not a form of colonial economic exploitation. It corresponded to the development of mainland trusts in the days before the New Deal. In its economy, based as it was on a few crops as well as in various features of its social and political structure, Hawaii in 1940 closely resembled the American South.

In company with other parts of the United States, Hawaii shared in the revolution in communications which has done so much to annihilate distances in the twentieth century. In 1889 an undersea cable was begun between Maui and Molokai. In 1899 Honolulu's first automobile appeared. In 1901 inter-island wireless service began to operate commercially. In 1902 cable communications linked Hawaii with San Francisco and robbed "boat day" of its previous glamor as the occasion to receive news from the outside world. But as late as 1917 cabled messages were expensive, $1.01 a word to China and forty-seven cents a word to New York. This situation led to an often repeated story about an Island boy who was sent to college on the mainland. To save money he agreed to cable the single word "Yes," if he passed all his examinations. By the time his father received the cryptic message many months later he had forgotten about the arrangement and cabled back, "Yes what?" The son respectfully replied, "Yes, sir."

In the 1920's a number of pioneer attempts were made to reach Hawaii by air. In 1925, John Rodgers led a flight of three navy seaplanes which left the West Coast for Hawaii. Two turned back, but Rodgers and his crew persevered until they ran out of gasoline about 200 miles from Pearl Harbor. They were finally rescued off Kauai after floating on the sea for nine days. On June 29, 1927, two army lieutenants, Lester J. Maitland and Albert F. Hegenberger, made the first flight between California and Honolulu in a trimotor Fokker. The trip took over 25 hours.

The first civilian flight from the West Coast almost ended in disaster. Ernest L. Smith and Emory B. Bronte left Oakland, California, on July 14, 1927, in a Travelair monoplane. When their auxiliary fuel pump failed they landed on the fifteenth in a *kiawe* tree at Keawanui near Kamalo on Molokai's south coast. One wing of the plane was wrecked but Smith and Bronte were not injured. A plaque marks the site of their landing, on the *makai* side of the road.

Thereafter aviation made rapid progress in Hawaii. Eight planes left California on August 16 in the "Dole Derby" transpacific race. Of these two cracked up at take-off, two turned back, and two vanished at sea. Only two planes reached Hawaii. The winners were Arthur C. Goebel and William Davis, with Martin Jensen and Paul Schluter in the other surviving plane. Despite this comparatively poor showing aviation enthusiasts remained undismayed. On November 11, 1929, Inter-Island Airways (later renamed Hawaiian Airlines) made the first commercial flight from Honolulu to the Big Island by way of Maui. In 1936, Pan American, which had instituted mail service to the West Coast the year before, received a license to carry passengers to and from Hawaii. (The company also flew regularly to the Orient by way of Midway, Wake, and Guam, and in 1937 opened service to New Zealand.)

Improved communications led to the development of Hawaii's third largest industry after sugar and pineapples, the tourist trade. This industry was slow in starting. Early in the twentieth century Jack London commented that Islanders were "poor boosters." Although Hawaii had, and has, few rivals as a glamorous vacation spot, comparatively few tourists came before World War II. In 1922 there were less than 10,000 visitors. In 1941, the peak prewar year, there were only 32,000. If you spoke to the Hawaiian orchestra leader in the Hawaiian Room of New York City's Lexington Hotel in the 1930's, and volunteered the information that you knew Hawaii, the chances were good that you would get a bored reply, "Army or Navy?" Before World War II tourism was an economic factor, but a comparatively minor one, in the Island's economy.

William R. Castle, Jr.'s *Hawaii Past and Present*, published in 1917, listed only five hotels in Honolulu. Of these, three were in the downtown area—the Alexander Young (from $1.50 a day, European plan), the Pleasanton ($2.50 to $5.00 a day, American plan), and the ("old") Royal Hawaiian (from $1.00 a day, European plan). The two hotels at Waikiki were the Moana ([literally, "Ocean"] from $5.00 a day, American plan) and the Seaside (from $2.50 a day, American plan).

A far-sighted promoter, Alexander Hume Ford, was a pioneer in developing Hawaii's tourist attractions. The son of a South Carolina rice planter, Ford became a newspaper reporter and toured the world in 1899. Eight years later he settled in Honolulu. At that time most of the Waikiki area was a swamp exploited by Chinese farmers who raised ducks and bananas. There were no facilities for surfing and no places to change clothing or take a shower after swimming. Ford had an active part in reviving the now famous sport of surfriding. On May 1, 1908, when the Outrigger Canoe Club was first organized at Waikiki, he became its first president. Other officers included L. H. Herbert, vice president; Henry O'Sullivan, secretary; and R. H. Trent, treasurer. J. P. Cooke, J. R. Galt, and Harry MacFarlane served as trustees. In those early days a grass shack served as a clubhouse. There were no showers. Ainahau Stream flowed through the premises, and it was customary to wash off the salt water by taking a dip in its beachside freshwater lagoon. Originally founded as a center of swimming, surfing, and canoeing, the club soon branched out to include football, track, volley ball, and other sports. A wooden clubhouse soon replaced the grass shack, and a new clubhouse was opened in June, 1941. Ford also founded the Pan-Pacific Union, designed to promote the dissemination of information and good will in the Pacific. The Union held its first international conference in 1916. Ford died in 1945.

Among the prominent Hawaiians associated with the Outrigger Canoe Club was "Duke" Kahanamoku, probably the best known Hawaiian after Queen Liliuokalani among the general public on the mainland. Duke Kahanamoku broke a world's record in 1913 by swimming 100 yards in 54.6 seconds. He said that he had learned the crawl stroke by watching older native swimmers. In 1917 he lowered the record time to 53.0 seconds. This record (shared with Pua Kealoha in 1921) stood until John Weissmuller broke it in 1922 by swimming 100 yards in 52.6 seconds. Duke Kahanamoku, who later served as sheriff of Honolulu, symbolized the glamor of the Islands and had much to do with making Hawaii a magnetic tourist center.

In the inter-war years tourist facilities improved greatly on

Oahu. Other major Waikiki hotels included the "new" Royal Hawaiian, a pink palace, and the incomparable Halekulani, both on the Ewa (west) side of the Outrigger Canoe Club. But tourist accommodations on windward Oahu and on the outlying islands left much to be desired.

Even in the 1930's some *kamaainas* deplored the intrusion of the tourists and spoke derisively of the Waikiki area as Coney Island, much as some residents of New York's fashionable upper East Side make a fetish of never going to Broadway except to the theatre. In retrospect the Honolulu of the 1920's and 1930's had the sleepy and gentle tempo of a charming small town, comparatively untouched by the slick and brassy ways of an expensive resort. It was, of course, far less crowded than it has since become, and such tourists as came to Hawaii then were generally people with fairly substantial means. But all of that was long ago. The New Deal and other social forces have long since made the rich poorer and the poor richer, in Hawaii as elsewhere in the United States. Whether the change is for the better is a question which many middle-aged people still debate. In any case, some *kamaainas* say that to see Hawaii as it was in the 1920's you have to go to Tahiti now. They also say it had better be done quickly, if it is to be done at all, for already jet planes are linking Tahiti with the outside world.

Meanwhile in Hawaii both Americanization and cultural enrichment proceeded apace. The public school system expanded and raised its standards. In the 1920's the "English Standard" schools appeared, limited to children with a stated proficiency in English, as a means of eradicating pidgin. Many high schools also appeared. An ambitious program was instituted in the 1930's, whereby Island teachers exchanged jobs for a year with teachers on the mainland. In 1908 the University of Hawaii, then called the College of Agriculture and Mechanic Arts, opened its doors. It moved to its present attractive site in Manoa Valley in 1912 and received its present name in 1920.

As was happening in other American communities, a number of organizations arose to perpetuate historical traditions and to encourage scholarship and the arts in the community. These included the Hawaiian Mission Children's Society (1852) and the Hawaiian Historical Society (1892), which share a library rich in printed and manuscript collections of Hawaiiana; the Bernice Pauahi Bishop Museum of Polynesian Ethnology and Natural History (1889), affiliated with Yale University and itself a unique center of scholarship about

Polynesia in general; and the Library of Hawaii (1913), mainly intended for the general reader.

In the 1920's Mrs. Charles M. Cooke and her family, missionary descendants, established the Honolulu Academy of Arts. This beautifully designed structure facing Thomas Square has extensive holdings of both Occidental and Oriental Art, including the Kress collection of Italian Renaissance painting and one of the best collections of Korean ceramics outside the Orient. It is a strange feeling to enter this cool and quiet spot and see there not only specimens of Greek-Indian statuary, the result of Alexander the Great's conquest of northwestern India in the fourth century B.C., but also incomparably older fragments of Egyptian stone carvings, still retaining clear traces of the original paint.

The ceremony dedicating the academy included an extraordinarily well-conceived statement of ideals:

"That our children of many nationalities and races, born far from the centers of art, may receive an intimation of their own cultural legacy and wake to the ideals embodied in the arts of their neighbors;

"That they may grasp the composite heritage accumulating for the new generations of Hawaii;

"That Hawaiians, Americans, Chinese, Japanese, Koreans, Filipinos, North Europeans, South Europeans, and all other peoples living here, contacting through the channel of art those deep intuitions common to all, may perceive a foundation on which a new culture, enriched by all the old strains, may be built in these islands;

"That it may contribute to understanding and mutual respect;

"The Honolulu Academy of Arts opens its doors to this community, so situated that it calls the East the West and the West the East, perhaps in happy continuance of that ancient Polynesian custom of exchanging the names of close friends."

Here is firm evidence indeed that although the old missionary spirit had entered a more secular channel, it was still certainly exerting a vigorous influence in the Islands.

Chapter 15

Hawaii in Literature

BEFORE THE OUTBREAK of World War II, Hawaii had achieved a prominent place in literature of various kinds. These included early accounts of voyages and travels, memoirs, histories, biographies, and collections of Hawaiian literature and folklore. This variegated mass of writing is somewhat uneven in tone, running the gamut from polemics on the part of moralists, imaginative fiction, and softly accented romantic journalism, to somber works of scholarship. In addition, a number of writers of first rank were inspired by Hawaii or visited the Islands, and left factual or fictionalized accounts of their experiences. In the years after 1941 this uneven flow of literature continued, especially as thousands of servicemen and others passed through the Islands on their way to the western (or is it eastern?) war zones, and returned to exploit Hawaii's rich reservoirs of local color. In short, many bibliophiles have found a happy hobby in collecting Hawaiiana, and a few have assumed the more difficult task of collecting manuscripts as well as printed works, for in many cases the manuscript accounts are far more interesting than those which have found their way into print. What follows is only a sample, of course, for a comprehensive survey would require a book in itself.

A number of distinguished but often neglected early narratives of voyages and travel exist which give authentic and clearly written descriptions of Hawaii. Many reveal that their authors had received a disciplined education, which produces good, and occasionally great, prose. It is a pleasure to browse through the shrewd and alert account of the voyage leading to Hawaii's discovery written in two volumes by Captain James Cook and continued in one volume by one of his subordinates, Lieutenant James King, entitled *A Voyage to the Pacific Ocean . . . in 1776-1780* (London, 1784). Vivid descriptions of Hawaii appear in the travel accounts of Jacques Arago (*Narrative of a Voyage Around the World*, London, 1823) and of William S. Ruschenberger (*A Voyage Round the World*, Philadelphia, 1838), and also in the later account of Charles Nordhoff (*Northern California, Oregon and the Sandwich Islands*, New York, 1874). Such works were extremely popular in the nineteenth century, as Western civilization overran the world and paused to record its expansion for the delectation of stay-at-homes. One of the most dramatic and penetrating of these early narratives was written by Charles Stewart, a missionary in the second company sent to Hawaii. The print is irritatingly small and the title is forbidding, *Private Journal of a Voyage to the Pacific Ocean and Residence at the Sandwich Islands in the Years 1822, 1823, 1824, and 1825* (New York, 1828). But the quality of the writing is so good that his book deserves an honored place in the field of informal literature.

Among early memoirs of Hawaii two are outstanding. Hiram Bingham left a long and somewhat heavy account of his years in the mission, *A Residence of Twenty-One Years in the Sandwich Islands* (Hartford, 1847). Nonetheless, at his best Bingham raged with the fervor of an Old Testament prophet and produced prose which is at the same time powerful and sensitive. In 1861, Laura Fish Judd finished her memoirs, *Honolulu: Sketches of the Life, Social, Political, and Religious, in the Hawaiian Islands from 1828 to 1861* (New York, 1880; reprinted, Honolulu, 1928). The most literate of the missionary wives, she had the temerity to quote Byron in her last letter written before leaving Boston for the Islands. As a writer she had a remarkable double gift, first of visualizing scenery and situations, and second of portraying them in musical prose. As is the case with the writings of others in the mission, her style has strong echoes of the prose rhythms of the King James Version of the Bible.

Among later memoirs, devotees of Hawaiiana have high praise for William R. Castle's *Hawaii, Past and Present* (New York, 1913, and later editions). This sincere, reliable, and unpretentious work has an honored place on the library shelves of *kamaainas*. A more recent and more professionally presented work is the autobiography of the Maui novelist, Armine von Tempski, entitled *Born in Paradise* (New York, 1940). For sheer charm and nostalgic evocation of the past this book has few peers in the literature of Hawaii.

Of the early histories of Hawaii, that of Sheldon Dibble, *A History of the Sandwich Islands* (Lahinaluna, 1843; reprinted, Honolulu, 1909), is a remarkably authentic work, since he collected much of his information at first hand from the chiefs. The journalist James Jackson Jarves published a *History of the Hawaiian or Sandwich Islands* (Boston, 1843) and a second book entitled *Scenes and Scenery in the Sandwich Islands* (Boston, 1843). In addition he wrote a semifictionalized autobiography, *Why and What Am I?* (London, 1857). All three treat fluently his experiences in Hawaii in the years 1837-48. Jarves then left the Islands and had a remarkable second career as an art collector. Of course, in later years historians and biographers, both amateur and professional, have dealt exhaustively with Hawaii's past.

During the nineteenth century a number of writers of renown learned about Hawaii, directly or indirectly, by visiting the Islands, by reading about them, or through acquaintance with Islanders, such as Kamehameha II, Queen Emma, King Kalakaua, and Queen Liliuokalani, who traveled abroad. Many found Hawaii a source of literary inspiration.

One of America's greatest novelists, Herman Melville, left Hawaii in August, 1843, after a sojourn of about six months. Melville was somewhat at a loose end during his stay in the Islands, which, in any case, were convulsed with the tensions surrounding their seizure by Lord George Paulet. Melville recorded his distaste for the missionaries in an appendix of *Typee* and in his later conversations with his friend, the author and editor, Evert Augustus Duyckinck, as recorded in Duyckinck's diary. Had he stayed, and learned to understand Hawaii better, it is possible that Melville would have written a great book about the Islands. But the course of human events can be strange indeed. Not every challenge has its response. Not every cause in history has its expected result. Melville left Hawaii in a dyspeptic mood, the privilege of any great writer, and he never took the opportunity to write the potential masterpiece about what he saw and experienced there.

In 1866, Mark Twain went to Hawaii. His extended tour took him to Maui and to the Big Island, where he visited the Kona Coast and the volcano of Kilauea. His lengthy recorded impressions appeared in the Sacramento *Union*, and form a substantial part of his travel book, *Roughing It*. In Hawaii he was at his best, and his narrative is studded with specimens of his wry humor. He wrote, with obvious delight, "At noon I observed a bevy of nude native young ladies bathing in the sea, and went and sat down on their clothes to keep them from being stolen. I begged them to come out, for the sea was rising, and I was satisfied that they were running some risk. But they were not afraid, and presently went on with their sport. They were finished swimmers and divers, and enjoyed themselves to the last degree." Mark Twain, it is clear, was also enjoying himself to the last degree. This passage sets the tone of his reporting. He also scooped his rivals by sending in the thrilling story of the loss of the clipper ship *Hornet* near the equator. Fifteen survivors reached Hawaii after forty-three days in an open boat.

In 1895, Mark Twain returned to Hawaii on a lecture tour, and wrote with anticipation: "On the seventh day out we saw a dim vast bulk standing up out of the wastes of the Pacific and knew that that spectral promontory was Diamond Head, a piece of this world which I had not seen before for twenty-nine years. So we were nearing Honolulu, the capital city of the Sandwich Islands—those islands which to me were Paradise; a Paradise which I had been longing all those years to see again. Not any other thing in the world would have stirred me as the sight of that great rock did." But he was due for a cruel disappointment. There was cholera in Honolulu, and passengers who went ashore could not continue their journey without facing detention in quarantine. Mark Twain found himself, therefore, trapped aboard ship anchored a mile from "Paradise." He looked longingly at the shoreline, and wrote: "We lay in luminous blue water; shoreward the water was green—green and brilliant; at the shore itself it broke in a long white ruffle, and with no crash, no sound that we could hear. The town was buried under a mat of foliage that looked like a cushion of moss. The silky mountains were clothed in soft, rich splendors of melting color, and some of the cliffs were veiled in slanting mists. I recognized it all. It was just as I had seen it long before, with nothing of its charm wanting."

On his departure from Honolulu on September 2, he reported a sight still to be seen in Hawaiian waters. "Flocks of flying fish—slim, shapely, graceful, and intensely white. With the sun on them they look like a flight of silver fruit-knives. They are able to fly a hundred yards."

A minor American author, Charles Warren Stoddard, left many pleasant descriptions of the Islands in his *South-Sea Idyls* (Boston, 1873) and other books. But he is best remembered for having inspired Stevenson to visit Hawaii and other islands of the mid-Pacific.

In January, 1889, Robert Louis Stevenson went to Hawaii and stayed until June. Despite poor health he found his visit to be pleasant and productive. He met King Kalakaua, Liliuokalani, and little Princess Kaiulani, whom he charmed by telling her stories about Scotland. Stevenson resisted the temptation to use his pen in favor of restoring autocratic government in Hawaii, and instead interested himself in studying Hawaii's traditions, in inter-island sightseeing, and in his own work. He visited the Big Island's Kona Coast and the leper settlement at Kalaupapa. In the Islands he finished his novel *The Master of Ballantrae* and began *The Bottle Imp*, a story in part inspired by Hawaiian lore.

After he left the Islands he read the Reverend Charles M. Hyde's attack on the lately deceased Father Damien of Molokai. At the risk of a libel suit he published his justly famous *An Open Letter to the Reverend Dr. Hyde*, one of the most spirited and furious attacks in any language. Hyde had the good sense to let the matter drop.

Stevenson made a five-week visit to Hawaii in the fall of 1893. He scorned the Provisional Government and called to pay his respects on Queen Liliuokalani, recently deposed by the revolution. When he left he wrote a note in the register of his hotel, the Sans Souci at Waikiki. It read: "If anyone desire such old-fashioned things as lovely scenery, quiet, pure air, clear sea water, good food, and heavenly sunsets hung out before his eyes over the Pacific and the distant hills of Waianae, I recommend him cordially to the 'Sans Souci.' Robert Louis Stevenson." The enterprising manager of the hotel ran this note for three days in the local press.

The dean of American historians, Henry Adams, visited Hawaii in 1890 on his way to the South Seas and had an audience with King Kalakaua. Adams was much impressed with the king's scholarly knowledge, and some of Adams' comments on Kalakaua have been published. Other material on his visit to Hawaii remains in manuscript and will probably be published at some future date.

Tennyson, who never visited Hawaii, nonetheless had a direct interest in the Islands, dating at least as far back as his meeting with Queen Emma in England in 1865. Twenty-seven years later in 1892, the year of his death, he wrote "Kapiolani," a poem purportedly set in the rhythm of a Hawaiian chant, to celebrate the courage of this chiefess in descending into the volcano to defy Pele. It is an interesting but far from great example of his lyric skill.

The self-educated socialist and writer of adventure stories, Jack London, arrived in Honolulu in 1907 in his small yacht, the *Snark*, on his projected trip around the world which ended in Australia. He spent four months in the Islands on this trip and in 1915 returned to spend nearly a year in Honolulu, where he was active in promoting the sport of surfboard riding. Hawaii fascinated Jack London, who at his best, when he was winning his battle against melancholia and alcoholism, wrote

some of America's finest short stories. One of his most success-
ful short stories set in the Islands was entitled "Koolau the
Leper," a haunting tale of courage and determination based
on fact, in which lepers in Kauai's precipitous Kalaulau Valley
heroically resisted efforts to send them to the settlement on
Molokai. London recorded his experiences and impressions of
Hawaii in *The Cruise of the 'Snark'* (New York, 1911), *The
House of Pride* (New York, 1912), and *On the Makaloa Mat*
(New York, 1919). His wife, Charmian, published *Our Hawaii*
(New York, 1922).

In 1913 the English poet Rupert Brooke began an extended
tour which took him to the United States mainland, Hawaii,
and the South Seas. This remarkable author, classically educated at Rugby and at King's College, Cambridge, is best remembered for his magnificent verses about the war in which
he lost his life in 1915. Island residents remember him with
particular fondness for his superb sonnet about Waikiki.

During World War I, Somerset Maugham visited the Islands.
Like other writers with a keen eye for local color and the
exotic in general, Maugham was intrigued by Honolulu, which
he described as the meeting ground of the East and West.
(Others using these vague terms have put the meeting ground
in such diverse locations as Venice, Vienna, Istanbul, and
Cairo.) Maugham relished his stay in Hawaii, which furnished
him with some material for his famous story "Rain," published
in 1921, and for other of his writings.

Genevieve Taggard (1894-1948) went to Hawaii with her
parents, both schoolteachers, when she was only two years old.
Her father taught in an outlying area of Oahu, and she grew
up among the children of plantation laborers, Chinese, Japanese, and part-Hawaiian. She had little contact with *haole*
children until she was sent to Punahou School. When she was
20 she left the Islands and never returned. After graduating
from the University of California, she went to the East Coast
to undertake a career of writing, editing, and college teaching.
Her childhood in the Islands provided her with much picturesque material, which she exploited with grace and sensitivity
in both poetry and prose.

In 1923 the Hawaiian legislature invited Padraic Colum, the
noted Irish poet and expert on Irish folklore, to make a study
of Hawaiian mythology and folk traditions to be used as children's stories. Fortunately Colum accepted. The result was two
charming volumes, *At the Gateways of the Day* (1924) and
The Bright Islands (1925), published for the Hawaiian Legend

and Folklore Commission by the Yale University Press. Many middle-aged *kamaainas* remember with gratitude their pleasure in reading these delightful books as children, and many have read them with equal pleasure to their children and grandchildren.

In an entirely different medium but one equally popular, Earl Derr Biggers (1884-1933), a Harvard graduate and former newspaperman originally from Ohio, found in Hawaii not only good living but a fertile source of literary material. His famous character, the Chinese detective Charlie Chan, first appeared in his *House Without a Key* (1925), and re-appeared in five other books. Millions who never read any of Biggers' novels became familiar with Charlie Chan in the movies. A persistent tradition has it that Charlie Chan's prototype was a Chinese-Hawaiian detective named Chang Apana. In any case, the famous fictional detective justly made his creator world famous, in those gentler days when detective fiction was just that, instead of its present welter of sex, smut, and sadism.

One of America's most distinguished novelists, John P. Marquand, lived in Honolulu in the 1930's, at the time he was writing his Mr. Moto stories. Marquand used the Hawaiian locale with his customary insight and balance as the background for some of his best writing.

Among Islanders devoted to fiction, Armine von Tempski (1899-1940) of Maui justly takes a prominent place. Unlike some of the others who have written notable fiction about the Islands, she shared with Genevieve Taggard the indisputable advantage of having learned her Hawaii at first hand in childhood. When she described the jingle of the *paniolo's* spurs, the pidgin of a Chinese servant, the courtesy of a Japanese nurse, or the sweet smell of sandalwood burning as a Christmas yule log, she was inventing nothing and making no guesses. In writing descriptions and setting a general tone, she was reproducing with inbred accuracy what Hawaii was really like, as the days passed softly and swiftly in those quiet times before 1941. Aside from her autobiography, *Born in Paradise* (1940), her many novels include *Hula* (1927), *Dust* (1928), *Fire* (1929), *Lava* (1930), *Hawaiian Harvest* (1933), and *Ripe Breadfruit* (1935).

For 157 years, then, from the publication of the account by Cook and King in 1784 to 1941, when America entered World War II, Hawaii has been the subject of a continuous stream of literature, some of it indifferent but much of it of first quality. By comparison, the literature about Hawaii published during the war years and in the postwar era generally has less merit. In any case, over the years Hawaiiana, far from being exotic lore, took its proper place as a vital part of Americana. No student of the American tradition can afford to by-pass Hawaii. Fortunately there is a rich body of literature about the Islands to awaken and sustain his interest.

Chapter 16

Pearl Harbor, December 7, 1941

EVERY AMERICAN over thirty, and some younger than that, remembers Pearl Harbor. Americans in Hawaii remember it particularly well. It is an amusing parlor game, now that the war is safely won and has been for a long time, to ask members of a group where they were and what they were doing on the "Day of Infamy," as President Roosevelt so aptly called it. Some were, as Walter Lord has reported in his brilliant anecdotal book on the subject, listening to radio station WOR's broadcast of the Giant-Dodger football game at New York's Polo Grounds, when at 2:26 P.M., EST, about an hour after the Japanese attack began, an announcer interrupted with the first flash-report. Others were having cocktails, doing the laundry, or engaging in a thousand other inconsequential occupations at the time, while in Hawaii many Americans were already dead or dying. Whatever the circumstances, and each person has a different story to tell, everyone remembers clearly just what he was doing when he heard the news.

At first, of course, there was much confusion and bewilderment. Except for a minority—mainly former tourists or military and naval personnel—few Americans were quite certain just where Pearl Harbor was. Many anecdotes, now remembered in tranquility, relate how so-and-so insisted that it was in the Caribbean, the Canal Zone, California, or the Philippines. It took a little while for Americans to agree that Pearl Harbor was in Hawaii, then universally pronounced "Hah-why-yuh," like a pun on "How are you."

But in any case the reaction was identical throughout the United States. Shock turned to cold fury at the sneak attack. Some men dropped what they were doing and headed for the nearest recruiting office. America's greatest defeat produced

America's greatest national unification. In retrospect, although it took almost four years of fighting, Japan had lost the war just as soon as news of the attack was made public.

Instantly a spotlight of interest was turned on Hawaii. Millions of Americans learned, on December 7, 1941, what they had never known, or had once known and forgotten, that in fact the territory of Hawaii was an "integral part" of the United States.

After the attack was over, and the stable door well locked, a series of investigations began which produced thousands of pages of testimony and documents. Obviously the armed forces had blundered somehow, and the Pacific Fleet had been crippled. Much buck-passing resulted, and much of the testimony was contradictory. In some cases high military officials, preoccupied with gigantic tasks and responsibilities, were honestly vague about details of exactly what they had done in the days and hours before the outbreak of the war. The responsibility for the disaster has not been fixed, and it may never be.

Nonetheless, careful investigation has produced a hard core of reasonably well-established fact, which is worth relating in summary form. Investigation also has scotched a number of nasty rumors, and it seems worthwhile to mention a few of these, for rumors die hard, especially among the former GI's who took the brunt of the holocaust, who were therefore emotionally involved in the events more directly than most Americans, and who may not have had the opportunity to inform themselves correctly in subsequent years.

Early in 1941 leaders in the Japanese navy began to plan the attack on Pearl Harbor, in order to destroy the American Pacific fleet should war break out between Japan and the United States. This plan matured during the summer and fall. In mid-November the Japanese task force began to assemble at Tankan (also known as Hitokappu or Shitokap) Bay of Etorofu Island in the cold and desolate Kuriles. This force left for Hawaii on November 26. It consisted of six aircraft carriers, two battleships, three cruisers, nine destroyers, three submarines, and eight tankers, under the command of Vice Admiral Chuichi Nagumo. In radio silence it proceeded eastward in waters far removed from ordinary shipping lanes. On December 2 it was told to climb Mount Niitaka, that is, to attack. A few days later it headed southeast and then south for Hawaii.

About 6:00 A.M. on December 7, when the Japanese task force was about 230 miles north of Oahu, it began to launch the first air strike. The Japanese had 432 planes—39 for air patrol, 40 in reserve, and 353 for the attack. The first attacking force consisted of 49 horizontal bombers, 51 dive bombers, 40 torpedo planes, and 43 fighters. The second consisted of 54 horizontal bombers, 80 dive bombers, and 36 fighters. The pilots, thoroughly trained and minutely briefed, had instructions to destroy the aircraft on Oahu's various military air stations and to attack the United States fleet in Pearl Harbor.

Meanwhile an advanced expeditionary force was already in Hawaiian waters. It consisted of twenty or more conventional submarines and five of the celebrated midget submarines. All five of these tiny craft were ultimately lost.

At 3:42 A.M. the American minesweeper *Condor* sighted the periscope of one of the Japanese submarines just outside Pearl Harbor. The destroyer *Ward* searched the area without success. At 6:30 A.M. the *Ward* made a second submarine contact in the area, and at 6:45 fired on the tiny craft, the first American shot to be fired in World War II. A navy PBY in the area assisted by dropping depth charges.

At 7:02 A.M. two army privates at the Opana Radar Station near Kahuku Point on northern Oahu picked up an airplane contact, which they plotted as 137 miles north and three degrees to the east. Here was well-advanced warning of the oncoming Japanese striking force. But the lieutenant in the Information Center assumed that it was a flight of B-17's, which he had reason to believe were scheduled to arrive from the West Coast about that time. Consequently, in this comedy of multiplied errors, he did not relay this priceless information. Meanwhile the two privates continued to trace the enemy force, until at 7:39 they lost it in so-called "dead zone" caused by the surrounding land masses. At 7:45 they left for breakfast at Kawaiola.

Authorities in Washington also had advance indications of the forthcoming attack. On the basis of intelligence reports and after consultation with President Roosevelt and others, General George Marshall, the Army Chief of Staff, sent the following message to the commanding generals in Manila, Panama, and Hawaii: "Japanese are presenting at 1:00 P.M. Eastern Standard Time today what amounts to an ultimatum. Also they are under orders to destroy their code machine immediately. Just what significance the hour set may have we do not know but be on alert accordingly. Inform naval authorities of this communication."

To preserve security Marshall did not use a scrambler telephone. He did not know that because of weather conditions the army's radio could not establish contact with Pearl Harbor, and that the message would be sent by commercial cable. The message was filed in the Army Signal Center at 12:01 P.M. (6:31 A.M. Honolulu time), and Honolulu's RCA received it at 7:33 A.M., just 22 minutes before the attack. But the messenger boy was delayed by the fighting, and did not reach the signal office in Fort Shafter until four hours later. The decoded message reached Walter C. Short, the commanding general, at 2:58 P.M. By that time, of course, it was a completely useless document.

The Japanese attack began about 7:55 A.M., Honolulu time. Aircraft bombed and strafed Oahu's various airfields, Hickham, Kaneohe, Wheeler, Ewa, and Bellows. The United States lost 188 aircraft, and an additional 159 were damaged. Between 8:00 and 9:00, Navy planes and the 11 B-17's from the mainland flew into the center of the fighting. No Navy plane was able to take off after the fighting started, but Army planes made 81 take-offs throughout the day. In general the surprise was so complete that American planes could offer little effective opposition.

At Pearl Harbor most of the damage came in the first attack, which began at 7:55 A.M. and lasted about half an hour. A second attack followed at 8:40 and ended about 9:45. The last Japanese plane reached its carrier about 1:00 P.M., and half an hour later the Japanese task force headed for home.

Of the ninety-six ships in Pearl Harbor, eighteen were sunk or severely damaged. The battleships *Arizona* and *Oklahoma* and the target ship *Utah* were total losses, along with the destroyers *Cassin* and *Downes*. Four ships were sunk or beached but later were salvaged: the battleships *California, Nevada,* and *West Virginia,* and the mine layer *Oglala*. Nine ships suffered major damage: the battleships *Maryland, Pennsylvania,* and *Tennessee;* the cruisers *Helena, Honolulu,* and *Raleigh;* the destroyer *Shaw;* the seaplane tender *Curtiss;* and the repair ship *Vestal*. Observers on Tantalus and other points of vantage overlooking Pearl Harbor later stated that the attack resembled the explosion of giant firecrackers.

The most serious single loss occurred about 8:10 A.M., when the battleship *Arizona* took a bomb in her forward magazines and exploded. A vast cloud of smoke and fire billowed 500 feet upwards, vividly described by witnesses at the time and fully recorded for posterity in many photographs. The battered hulk of the *Arizona* still lies in Pearl Harbor as a gruesome memento of the attack and the honored grave of 1,102 sailors.

The raid killed 2,403 Americans and wounded 1,178. The

Navy lost 2,008; the Army, 218; the Marine Corps, 109; and the civilian population, 68. Of the wounded, 710 were from the Navy, 364 from the Army, 69 from the Marine Corps, and 35 from the civilian population.

In addition, there were about 40 recorded explosions in the city of Honolulu, of which all but one resulted from American antiaircraft fire. These explosions caused about $500,000 worth of damage.

In comparison, the Japanese losses were trivial. The striking force lost only 29 planes—15 dive bombers, 9 fighters, and 5 torpedo planes. The advanced expeditionary force lost 1 conventional and 5 midget submarines. The total Japanese loss in military personnel was probably less than 100 men: 55 fliers, 9 crew members of the midget submarines, and an unknown number on the conventional submarine.

Quite naturally an atmosphere of shock, near-hysteria, and rage prevailed in Honolulu. Radio station KGMB first announced the attack at 8:40 A.M., and Honolulu residents still remember well how the announcer kept insisting that it was "the Real McCoy." But under Army orders both this station and KGU went off the air at 11:42 A.M. to prevent enemy planes from navigating from their broadcast beams. Thereafter they were silent, except for occasional terse announcements. Eager residents tuned in the police radio, where they heard hundreds of garbled reports.

Under the circumstances, wild rumors multiplied. They reached such serious proportions that on December 11 Colonel (later Brigadier General) Kendall J. Fielder, assistant chief of staff to the commanding general, warned in a radio address, "It is important for you to be alert but you must beware of unfounded rumors and fantastic flights of your imagination. Check carefully the authenticity and accuracy of the rumor you may hear. Promiscuous spreading of wild rumors will only contribute to confusion."

One of the most persistent false rumors was that Island residents of Japanese descent had helped the attack with acts of sabotage. Navy wives evacuated to the West Coast spread such nonsense far and wide. Even Frank Knox, the Secretary of the Navy, who visited Pearl Harbor shortly after the attack, stated in a press conference that Hawaii had been subjected to "the most effective fifth column work that has come out of this war except in Norway."

On January 15, 1946, Robert L. Shivers, agent in charge of the Federal Bureau of Investigation in Hawaii, stated before a Congressional committee:

"I am sure you gentlemen have heard of one hundred and one rumors that have been spread throughout this Territory and the mainland United States since the day of the attack. One of these stories was to the effect that some of the Japanese aviators who were shot down over Oahu that morning were wearing class rings of McKinley High School (of Honolulu). Another was that arrows had been cut in the cane fields by the Japanese population which pointed toward Pearl Harbor and guided the attacking force to their targets. Another was that a transmitter had been discovered in the possession of some Japanese who were transmitting information to the enemy. Another was that the sides of a milk truck at Schofield Barracks suddenly collapsed and machine guns manned by Japanese opened fire on the soldiers at the post. There were many more rumors with which you are familiar. *There was not an iota of truth in any of them.* . . . There was not one single act of sabotage committed against the war effort in the Hawaiian Islands during the course of the entire war. Nor was there any fifth-column activity in existence or in evidence here. . . . *I want to emphasize that there was no such activity in Hawaii, before, during, or after the attack on Pearl Harbor.* Consequently there was no confusion in Hawaii as a result of fifth-column activities. I was in a position to know this fact, and I speak with authority when I say that the confusion in Hawaii was in the minds of the confused, and not because of fifth-column activities. No amount of repetition before the investigating committee will alter the fact that *sabotage and fifth-column activity was never engaged in at any time prior, during, or subsequent to the attack on Pearl Harbor.*"

On March 14, 1942, W. A. Gabrielson, Honolulu's chief of police, stated in a telegram, "There were no acts of sabotage committed in city and county of Honolulu December 7 nor have there been any acts of sabotage reported to police department since that date."

In March, 1943, Colonel Fielder stated, "Having been in charge of military intelligence activities since June, 1941, I am in position to know what has happened. There have been no known acts of sabotage, espionage, or fifth column activities committed by the Japanese in Hawaii either on or subsequent to December 7, 1941."

Gwenfread Allen's authoritative book, *Hawaii's War Years, 1941-1945* (Honolulu, 1950) has an illuminating analysis of the four rumors mentioned by Shivers and of many others in circulation at the time. The story about the McKinley High School rings had several variants, including rings from the University of Hawaii, the University of Oregon, and the University of Southern California. No evidence corroborates it. Besides, Japanese military discipline prohibited the wearing of rings. No arrows in the cane fields were found, although a bare spot harvested in October, 1941, in an experimental field pointed toward Pearl Harbor. The Federal Communications Commission reported, "There were no illegal radio stations operating in Hawaii on December 7 or afterwards throughout the war." Japanese voices heard over the radio came from a station in Argentina whose beam to Japan came close to Oahu. The story about the milk truck was just that—a story.

Other rumors appeared: that epidemics had spread among evacuees (undoubtedly stomach-aches from upset nerves); that Japanese in Hawaii knew about the attack in advance (pure fabrication); that commando detachments had landed (more fabrication); that plantation workers had fired on sentries (probably sentries firing on one another in the darkness); that signal lights guided ships or planes (dozens of such reports, all unverified). The otherwise staid New York *Times* in its December 8 issue mentioned unconfirmed reports that German raiders had participated in the attack. But this was mild in comparison to other rumors sweeping throughout Hawaii, among them that the Panama Canal had been bombed and that the Japanese had landed in California.

A week or so after the attack it became known that one of the Hawaiian Islands, remote Niihau, had been invaded. The story of the "Battle of Niihau" instantly caught the public fancy and in time gave rise to a saying which forever will be a part of Hawaiian lore.

About 2 P.M. on December 7 a Japanese plane made a crash landing on Niihau near the house of a Hawaiian, Hawila (Howard) Kaleohano. Instantly Kaleohano disarmed the pilot and seized his papers. As a crowd gathered, Kaleohano sent for the only two Japanese residents of the island, Ishimatsu Shintani, an alien employed as head beekeeper for the Robinson family, and his assistant, a Nisei, Yoshio Harada, to act as interpreters.

Throughout the week the Hawaiians guarded their captive, somewhat puzzled that the regular weekly sampan from Kauai, scheduled to arrive on Monday, had not appeared. (The army had prevented it from making the trip.)

On Friday, December 12, the Hawaiians built a huge fire as a pre-arranged distress signal to get help from nearby Kauai. That same day the pilot persuaded the two Japanese on Niihau to help him. After careful investigation it was established that they acted from fear rather than from loyalty to Japan. With a pistol and shotgun, taken from the Robinson house, they freed the pilot from his lone guard and began to terrorize the island.

They searched Kaleohano's house for the pilot's papers, and set up the machine guns from the plane in the village of Puuwai. The women and children fled to caves or hid throughout the night in *kiawe* forests. The three conspirators threatened to kill Mrs. Huluoulani, who was too old to hide with the others, if she would not reveal where Kaleohano was hiding. She answered that only God had control over life and death, and continued to read her Bible. The frustrated conspirators vainly searched Kaleohano's house again for the papers, and then burned it in the hope of destroying them. They then burned the plane.

Meanwhile about midnight Kaleohano and four others began to row in a whaleboat across the rough channel to Kauai. After rowing continuously for sixteen hours they reached their destination about 3 P.M. on Saturday afternoon. They returned to Niihau at 7:30 Sunday morning with Aylmer Robinson and a military detachment on board the lighthouse tender *Kukui*.

By that time the "Battle of Niihau" had ended. Shortly after 7:00 A.M. on Saturday morning, Benehakaka (Benjamin) Kanahele and his wife attacked the pilot and his ally, Harada. In the scuffle the pilot shot Kanahele three times, in the thigh, groin and stomach. "Then I got mad," Kanahele later reported. Although badly wounded he picked up the pilot by the leg and neck and beat out his brains against a stone wall. Harada then shot himself and died several hours later.

Kanahele later received the Medal of Merit and also, by special dispensation because he was a civilian, the Purple Heart. Kaleohano received the Medal of Freedom.

The "Battle of Niihau" has given rise to a classic saying, "Never shoot a Hawaiian three times (or more than twice). He will get mad at you!"

Chapter 17

Hawaii in World War II

FOR RESIDENTS of the Hawaiian Islands, World War II was a mélange of terror, shock, hard work, overcrowding, heroism, rage, and all the other accelerated changes in attitudes and habits that came to other Americans. Hawaii was at one time a battleground and for many months a haven on the fringe of the actual war zone. The great American campaigns in the Pacific were funneled through the Islands, and the backwash of this surge of raw energy created turbulence and friction comparable to the slower surge of Western civilization through Hawaii to Oceania in the nineteenth century.

In the beginning there was terror. No one knew, or had the means of knowing, that the original intention of the Japanese attack was to knock out the United States Pacific Fleet and then withdraw for the more immediate objectives of imperial conquest in the Philippines, Malaya, and the Netherlands East Indies. In the hours of blackout and uncertainty which followed the original raid, Island residents worked frantically at tasks presented by the emergency (doctors in makeshift surroundings operated around the clock), or in solitude and inaction braced themselves for the expected assault and made many personal hypothetical decisions: should I shoot my wife and children to prevent them from becoming victims of the "yellow peril," or should we merely wait and hope (and pray) together and take our chances in a world coming apart at the seams? Citizens in Poland two years before had faced a similar crisis and had made similar resolutions. It is all very well, in the safe light of hindsight, to say that the fears of Hawaii's population were groundless. At the moment, as night fell swiftly (there is little twilight in the semitropics), few people slept and many searched their hearts. Only people who have experienced this moment of desperation will truly understand its impact. The others may imagine what it was like, and sympathize with the many hundreds who clutched their rifles with sweaty fingers and waited tensely for the invasion which never came.

Immediately Hawaii went on a war footing. Governor Poindexter declared martial law. The Army closed all saloons, liquor stores, and places of amusement, and put into effect a curfew and blackout. Barbed wire appeared on the beaches, and slit trenches were dug at various inland points. Adhesive tape criss-crossed plate-glass windows to prevent their shattering danger-ously in an air attack. Gas masks were issued, and people began to dig "scare *pukas*" (holes) as bomb shelters. Meanwhile in the early hours and days hundreds of volunteers assembled, including American Legionnaires, veterans of 1898 and 1918.

Although the Japanese, occupied as they were with their suc-cessful amphibious operations to the west, did not invade Ha-waii, their submarines operated in Hawaiian waters throughout the rest of December, 1941, and in January, 1942. Survivors from several torpedoed merchantmen reached the Islands, and on January 28 a Japanese submarine sank the army transport *Royal T. Frank* in the channel between Hawaii and Maui. In December submarines shelled Hilo on the Big Island, Kahului on Maui, and Nawiliwili on Kauai, but caused only slight damage. On October 17, 1943, a Japanese plane launched from a submarine made a successful reconnaissance of Pearl Harbor.

Aside from frantic and improvised measures to repulse an invasion, the main immediate war effort centered in Pearl Har-bor, where workers toiled to exhaustion to repair battle damage and to salvage vessels of war which had been sunk or beached. By December 20 the battleships *Maryland, Pennsylvania,* and *Tennessee* were operational. The *California* in October, 1942, and the *West Virginia* in May, 1943, left for refitting on the West Coast. The *Arizona, Oklahoma,* and *Utah* were beyond repair, although salvage workers took much equipment and a million gallons of precious oil from the *Arizona.* Fortunately, important installations such as oil storage tanks and drydocks had not been attacked.

In the months to come Oahu became a gigantic staging area from which the mounting offensive in the Pacific was launched. Hundreds of new buildings supplemented the older ones which were "pock-marked," as it was observed, by Japanese machine-gun bullets. The Navy's facilities expanded almost sevenfold at Pearl Harbor. Throughout the war years over 7,000 ships were repaired there, and at its peak the harbor contained 528 ships.

Thousands of troops swarmed over "the Rock," as the GI's called Oahu, on their way to and from the forward combat zones. Over a million men went through Schofield Barracks. In June, 1945, there were 253,000 soldiers on Oahu, as compared to 43,000 on December 7, 1941. In the peak month of December, 1944, the navy had 137,000 men in the Islands. In August, 1945, there were 116,000 marines in Hawaii.

Aside from operating as a staging area the Islands provided camps for basic and special training, immense and efficient hospitalization facilities for the wounded flown in from the battle zones, a number of intelligence and operation centers, and the thousand-and-one other installations necessary in fighting a mechanized war over a huge seagirt field of battle.

The war, of course, placed an enormous strain on Hawaii's resources. A peak total of 82,000 skilled war workers from the mainland ran head-on into a critical housing shortage. Restrictions on inter-island transport caused much food to rot on the piers and in the fields. Overcrowding, the annoyance of the curfew and blackout, and the general psychological strain of fighting the war caused tempers to flare high upon occasion. At times there were nasty brawls between servicemen and Island youths, known contemptuously to the GI's as "Gooks."

On the other hand many Islanders went out of their way to extend traditional Hawaiian hospitality to servicemen. Many opened their homes to aviators, submarine personnel, and others suffering from combat fatigue. Hawaii seemed incredibly peaceful, and beautiful too, to men temporarily out of combat. Some servicemen formed lasting friendships with Island residents during the war, and several thousand returned to live in the Islands when the hostilities ended.

In some respects Hawaii's war years have their counterpart elsewhere, but in some ways what happened to Hawaii in those troubled times was unique in American experience. In the first place the war began for Hawaii with a devastating air attack and the numbing fear of invasion. Second, Hawaii had difficulties with the military authorities in what some people have described as the only real instance of fascism in the history of the United States. Third, in Hawaii a racial minority, the Nisei Japanese, fought a heroic and often heralded crusade to prove to the world that they were first-class American citizens.

About noon on December 7, 1941, Lieutenant General Walter C. Short, the commanding general of the Hawaiian Department, called on Governor Poindexter and urged the immediate institution of martial law. He assured Poindexter that if no invasion came martial law would be lifted "within a reasonably short time." Reluctantly Poindexter agreed, and at 3:30 P.M. he issued a proclamation putting Hawaii under martial law. At the same time General Short proclaimed, "I have this day assumed the position of military governor of Hawaii, and have taken charge of the government of the Territory." Both proclamations had been in Army files since the previous March.

Poindexter based his action on Section 67 of the Hawaiian Organic Act which authorized martial law "in case of rebellion or invasion or imminent danger thereof." But, as Joseph Garner Anthony, later Hawaii's attorney-general, has stated in his well-documented book on the subject (*Hawaii Under Army Rule*, Stanford, 1955), Poindexter went beyond the provision of Section 67 by handing over in his proclamation the executive and judicial powers of the territorial government to the commanding general.

Martial law, along with the suspension of the writ of habeas corpus, functioned in Hawaii through a military commission—at first a combined civilian-military body and then an all-military body, which tried a few important cases—and through a network of provost (drumhead) courts. General Orders No. 4 (December 7, 1941) authorized the trial of civilians before these military courts, which were to be "guided by, but not limited to the penalties authorized by the courts-martial manual, the laws of the United States, the Territory of Hawaii, the District of Columbia, and the customs of laws in like cases."

In sum, fixed law was suspended for the duration of the emergency, and Island residents found themselves in the awkward predicament of having lost many of their traditional civil liberties. Workers were frozen in their jobs. Hawaii's provost courts collected over one million dollars in fines, imposed hundreds of prison sentences on civilians, and in many cases inflicted extraordinary punishments such as the enforced purchase of war bonds and the enforced donation of blood. In some instances, provost court officers were not legal specialists. As Garner Anthony stated, "Even the military governments imposed on the South during the Civil War did not cover the sweep of power that was exercised in Hawaii by the military arm from December 7, 1941, to March 10, 1943."

In the beginning few objected to martial law, which seemed mandatory to cope with a major military crisis. Under the circumstances it seemed unpatriotic to object. But the crisis, the "imminent danger" of invasion mentioned in Section 67, soon passed. The Army permitted the reopening of places of amusement on December 24, 1941, and the reopening of bars and liquor stores on February 4, 1942. In any case, the United States victory at the Battle of Midway of June 4-5, 1942, removed whatever shred of "imminent danger" to Hawaii which might have remained.

Nonetheless martial law continued. So did the blackout and 10:00 P.M. curfew, which were not removed until July 11, 1945. Honolulu civilians became increasingly annoyed that military installations were exempted from blackout regulations, just as servicemen returning from brightly lit places like Guadalcanal were astonished to find Honolulu's civilian areas in total darkness.

As Garner Anthony has commented, "It was plainly the desire of the high command in Hawaii to maintain the military government of Hawaii for as long a period as it could be maintained." In 1946 Judge J. Frank McLaughlin castigated the army authorities for this arbitrary rule: "They did it in knowing disregard of the Constitution. They did it because Hawaii is not a state. They did it because they did not have faith that Americanism transcends race, class and creed."

For a number of reasons there was comparatively little complaint. Ignorance and honest patriotism caused many to accept military rule. Others felt compensated for the loss of their liberty because the war brought much inflated prosperity. Students of the modern totalitarian state will recognize here a familiar and sickening pattern.

A change took place with the appointment on August 24, 1942, of Ingram M. Stainback as the ninth governor of the Territory of Hawaii. Stainback appointed Garner Anthony as Hawaii's attorney-general. In December they went to Washington to try to put an end to martial law. After conferences with civilian and military officials a compromise was reached.

On February 8, 1943, the governor and the commanding general issued proclamations to go into effect on March 10. Eighteen functions were restored to the territorial government. Jury indictment and trial, for example, replaced the provost courts in cases dealing with violations of federal and territorial law. But the military authorities retained jurisdiction over criminal cases dealing with violations of military orders and also kept control over the "frozen" laborers working on Army and Navy projects. Later arguments raised doubts as to whether the proclamations had restored the habeas corpus. In any case, appropriate ceremonies marked "Restoration Day" at Iolani palace on March 10.

Nonetheless friction with the military authorities continued. On August 16, 1943, Judge Delbert E. Metzger issued a writ of habeas corpus on behalf of Walter Glockner and Edwin R. Seifert, held in custody by the military authorities without charges. That same day a middle-aged deputy United States marshal, attempting to serve the writ on the commanding general, Robert C. Richardson, Jr., was manhandled by military police and prevented from doing his duty. Richardson accepted service on August 20, but on orders from General Marshall, the Army Chief of Staff, refused to produce the prisoners. Judge Metzger on August 25 found him guilty of contempt and fined him $5,000. That same day Richardson issued his famous General Orders No. 31, which forbade courts in the territory to accept applications for writs of habeas corpus, and specifically ordered Judge Metzger to stop proceedings in the case of Glockner and Seifert, under penalty of a $5,000 fine or five years' imprisonment, or both.

In a compromise Richardson withdrew his order. Judge Metzger reduced the fine to $100 but refused to rescind the contempt charge. President Roosevelt later granted Richardson a pardon and remitted the fine.

Five cases tested the legality of martial law as exercised in Hawaii. In two cases (Zimmerman's and that of Glockner and Seifert) the Army prevented a full-scale judicial review of their constitutionality by taking the prisoners to the mainland and releasing them there. In a third case (Spurlock's) the Army prevented an appeal to the Supreme Court by remitting the rest of his sentence.

Martial law ended in Hawaii on October 24, 1944, by presidential proclamation. But meanwhile two cases (Duncan's and White's) were combined and taken to the United States Circuit Court in San Francisco, where the petitioners had the support of the Bar Association of Hawaii and the American Civil Liberties Union. On December 7, 1945 (a significant anniversary), this case came before the United States Supreme Court, which ruled on February 25, 1946, that martial law as exercised in the Islands exceeded the authority as stated in the Organic Act.

One view of the matter appeared in the platform of Hawaii's Democratic party in 1944: "Hawaii is not a conquered nation but as a part of the United States is justly proud of its role in this war and is entitled to the kind of government prescribed by the constitution and laws of the Congress of the United States, and that the imposition of a military government over this loyal American territory is contrary to every tradition of America from its very beginnings."

While Hawaii smarted under the military government, one

group of Americans, like their counterparts on the mainland, felt not only shock and rage but shame at the sneak attack. On December 7, 1941, there were about 158,000 people of Japanese descent in Hawaii, of whom about 120,000 were Americans by birth. These AJA's (Americans of Japanese Ancestry) had a particularly hard ordeal in the war to prove their loyalty as Americans.

Color prejudice and echoes of the "yellow peril" myth created in some quarters suspicion and outright hostility toward the AJA's. *Haole* leaders, who lived apart from their Japanese neighbors, were not in a position to vouch for their loyalty. In his telephone conversation with President Roosevelt on December 7, 1941, Governor Poindexter reportedly stated that Hawaii's main danger was from the "local Japs." The United States Navy accepted (until 1947) no *Nisei* enlistments, and naval officers justified this policy on the ground that "Once a Jap, always a Jap." Early in 1943 a Honolulu businessman, John R. Balch, published a pamphlet entitled *Shall the Japanese Be Allowed to Dominate Hawaii?* Balch also urged the evacuation to the mainland of all Island residents of Japanese descent.

Meanwhile these unfortunate people made themselves as inconspicuous as possible. (Their critics accordingly accused them of being sullen.) They stopped wearing kimonos, destroyed everything Japanese in their homes, and stopped speaking Japanese to their parents. They also abandoned Japanese customs and festivals and stopped drinking sake. Instantly leadership in the Japanese community passed from the alien elders to the American-born Nisei.

The AJA's did not lack defenders. Charles R. Hemenway, long a member of the board of regents of the University of Hawaii, was outspoken in insisting on their loyalty. Hawaii's delegate to Congress, Samuel Wilder King, stated early in 1941, "I have felt and said repeatedly that those who believe they can return any loyalty towards Japan after having been born and brought up in an American environment, belittle the value of our American institutions and the great benefits our American democracy offers to the individual. I have not the slightest doubt that the overwhelming majority of our citizens of Japanese ancestry are loyal to the United States, and are making every effort to make themselves completely American."

Six months before the attack on Pearl Harbor Dr. Shunzo Sakamaki of the University of Hawaii stated, "We cherish our heritage as Americans, and we realize how fortunate we are to be living in this of all the lands of the earth. It is only natural and proper, therefore, that our loyalty to the United States should be true and deep-rooted. These are not mere words spoken for effect, with tongue in cheek. We are fully conscious of their import, and we mean every word. And we wish to add, in unmistakable language, that if and when war comes, no matter with what other country, we will do everything we possibly can, giving our lives if necessary, in defense of those democratic principles which other Americans have lived, and fought, and died for."

Nonetheless, there were Doubting Thomases in high military places. On January 21, 1942, the 317 AJA's in Hawaii's Territorial Guard were dismissed without explanation. Here was the challenge. The response came in the form of a letter from the dismissed men to Lieutenant General Delos C. Emmons, the commanding general of the Hawaiian Department, which stated in part, "Hawaii is our home; the United States, our country. We know but one loyalty and that is to the Stars and Stripes. We wish to do our part as loyal Americans in every way possible and we hereby offer ourselves for whatever service you may see fit to use us."

The army responded by inviting the AJA's to form a labor unit under the Corps of Engineers. Over 150 AJA's signed up at $90 a month, in preference to taking other war work which was much more highly paid. Most of the boys were students or graduates of the University of Hawaii, and the unit became known popularly as the Varsity Victory Volunteers (VVV).

On June 5, 1942, the 1,406 AJA's in the army left Hawaii for training on the mainland, where they formed the famous 100th Infantry Battalion. This group, known to its members as the "One *puka puka*" (*puka* means "hole," therefore "zero" in Hawaiian), left for North Africa and Italy in the summer of 1943.

Meanwhile on January 28, 1943, General Emmons called for 1,500 AJA volunteers, and the VVV labor unit was disbanded so that its members could enter the army. Within a few weeks almost 10,000 AJA's volunteered. Ultimately about 2,600 were accepted and sent for training to the mainland, where they joined about 2,000 AJA's from other parts of the United States. This group, known as the 442nd Regimental Combat Team, sailed for Europe on May 1, 1944, and a month later, at Civitavecchia, Italy, absorbed the 100th Battalion.

The war record of these Nisei soldiers has become a military legend. In Italy and France the 100th and the 442nd became known as the "Purple-Heart Regiment." They had over 4,000 casualties, including 650 killed and 67 listed as missing in action. Those who visited these troops in the Walter Reed or some other hospital will never be able to forget that the term "wounded" may refer to a multiple amputee case. Their honors included 1 Congressional Medal of Honor, 7 Presidential Distinguished Unit Citations, 47 Distinguished Service Crosses, 1 Distinguished Service Medal, 12 Oak Leaf Clusters to the Silver Star, 350 Silver Stars, 18 Legion of Merits, 16 Soldier's Medals, 41 Oak Leaf Clusters to the Bronze Star Medal, 823 Bronze Star Medals, one Air Medal, 500 Oak Leaf Clusters to the Purple Heart Medal, and 3,600 Purple Heart Medals. In addition they received 18 foreign decorations, including the *Croix de guerre*. Their record fully entitles them to take an honored place among other brave Americans who served in places such as Valley Forge, Gettysburg, San Juan Hill, the Argonne, and Guadalcanal.

Other American troops overseas recognized their fighting qualities. In August, 1945, every man in Company D, 168th Infantry, which had advanced with the AJA's from Salerno to the Arno River, signed a statement: "We do hereby assert that our help can be counted upon to convince the folks back home that you are fully deserving of all the privileges with which we are ourselves bestowed. It is a privilege and honor to acknowledge the members of the 100th Battalion and the 442nd Regiment as fellow Americans. We are duly proud to say 'Well Done' to you and yours."

Particularly as translators and intelligence agents, the AJA's served, not only in Italy and France, but also in every Pacific campaign from Guadalcanal to Okinawa. A few were in Burma with Merrill's Marauders, and they also served elsewhere in the China-Burma-India theater of operations. For security reasons these troops received no publicity, but in recognition of their valuable services a high ranking officer called them "America's secret weapon."

Meanwhile, on the home front, Hawaiian residents of Japanese descent did what they could to demonstrate their loyalty. On June 5, 1943, over 1,700 of them contributed a total of $10,340.16 to the United States Treasury, and wrote bluntly, "We are real Americans and we are going to act and fight like Americans. We hope that this money will be used for bombs which will give Tojo and his cutthroats bloody hell."

For the AJA's in general the war became a kind of latter-day crusade, to prove to a doubting world that they were really Americans. As Captain Spark Masayuki Matsunaga, who fought with the 100th in Italy, testified before a Senate committee in May, 1950, "Those men whom I saw die at the front did die for ideals—died so that those whom they left behind would have a better life and might enjoy the full status of American citizenship despite their racial ancestry."

The tremendous drama of the AJA crusade has tended, somewhat unfortunately, to obscure the war service of other Americans in Hawaii. In the early months of the war Selective Service inductions were suspended in the Islands for a number of reasons, among them the imagined need for young and healthy young men in case of an invasion, and the real need for war workers in military installations such as Pearl Harbor. Consequently, although 40,000 served, the over-all proportion of Island residents in uniform was lower than in some of the states. Nonetheless in the various branches of the armed services 806 Hawaiian residents were killed and over 2,000 were permanently disabled.

They served with distinction in every theater of war. One was with Doolittle's raid on Tokyo. Another was a navigator in the B-17 raids on Germany. A third fought in Austria. A fourth lost his life as a paratrooper in France on D-Day. Others served in such diverse locations as New Guinea, the Philippines, Burma, North Africa, and Attu.

News of peace with Japan came to Hawaii, as to other parts of the United States, on August 14, 1945. A typical jubilant and near-hysterical demonstration followed receipt of the news at 1:42 P.M.

Official V-J Day came on September 1, when the Japanese authorities formally surrendered on board the *Missouri* in Tokyo harbor. That day something weird and pathetic occurred in Honolulu. Scores of Issei Japanese, convinced by their earlier training that Imperial Japan could never lose a war, gathered on Aiea Heights to watch the Japanese navy enter Pearl Harbor.

Chapter 18

The Postwar Years, 1945-59

AFTER THE WAR ended, Hawaii shared with other parts of the United States the enormous problems of readjusting to peace. A highly complicated war-making machine, with its roots in industry under government controls, had slowly to be disassembled. Hundreds of thousands of troops wanted "out," and fast, although some found in military life a pattern of living which exactly suited them, and consequently stayed in uniform while their fellows left for thousands of places called "home." Hawaii's many servicemen streamed back to the Islands, wore *leis* and smiles in warm-hearted welcoming celebrations, and settled back to the far less hectic routine of being just plain Mr. Civilian again. Meanwhile many more servicemen passed through the Islands briefly and with torn feelings on their way eastward to the mainland.

At last the final vestiges of military rule vanished, and the wheels of politics turned in areas of more peaceful concern. Governor Ingram M. Stainback, appointed by President Roosevelt in 1942, continued in office until 1951. At that time President Truman appointed Oren E. Long as Hawaii's tenth territorial governor. Long, who served until 1953, was born in Altoona, Kansas, and came to Hawaii in 1917. In the Islands he had a distinguished career as an educator and as a member of the territorial senate. In 1953 he was succeeded by Samuel Wilder King, a *kamaaina* with a long record of devoted service as Hawaii's delegate to Congress. Hawaii's last territorial governor was William Francis Quinn, appointed in 1957. Quinn, born in Rochester, New York, served with the Navy in World War II and after graduating from Harvard Law School settled in the Islands in 1947. These men performed well the difficult and delicate task of directing Hawaii's political adjustment to the postwar world.

In 1950 the outbreak of the Korean "conflict" interrupted the postwar recovery and brought misery and sacrifice to Hawaii as to other parts of the United States. Island troops at first served mainly in the 5th Regimental Combat Team (sometimes called "Hawaii's Own"), the 24th and 25th Divisions, the 1st Cavalry Division, and the 7th Infantry Division, but in time they were scattered widely among other units engaged in this cruel and frustrating holocaust. Some AJA's from the 100th and 442nd were among the 17,000 Island residents serving in the Korean War.

General J. Lawton Collins has stated: "The splendid part played by Hawaii in the Korean war is entirely in keeping with the distinguished record it established in World War II. The record of the Korean war can be summarized as follows: Not one case of cowardice by a Hawaii soldier in the face of the Communist enemy was recorded in Korea. Not one successful

Red "brainwashing" of any Hawaii soldier was recorded. Not one case of a Hawaii soldier's desertion to the enemy was recorded. Of the 22 American servicemen who refused repatriation after the Korean war in favor of remaining with the Communists . . . there was not one from Hawaii. There were 426 Hawaii boys killed in Korea action, a death toll 4½ times the killed-in-action average for the rest of the United States. There were 1,352 total battle casualties from Hawaii, a rate three times as great as the casualty rate per capita for the rest of the nation."

Meanwhile, and despite this savage interlude, Islanders went about their daily tasks to rebuild and advance their productive resources. In the years 1950-59 the annual value of sugar produced rose from $124 million to $131 million on Hawaii's twenty-seven plantations and the annual value of pineapples rose from $101 million to $127 million. In keeping with its previous tradition of scientific agriculture, the sugar industry spent $2 million on research in 1959, and the pineapple industry spent nearly $1 million.

A striking economic development occurred in diversified agriculture, which rose in value from $28 million in 1950 to over $43 million in 1959. Major items in diversified agriculture in 1959 included beef ($11.2 million), dairy milk ($9.4 million), vegetables ($5.9 million), eggs ($5.8 million), hogs ($3.7 million, coffee ($2.9 million), tropical fruit and nuts ($2.4 million), and poultry ($1.8 million). In 1959 the Islands also produced 148 tons of honey and beeswax valued at $36,000. In addition the Big Island has developed a flourishing trade in the export of orchids. Despite the introduction of the destructive Oriental fruit fly by troops from Saipan in 1944 or 1945, there is much opportunity for truck farming in Hawaii, since crops grow continuously every day. With proper fertilization it is possible to grow eight or more vegetable crops in a year.

The rise in diversified farming is a symptom of the way Hawaii's economic base is broadening. In Oahu, which accounts for almost four-fifths of Hawaii's population, the dollar volume of construction rose from $97 million in 1955 to $216 million in 1959. In the latter year a large oil refinery, a steel mill, and two cement mills were under construction, and manufactures reached an annual value of $129 million. A striking example of this boom in diversified manufacture was Hawaii's garment industry, which rose in value from $10 million in 1959 to about $18 million in 1960.

Most striking of all was the increase in the tourist industry.

The number of tourists coming to Hawaii rose from 46,000 in 1950 to 243,000 in 1959, more than a fivefold increase. In these years the revenues from the tourist trade increased from $24 million to $109 million. To encourage and serve this huge influx the prewar Hawaii Tourist Bureau was revived as the new and enlarged Hawaii Visitors Bureau.

Another feature of the postwar tourist trade was the construction of a number of lavish and lovely large resort hotels on the outlying islands, mainly Hawaii, Maui, and Kauai. Of these one of the most magnificent is the Hotel King Kamehameha on the Big Island's Kona Coast. It serves tropical drinks in its attractive Splintered Paddle Bar. One wonders what Kamehameha the Great would make of all this. There is an even chance that he would approve.

Except for a small number of cabins on unscheduled freighters, inter-island travel by sea is a thing of the past. Currently almost everyone travels among the islands by air. Hawaii's regularly scheduled airlines and charter planes carried over 800,000 passengers in 1959. *Kamaainas* have become quite casual about inter-island air travel. Some of them refer to the trip as a "trolley-car ride."

A major factor in the expansion of Hawaii's tourist industry was the industrial and shipping magnate, Henry John Kaiser, who first came to Honolulu on a short visit in 1954. When he was unable to find a hotel room, so it is said, he decided to do something about the shortage. He began by buying an undeveloped area just west of Fort De Russy and building there the modernistic and domed Hawaiian Village Hotel. After much protracted negotiation he reclaimed submerged lands off his acreage and constructed a beach and tropical lagoon. Already Kaiser has built over $50 million worth of hotels, hospitals, housing developments, and other installations including a cement plant and a radio and television station.

Kaiser then undertook a gigantic project called Hawaii Kai ("Sea" in Hawaiian) on the east and southeast coasts of Oahu. This huge development will cover some 6,000 acres leased from the Bishop Estate and is designated to become the home of 75,000 people. It will include twenty miles of marina frontage, with hotels, beaches, golf courses, parks, and other recreation facilities. Its ultimate cost is estimated at one billion dollars. Some houses in the development have already been constructed in Portlock at the base of Koko Head.

Although some *kamaainas* have grumbled that Kaiser is ruining (or has already ruined) the Islands, they are really being nostalgic and somewhat unrealistic. Kaiser and others like him from the mainland, now active as promoters, investors, and workers in Island industries, are merely the symptoms and agents of Hawaii's broadening economic base. The total mainland investment in Hawaii was approaching one billion dollars in 1960. At this time, there were several Sheraton hotels at Waikiki. Several mainland investment firms have established branches in downtown Honolulu. These include Francis I. Dupont; Warner, Jenning, Mandel and Longstreth of Philadelphia; and Schwabacher and Company. In sum, Hawaii's economy has become increasingly integrated with the mainland, and with the Orient also. Capital from without has quickened Hawaii's economy, and capital from Hawaii has found investment outlets far from the Crossroads of the Pacific.

The influx of mainland capital and industry to Hawaii has, of course, presented a serious challenge to the Big Five, just as the influx of executives from the mainland has presented a serious challenge to the scions of *kamaaina* families. At the same time the second and third generations of men and women of Oriental descent have presented an increasing economic challenge to island-born and other *haoles*. Something approaching a three-way equilibrium among these groups seems to be in process of formation. The issue, as yet far from settled, must, of course, be left for the future to decide.

Nonetheless, under vigorous and enlightened management the Big Five have kept pace with the times. Here Castle and Cooke, the biggest of the Big Five, with stated assets of $117 million in 1960, may serve as an illustration. With 156,000 acres of land, Castle and Cooke is the third largest landowner in Hawaii (after the Bishop Estate and the Parker Ranch). The company has an interest in three sugar plantations, Kohala on the Big Island (wholly owned), Waialua on Oahu (52 per cent ownership), and Ewa on Oahu (30 per cent ownership). In addition it has an interest in the California and Hawaiian (C & H) Sugar Refining Corporation in San Francisco. It wholly owns the Dole Corporation, formerly the Hawaiian Pineapple Company, which produces almost 40 per cent of Hawaii's pineapples and also packs fruit and vegetables on the West Coast. Castle and Cooke owns 24 per cent of the stock of the Matson Navigation Company and serves as the Honolulu freight agent of that company and other carriers, among them Isthmian Lines and Nippon Yusen Kaisha. It has a 55 per cent interest in Kawaihae Terminals, Inc., which operates storage and loading facilities at the new port of Kawaihae on the Big Island. Its wholly owned subsidiary, Castle and Cooke Terminals, Ltd., handles about 80 per cent of the stevedoring at the port of Honolulu. Its wholly owned subsidiary, Hawaiian Equipment Co., Ltd., is a wholesale distributor of much agricultural and industrial equipment for firms such as International Harvester, Ingersoll-Rand, and Fruehauf Trailers. It has a 40 per cent interest in the First (before 1961, Home) Insurance Company of Hawaii, Ltd., which annually collects gross premiums of about $10 million.

Castle and Cooke has recently made an effort to diversify further its interests in order to broaden its economic base. It has absorbed Bumble Bee Seafoods, Inc. (formerly Columbia River Packers Association, Inc.), one of the largest packers of sea food in the United States. It has about 1,500 acres planted in macadamia nuts, which it sells under the brand name of Royal Hawaiian Macadamia Nuts. In addition, Castle and Cooke holds as a speculation the self-supporting 6,500 acre Blackhawk Ranch in Contra Costa County, California, near San Francisco. With an eye to the future, Castle and Cooke is alert to the possibility that some of its extensive land in the Islands may be suitable as resorts for the tourist trade.

A vast unionization movement, somewhat like a belated New Deal, accompanied and agitated Hawaii's postwar economic development. Before the war there were few union members in the Islands, about 500 in 1935 and only 10,000 in 1941. The great plantations, with docile peasant labor imported under contract, operated in a thoroughly paternalistic fashion, with low cash wages, while the plantations generally supplied food, housing, and medical care.

The war brought about 25,000 unionized workers to Hawaii who spread much pro-union sentiment in the Islands. The arbitrary "freezing" of workers in their jobs for the duration created much discontent which also prepared the way for unionization after the controls were removed. By 1947, Hawaii had about 40,000 union members, mainly belonging to the International Longshoremen's and Warehousemen's Union (ILWU). The old paternalism vanished, as plantation owners raised wages and began to charge nominal sums for food, housing, and medical care. The higher wages associated with unionization also encouraged the further development of mechanical equipment on the plantations to keep costs down, among them a mechanical harvester for pineapples. In more general terms, Hawaii's big union, the ILWU, taken in conjunction with smaller unions, has created in some degree an economic counterpoise to Hawaii's big businesses. Much the same, of course, has happened on the mainland.

A number of crippling strikes accompanied the unionization process—a phenomenon not at all unusual in the United States. In 1946, Hawaii's sugar workers were on strike for over ten weeks, with high losses both in production and in wages. An even more serious strike occurred in 1949, when for 178 days, the ILWU tied up shipping between Hawaii and the West Coast. In 1958 a long and disastrous sugar strike ended in partial victory for labor, which won a slight increase in hourly wages. The net result, especially from the shipping strike, was to encourage agitation for statehood, so that Hawaii might have broader powers to protect its economy. A second result was the movement for further diversification of business, particularly on the part of the Big Five, to prevent the disaster of having too many eggs in a small number of vulnerable economic baskets.

Some Communist activity accompanied Hawaii's unionization, as elsewhere in the United States. To combat communism the legislature established in 1949 a tax-supported Territorial Commission on Subversive Activities. In addition public-spirited residents of the Islands organized a privately supported anti-Communist agency known as Imua (in Hawaiian, "Forward"), which had a budget of $92,000 in 1958. These two organizations have been singularly successful. In 1959, Stewart French, chief counsel of the United States Senate's Committee on Interior and Insular Affairs, after investigation, spoke plainly of "the vigilance, resourcefulness, and energy of the people of Hawaii in combating communism in their midst, despite the handicap of Territorial status."

The over-all growth of, and internal shifts in, Hawaii's population may be seen in the following table:

POPULATION OF HAWAII, 1950-60

(By Numbers)

	1950	1960
Japanese	184,611	203,455
Caucasian	114,793	202,230
Filipino	61,071	69,070
Chinese	32,376	38,197
Negro	2,651	4,943
Other	104,292	114,877
Total	499,794	632,772

(By Percentages)

Japanese	36.9	32.2
Caucasian	23.0	32.0
Filipino	12.2	10.9
Chinese	6.5	6.0
Negro	0.5	0.8
Other	20.9	18.1
Total	100.0	100.0

These statistics reveal that in the years 1950-60 Hawaii's total population increased by over 25 per cent. The most significant increase among racial and ethnic groups was in the Caucasian, which almost doubled in these years, largely from immigration to the Islands. The numerical relationship of the Caucasians to the Japanese has shifted sharply. The Japanese outnumbered the Caucasians two to one in 1920 and almost three to two in 1950, but in 1960 their numbers were about the same. Some statisticians, who find little significant differences in the birth rates of these groups, expect the Caucasian element in Hawaii to grow more rapidly than the Japanese, since many Caucasians are coming to Hawaii, while few Japanese are entering the Islands and some are leaving. In any case, here is an answer to those false prophets who predicted a generation ago that ultimately the Japanese would dominate Hawaii. On the other hand, this whole train of argument has little importance, for most of Hawaii's "Japanese" are really Americans, including over 10,000 naturalized after 1952.

The "other" category in the statistics consists mainly of Hawaiians and Part-Hawaiians. In recent years about one-third of the marriages in Hawaii have crossed racial and ethnic lines, and sociologists accordingly expect the Part-Hawaiian group to increase sharply. Even the Japanese, who traditionally married almost entirely within their own community, are crossing racial lines. In 1959 about one-fifth of the Japanese women and about one-tenth of the Japanese men married out of their race. Further, sociologists have pointed out that basic differences among Hawaii's racial and ethnic groups are declining. The birth, death, and infant mortality rates of Hawaii's various peoples do not differ significantly. Increasingly the "racial" factor is declining, as group activities are based more and more on similarities of interest of a religious, socio-economic, professional, or recreational character.

In addition, Hawaii's class structure has shifted. Descendants of immigrant aliens, fortified by sound education, have prospered. Some have achieved great wealth. The net result has been to strengthen Hawaii's middle class, and with this phenomenon has come a quite normal change of attitude. The original alien immigrants to Hawaii resembled other alien immigrants to the United States. They were deeply appreciative of the higher standard of living and freedom which they found in their new home, and they generally made a great effort to conform to American ways. In gratitude and humility they worked hard and tried hard to please, while the language barrier kept them somewhat apart from more established and more privileged groups. But their children and grandchildren, with no language barrier and an education in the American tradition of democracy and equality of opportunity, aspired to be first-class citizens. The Nisei Japanese in particular felt that they had earned such equal status because of their magnificent war record. What some *haoles* regard as a "cocky" attitude on their part is merely their pride and their wish to be accepted on an equal footing with all other members of the Hawaiian community.

In any case, Hawaiian residents of Oriental descent have achieved much greater weight than before in the Islands. In postwar politics a number of AJA's, for example, received unprecedented appointments to high public office. In 1952, Sakae Takahashi, a lawyer and former captain in the 100th Battalion, was appointed treasurer of the territory, the first AJA to become a cabinet member. In 1953, Howard K. Hiroki, another veteran of the 100th, became auditor of the territory, Dr. Katsumi Kometani became chairman of the Board of Commissioners of Public Instruction, and Jack Mizuha became a member of the board of regents of the University of Hawaii.

Hawaii's shifting social structure has had other repercussions in politics. In 1954 Islanders broke a tradition of long standing by electing a Democratic legislature. In 1956 the legislature was again Democratic, by a somewhat lesser majority. But in that year another upset occurred when the Democratic candidate John A. Burns defeated Mrs. Farrington, the widow of former delegate Joseph R. Farrington, in the election for Hawaii's delegate to Congress. Some observers have interpreted these election results as the political defeat of the Big Five.

Chapter 19

The Fiftieth State

THE POSTWAR YEARS brought to a climax Hawaii's long struggle to become a state. The drive behind the statehood campaign was a phase of nationalism, as Islanders developed chauvinistic pride in being residents of Hawaii. On one occasion in the 1930's the headmaster of a boy's select prep school in New England, in speaking to the middle-aged granddaughter of one of the missionaries, characterized Hawaii as being in "the backwaters of civilization." His tactless remark provoked fury, and she often told the story in her family circle. In seeking statehood Hawaii was really seeking freedom, not in the sense of becoming independent of the United States, but in the liberal-national sense of becoming a first-class instead of a second-class American community.

As citizens of a territory, Islanders lacked certain fundamental rights. A United States Senate committee recommending statehood in 1959 summarized these as follows:

"1. The right to voting representation in both the Senate and the House of Representatives;

"2. The right to vote for the President and Vice President of the United States;

"3. The right to choose their own Governor and to carry on functions of government by their own elected officials instead of Federal administrators;

"4. The right to determine the extent of the powers to be exercised by their own legislature;

"5. The right to have local justice administered by judges selected under local authority rather than by Federal appointees;

"6. The right to freedom from overlapping Federal and local authority; and

"7. The right to a voice in any proposed amendment of the Federal Constitution, as well as on the taxes which they must pay."

In essence the issue was the British-derived American cry of "No taxation without representation," and in sounding this note the American citizens of Hawaii were evoking the basic demand of the American colonists in 1776. Former Governor Lawrence M. Judd was quoted in 1953 as having stated, "I do definitely feel that until such time as Hawaii is granted statehood, the United States government should desist from collecting all federal income and other taxes from residents of Hawaii. In other words, grant us statehood now. If not, then stop taking our money until you do." Unquestionably Thomas Jefferson would have endorsed the spirit of those remarks.

Over the years Island residents accumulated a long list of real grievances. It took eight years of fighting to get part of the benefit of the Federal Road Act of 1916, and Hawaii had similar difficulty in obtaining federal support of its territorial university. One of the main tasks of Hawaii's voteless delegate to Congress was to try to add the words "and Territories" to bills pertaining to "the several States." Hawaii was omitted, for example, from the original Social Security bill. Hawaii paid the higher gasoline and excise taxes for the construction of interstate highways, yet received none of this money for Island roads. In the five years before 1952, Hawaii paid $485 million in federal taxes but received only $50 million in federal grants.

There were other grievances. Island residents remembered the discriminatory Jones-Costigan Sugar Control Act of 1934; Franklin Roosevelt's attempt to introduce a carpetbag regime; the attempt on the part of the armed services to institute a commission form of government as a reaction to the controversial Massie case; California's discrimination against Hawaii's honey; and the Army's illegal regime of martial law during World War II. There were other difficulties. The Immigration and Naturalization Service of the U.S. Justice Department stubbornly refused to admit that Hawaii, although only a territory, was an "integral part" of the United States. It was infuriating when thick-headed and self-important immigration officials made it difficult for aliens holding United States permanent resident visas to return from Hawaii to the mainland.

Following the abortive annexation and statehood proposals in the mid-nineteenth century, agitation for statehood was resumed in 1903, when the Hawaiian legislature sent a petition for statehood to the United States Congress. Many other similar petitions followed in later years. In 1919, Prince Kuhio Kalanianaole introduced the first statehood bill to the 65th Congress, but the bill was sent to committee and no action followed.

In 1935, in reaction to the Jones-Costigan Act, strong agitation for statehood was revived. In that year Congress began the first of twenty-four hearings on statehood, the reports of

which fill 6,690 pages in thirty-four volumes. In 1940 a plebiscite in Hawaii voted two to one in favor of statehood.

After the war the clamor for statehood continued. In 1947,
Hawaii created a tax-supported commission to promote statehood, and in that year the United States House of Representatives passed a bill granting it. President Truman indicated his
approval, but the Senate insisted on further investigation.

In 1950 a convention drafted and a plebiscite approved by
three to one a proposed constitution for the state of Hawaii.
Its preamble stated, in language which would have delighted
Hiram Bingham, "We, the people of the State of Hawaii, grateful for Divine Guidance, and mindful of our Hawaiian heritage,
reaffirm our belief in a government of the people, by the people
and for the people, and with an understanding heart toward all
the peoples of the earth, do hereby ordain and establish this
constitution for the State of Hawaii."

Disappointments followed. In 1948 and in 1952 the national
platforms of both the Republican and Democratic parties
favored statehood for Hawaii. President Eisenhower supported
statehood and said in 1959, "May I voice the hope that before
my term of office is ended I shall have the opportunity and
great satisfaction of seeing the 50th star in our national flag."
But the statehood bills met consistent and successful opposition,
primarily from Southern Democrats, fearful that they would
lose strength if Hawaii elected Republicans to Congress.

Meanwhile Island residents kept up their agitation. In 1954
a roll of newsprint paper six feet wide and almost a mile long
was rolled out on a downtown street in Honolulu as a statehood
petition. In a few days 116,000 people signed it.

Quite naturally, during all these heated proceedings, a great
debate arose. Supporters of statehood argued that Hawaii was
geographically larger than three states (Connecticut, Delaware,
and Rhode Island); that it had a greater population than
six states (New Hampshire, Delaware, Vermont, Wyoming,
Nevada, and Alaska); and that it paid higher federal taxes
than 10 states (New Hampshire, Vermont, North Dakota,
South Dakota, Montana, Idaho, Wyoming, New Mexico,
Nevada, and Alaska).

In studying the question a Senate committee decided in 1959
that there were three customary requirements for statehood:
that the inhabitants of a territory believed in and practiced a
democratic way of life; that a majority desired statehood; and
that the territory had enough population and resources to support itself and pay its share of federal costs.

The committee concluded that Hawaii was truly democratic and cited the liberal 1840 constitution, the democratic proposed constitution of 1950, and Hawaii's record in World War II and the Korean conflict. Hawaii's plebiscites in support of statehood in 1940 and of the proposed state constitution ten years later met the second requirement. A survey of Hawaii's economy, the fact that Hawaii had more population than six states and paid more federal taxes than ten, satisfied the third.

The committee then raised and answered four main arguments against statehood: "(1) That communism is a threat to the political stability of the Territory . . .; (2) That the so-called Caucasians are outnumbered by groups of different ancestry; (3) That the Territory is noncontiguous and hence outside the pattern of the present United States; (4) That two senators from Hawaii would give the new State representation in Congress disproportionate to its population in comparison with other states."

In reply to these arguments the committee cited evidence from the Department of Justice and the Department of Defense and stated "that a grant of statehood will not in any way decrease the ability of the Nation or the people of Hawaii to combat the malignancy of communism. On the contrary, the people of Hawaii have taken unprecedented steps to protect themselves and have shown superior recognition of the menace."

On the racial issue the committee took a firm stand. "The committee does not believe that the 86th Congress will deny full political equality to a group of its own citizens who have met every historic test of qualifying for statehood merely because of the ancestry of a part of that group. Hawaii has been thoroughly American in word, thought, and deed for a half century and longer. Its American institutions and school systems have produced American citizens worthy to stand on a basis of full equality with the best citizens of any State in the Union."

On the issue of noncontiguity the committee stated, "Physical contiguity is not, and never in all our history has ever been, one of the requirements for statehood." On this point supporters of statehood stated elsewhere that California in 1850 was not contiguous to any other state, nor was Alaska when it became a state in 1958. The committee stated further, "In terms of modern communication and transportation Hawaii is today far closer to Washington than were many of the Original Thirteen States when the Constitution was adopted. . . . The argument that Hawaii is noncontiguous can carry little weight. Hawaii is in fact contiguous to the mainland for all practical purposes." On this point there was general agreement. With California a little over five hours by jet plane from the East Coast and Hawaii a little over four hours from California, it would today be possible to have breakfast in New York City and (considering the time change) have lunch at the Hale-kulani Hotel on Waikiki Beach.

Finally, on the issue of representation, the committee stated tersely, "The last argument, which asserts that two Senators would dilute the representation of large States, seems . . . to have been wisely and finally settled 172 years ago by the Founding Fathers."

The Senate committee accordingly made a strong recommendation for statehood. "More than one-half million Americans in Hawaii are asking for the responsibilities that go with the kind of government which we know to be best for the Nation and best for individual Americans. The committee believes that Hawaii has proved all qualities that the Nation traditionally demands. Now is the time to prove to all the world that self-determination applies in the United States just as it must apply wherever in the world human nature can be free to follow its course."

On an issue of such magnitude not everyone agreed. Former Governor Stainback argued eloquently, not for statehood, but for commonwealth status, without federal taxes, which Puerto Rico received in 1952. Stainback argued that because of high costs of production sugar in Hawaii was a "dying industry," that the pineapple industry was threatened by foreign competition, that the tourist industry was a luxury business vulnerable to recessions, and that Hawaii had little land available for homesteading and no large deposits of minerals. (Presumably he was unaware of Hawaii's bauxite deposits.) Accordingly he opposed statehood "not only on the ground our economic development requires a commonwealth-type government so the Territory can offer inducements to new industries to supply jobs for our rapidly increasing population and decreasing jobs but, further, because the communist menace is real. . . . As long as Hawaii remains a Territory . . . Congress could alter the Territorial form of government in such manner as might afford protection against the Communists."

Another strong opponent of statehood was Benjamin F. Dillingham II of a prominent *kamaaina* family. He was quoted as stating, "I formerly favored statehood for Hawaii but the

1955 Territorial legislature, in which I served as a member of the senate, changed my mind. As I observed the legislature I decided we were not politically mature and should wait for statehood." In speaking of his fellow legislators he reportedly commented, "I found too many of them tainted with New Dealism." This segment of opinion represented the conservative wing of some of Hawaii's *kamaaina* families, which apparently refused to recognize the fact that, whether they liked it or not, the New Deal had become a basic part of American political and economic life 22 years before Hawaii's 1955 legislature convened. Other conservative *haoles* viewed with alarm the possibility that Hawaii's representatives in Washington might be "Japanese."

Nonetheless, such voices found themselves in the minority. On March 11, 1959, the United States Senate passed the statehood enabling act, and the House passed it on March 12. That day Governor Quinn telephoned the good news from Washington. Sirens screamed, firecrackers went off, and people danced in the streets in the greatest celebration since VJ day. A plebiscite on June 28 voted for statehood by a majority of seventeen to one, and on August 21 President Eisenhower declared in an official proclamation that Hawaii was the fiftieth state.

In the elections which followed, over 93 per cent of Hawaii's registered voters went to the polls. William F. Quinn, Hawaii's last territorial governor, became Hawaii's first state governor. Hiram Leong Fong, a Republican and a lawyer (Harvard Law School) of Chinese descent, and former governor Oren E. Long became Hawaii's two senators. Fong was the first person of Asian ancestry to sit in the upper house of the United States Congress. Hawaii's congressman in the House of Representatives, a Democrat and a lawyer (George Washington University), was Daniel Ken Inouye, a Nisei veteran of World War II who had lost an arm in combat.

An immediate economic effect of statehood was a phenomenal increase in the tourist trade, as thousands of visitors flocked to Hawaii to see for themselves America's newest state. Tourists going to Hawaii rose from 171,000 in 1958 to 243,000 in 1959 and 296,000 in 1960. At the Governors' Conference held in Honolulu in June, 1961, James H. Shoemaker of the Bank of Hawaii said, "Statehood had the effect of a multi-million-dollar advertising campaign—for free. Everyone suddenly discovered Hawaii." He called the 42 per cent increase in tourist arrivals of 1959 over 1958 "unprecedented in history." The 22 per cent increase in tourist arrivals of 1960 over 1959 represented, as he stated in another report, "a marked increase." The $131 million spent by tourists in Hawaii in 1960 put the tourist trade first in Hawaii's economy, above both sugar and pineapples.

The boom in the tourist trade has created an unprecedented real-estate boom. In 1961 prime land in Waikiki sold for about $100 a square foot. By the middle of 1961 indications appeared that the peak of the boom was passing, with second-class hotels in Waikiki encountering financial difficulties. Nonetheless the Hawaii Visitors Bureau has taken an optimistic view of the long-range prospects of Hawaii's tourist industry. The Bureau has reported plans for the creation of resort areas on windward Oahu, in particular at Kahala, Waianae, and Haleiwa-Waimea, in addition to further expansion of existing facilities on the Big Island, Maui, and Kauai. Plans are maturing to build a 125-acre resort on the pineapple island of Lanai and to build a ridge highway to exploit the magnificent scenery of Molokai's windward valleys. On the basis of a report by the Pacific Area Travel Association, the bureau believes that it is possible to quadruple Hawaii's tourist trade by 1970; that is, to increase the number of tourists to a million a year and the revenue from tourist expenditures to half a billion dollars annually. These expectations may appear sanguine, but in any case some *kamaainas* expect that in time the tourist trade will exceed the combined revenues from sugar and pineapples.

Recently bauxite, the raw material for aluminum, was discovered in the Islands. Preliminary studies indicate that the deposits, mainly on Kauai, may yield as much as 600 million tons of aluminum oxide, with some titanium and much iron as by-products. The ore itself is not of first quality, but some Island economists believe that it would be highly suitable for export to Japan.

Plans are also going forward to exploit Hawaii's 500,000 acres of timberland. In the past timber was planted mainly to safeguard water reserves and to check soil erosion. Island promoters now see Hawaii's timber as a source of wood pulp, possibly for export to Japan for use in the manufacture of bagasse paper.

A direct result of statehood was the appropriation by the United States Congress in 1960 of $10 million to establish in Hawaii a Center for Cultural and Technical Interchange between East and West. This organization (known familiarly as the East-West Center), under the United States State Department, is to be administered by the University of Hawaii, long a meeting place for Western-Oriental scholarly conferences. Plans call for a total of 2,000 students in the sixth year of its operation, four-fifths of them foreign. Such an intercultural center has vast possibilities for research and mutual understanding. Possibly under its auspices the twain will actually meet.

In this connection Governor Quinn echoed the spirit of the dedication of the Honolulu Academy of Arts when he stated in his inaugural address in 1957, "The man of the Pacific, Hawaii's citizen, stands like Atlas astride the ocean joining East and West. He is as Western and up-to-date as the San Francisco Giants. And yet, through association, and often through family tradition, he understands the culture and thinking of the East. Our importance as a cultural link is heightened by our location. We sit at the hub of the great circle of the Pacific—at the center of a wheel with spokes connecting all the great nations on the mighty ocean. Our destiny as the Pacific center has not yet been achieved."

Perhaps the greatest immediate result of statehood for Hawaii was psychological, as its residents realized that they were no longer second-class citizens of the United States. How has statehood affected Hawaii's much-vaunted race relations?

Hawaii's race relations are not perfect, Hawaii not being Utopia and its residents not being superfolk. Certainly there are tensions and animosities among Hawaii's various racial and ethnic groups. In the popular image the *Pakes* (Chinese) are money-mad, the Buddha-heads (Japanese) boast too much about their war record, the Hawaiians are lazy, and the Filipinos make too much noise in general. *Kamaainas* look askance at *malihinis*, and at times the military and civilian populations become mutually irritated.

The greatest single cleavage is still between the *haoles* on the one hand, and all other groups on the other. The *haoles*, with superior education and wealth, enjoy definite privileges and evoke some resentment from the other residents. Especially this is the case with mainland *haoles*, newly arrived and unfamiliar with Hawaii's traditions. *Kamaaina haoles* (excluding the Portuguese), although entirely tolerant, generally live apart and exclude Hawaiians of Oriental descent from their most fashionable clubs. Until recently they seldom entertained Orientals in their homes, and they still seldom marry out of their race.

But to stop here is to miss the point. Ever since the coming of the first foreigners Hawaii has maintained a genuine and sincere tradition of racial tolerance. The tensions and animosities are skin deep, like family quarrels. No member of any racial or ethnic group is debarred from entering any public place, and certainly there is no segregation in the public schools. Privileged *haoles* who marry out of their race (this happens often enough so that a general statement is possible) do so without loss of social status.

It is much too early to estimate what effect (if any) statehood will have on Hawaii's race relationships. But one fact is clear. It removed Hawaii's feeling of political inferiority and created a new sense of pride among the citizenry as a whole. The day after Hawaii received statehood a full-page grocery advertisement carried a headline which read, "Statehood for Hawaii. We're all haoles now."

APPENDIX A

Unpublished Journal of Laura Fish Judd, 1827-28

What follows is the hitherto unpublished journal of Laura Fish Judd, wife of Dr. G. P. Judd, written during her journey to Hawaii on board the Parthian, *a wooden sailing ship. She left Boston as a member of the third missionary company on November 3, 1827, and reached Honolulu by way of Cape Horn on March 30, 1828, three days before her twenty-fourth birthday, after a journey of 148 days and 16,000 miles. The journal was later sent home to her sister as an extended letter. Both the beginning and the end of the journal are damaged and parts of it are almost impossible to read.*

The journal is published with the gracious permission of its owner, Mrs. Mary H. Marks of Old Forge, New York.

* * * * * * * * * * * * * *

emphatic "O dear"—! The natives were very attentive and kind. Phelps took care of Mr. and Mrs. Shepard. Mills and Henry assisted Mrs. Green in cabin, and Tyler took care of Dr. Judd and myself.

Monday morning with great exertion I got on deck. Waves running mountains high. I had been seated but a few minutes when one broke over deck, and wet me completely, my mouth and eyes and ears filled with salt water. The effect was salutary. My sea sickness left me and returned not again. I felt quite like another being. It seemed to me as if awakened from some strange dream. I went into the cabin and visited the sick, but the ship rolled so violently I was obliged to keep still as possible in some place where I could hold fast with both hands. O! methought, what would our friends say if they could take a peep into the *Parthian* and see the situation of its inmates. The cabin is only ten or twelve feet square, you cannot see the floor [for] trunks, boxes, bags and bundles of various descriptions. Four or five constantly vomiting. Vessel rocking so that table, chairs, and folks (if out of their berths) are thrown indiscriminately from side to side, not one murmur, the most of them are deadly seasick. All they can eat is a little water gruel which the natives make twice a day. But the smell is most killing of all. The sea is so rough the windows and dead-lights are in, and it would seem as tho' all must suffocate.

Tuesday Nov. 6th. In the gulph-stream, seas higher still and frequently break over deck. The cabin floor is constantly covered with water. We go ten knots an hour, steering directly eastward as tho' going to Europe.

A dear little bird visited today. It had flown till its wings were weary, and ligh[t]ed amongst the ropes. Little Peero (a Sandwich Island boy belonging to the ship) caught it and brought it to me. It seemed quite tame. I took it, and wept over it, for I knew it cam[e] from America, and Oh how I wished it could have brought me a billet under its [wing] that I might know [that] all are well— [flut]tered about in cabin all day and this evening *wicked* puss devoured it.

Thursday 8th. Yesterday about noon, the wind shifted, the sky darkened and there was every appearance of a tremendous gale. I was on deck. Capt. Blinn says, "Boys not a minute to lose." Things on deck were lashed with double caution, sails taken in or reefed closely. Orders were given and obeyed with the greatest alacrity, and many a fearful and anxious glance was cast to that part of the horizon where the storm was gathering. I remained on deck as long as my sensitive nerves could endure it. About 3 o'clock I went below and the hatchways were closed, the dead light put in, and the cabin converted into a perfect prison. All, excepting Mrs. Green and myself were too sick to realize the danger of our situation. O my sister, if I could tell you how I felt. It seemed every moment as if my breath would stop. I could not endure the confinement, and every few minutes went up the stair in the companion way, to breathe as well as look and listen. I had heard of "angry floods" of "roaring billows" of "mounting up to heaven and going down again into the depths, of reeling to and fro, and staggering like a drunken man," but now, I saw, and felt it, and of all the descriptions of storms at sea, I had ever read or heard, I could say, the half was not told me. The gloomy dismal sound of the wind roaring thro' the naked ropes had terror enough in it to unnerve the most hardened son of Neptune. As soon as dark, I retired to my stateroom, which is away from the others, laid myself down on my pillow with little expectation of seeing the light of another morning or the dawning of another sun. I was sensibly alive to all that passed. I lay and heard wave after wave dash and roll over deck; the timbers creaked and groaned like a human being in dying agonies. Three thunder showers followed each other in rapid succession, accompanied with lightning so vivid that the little which could enter my sky light (two inches bro[a]d and four long) almost blinded me. Once in a while between the gusts of wind I could distinguish the captain's voice giving orders. About midnight the little green boat that we left the wharf in, was carried away and the railing on the side of the ship to which it was lashed with sixteen of our chairs in it; (leaving eight, for six families beside the young ladies and natives.) And it seemed as if the ship must rock to pieces. Never before did I feel so much the exceeding weakness and impotency of human will and human skill. It appeared to me as if God has cast us right out into the midst of the ocean, let go his grasp upon the winds and said, "Now at the beginning, feel your helplessness, your insufficiency and learn your dependence on me. Your little barque is too frail, an arm of flesh too feeble to trust. Stay your souls on me for in my arm is everlasting strength." And I felt as if he threw his Almighty arm around us and held our little barque together, and said to the winds and waves hitherto shalt thou come and no farther and here shalt thy proud waves be stayed. Another morning dawned upon us on the waters (if not on the land) of the living. Towards noon the winds were entirely hushed, and this afternoon there is a great calm. Our language is, O give thanks unto the Lord for he is good, for his mercy endureth forever. Capt. Blinn (tho' an old and constant navigator) says he has not seen such a gale in ten years, and not one ship in fifty could have rode it. He had axes all night to cut away the masts if she capsized, so that she might possibly be righted again. What a perilous condition! We feel as tho' God had wrought a great deliverance for us and may we never more distrust him.

Friday. The winds died away entirely last night and left us rolling and tossing in the heavy dead seas. The vessel leaned [?] one way on her very beam-ends and back again the other way so that the railing lay flat in the water and often seemed to belance on a pivot and we could not guess whether she would strike on the bottom or [r]oll over in the water. You cannot imagine how distressing such motion is when continued hour after hour with no intermissions of rest. The wind to day is fair, but high sea and cabin floor constantly wet. Dr. Judd is yet very si[ck].

Sat. 10th. This is by far the calmest day we have had. Dr. J. is better. He with Miss Patten and Mr. Andrews and myself have our desks on deck trying to write. We are obliged to sit flat down and hold on with one hand. Now and then a spray of salt water comes over us but we do not mind trifles. Invalids recovering. We do not set table, but take a bit[e] in our hands, and eat and live more like barbarians than teachers of civilization.

Sab. 11th. A prayer meeting in cabin. Most of our family able to sit up.

Monday 12th. We are now nearly eighteen hundred miles from Boston Harbor and have made rapid progress on our voyage. I wish you could look into my stateroom and see me at my writing desk. It is just long enough for my berth, nearly as wide as it is long, a stand in the corner upon which is my desk. I can set a chair before it, which leave[s] just room enough for an entrance. Our trunks and Dr J——'s medicine chest are under the berth. I have a fine little shelf for the books we use on the way, and my work baskets etc., a nail for the clothes' brush and one for the thermometer. I cannot endure the door shut and have me a curtain of unbleached factory cloth. It opens, not into the cabin but what should be a dining room, tho' now so filled with bags, barrels, sails and lumber of every kind that I am obliged to get to my room in a very humble posture. My next neighbor is Mrs. Shepard. Opposite is Mr. Marshall (son of the owner of the ship.) Opposite Mrs. S. is Mr. Taylor's room, a passenger, who is to command a ship from the Islands to the Northwest Coast, and the backside of the room, is another for the mates. We expect it will be cleared when it comes good weather. Between us and the cabin is the Captain's room, pantry and stairs to go on deck. My room is larger than any others, for they have no room to sit down at all. I am writing by a lamp that I am obliged to hold, or it will fall. We hope by and bye to have better weather and things in better order.

Tues. 13th. A Brig in sight this morning in hopes to speak it, and send letters. Seems to be making towards us. Capt. think[s] she may be in want of water or provisions. It is fine weather almost no wind, but considerable sea, so much motion it is yet difficult to write. I wish you knew how much I want to see you. I feel sometimes almost sorry I did not visit Lyme at all events, but I try not to think about [it] as it avails nothing. All the members of the mission family better this morning. I succeeded in getting the ladies on deck. The voyage thus far has been uncommonly tedious, but our spirits and courage hold out. I am looking forward with much anxiety to the joyful day that will land us among the sea-girt isles. I find much less to interest at sea than I expected, nought but sky and water, water and sky day after day. I cannot yet sit down and think I am never to see any of you again in this world, and be composed. The thought is too painful, but I am willing to leave it with God. I love to think of the precious promises made to those who forsake all for Christ.

Wed. 14th. Beautiful weather today. Mr. Andrews [has] been playing the flute on deck this evening. Everybody knows how delightful music is on water. We begin to have things in better order. I feel the need of a grateful heart.

Thurs. 15th. Today Peero brought me some seaweed which he caught with a hook and line. It comes in the gulph-stream from Florida. I have preserved it to send home to America. We are now directly east of New Orleans near the parallel of fifty and thirty. We did not speak the ship we saw day before yesterday, tho' in sight all day. Capt. thought it a British East India Man homeward bound. Another sail in sight today. Sailing in the same direction and gaining upon us very fast. Capt. fears it may be one of the "*red* or *black flag*" gentlemen. Accordingly all the fire arms put in order—says the ladies must put on hats and pea jackets, go on deck and the sight of so many persons would confound them. They would think it must be a man of war, disguised instead of a Merchant man. My sensitive nerves are some disquieted by the thought of such a contact, but the name of the Lord is a strong tower into which the righteous may run and be safe. Evening has set in and we have almost lost sight of the dreaded vessel.

Friday 16th. This a most lovely morning. The vast expanse of blue waters, the clear sky with light turban clouds, present themselves in all their beauty and purity. The Parthian glides along majestically thro' the deep never weary never halting. Been sewing on deck, feel as quiet as on land, but that my ears are annoyed with oaths.

Sat. 17th. Alarmed at a water spout this morning. They occur at sea very frequently, are much dreaded tear ships into atoms if they strike them, guns were loaded to fire into it, (which is the only preventive) but winds sprang up and soon bore us beyond its influence. The Lord provides a way of escape from every danger, our little hearts can do nothing but trust in him. Pleasant weather, but contrary winds, rainbow more brilliant this morning than I ever saw it on land. Two weeks today since we left Bos[ton]. My nerves are not as sensitive as at first, suffer much less. We are nearer Europe than America. It would take but a few days to reach Gibraltar. Seen porpoises playing under the bow of the vessel.

Sabbath. I cannot but regret we did not have service on deck that the seamen might be benefited, but it was left for those to direct who are older and more prudent than myself.

Monday 19th. Wind more favorable. My mind still dwells on my friends and native land and tears flow freely, but Oh if I may be the means of leading one benighted soul to the knowledge of Christ, or ameliorate the condition of one degraded female, how small my sacrifice.

Wed. 21st. Sailing eight knots an hour. We observe today a season of prayer for the favor of God especially on the present voyage, that we may be kept from ship[w]reck and sudden death. Another British ship came near, and hoisted their colours which we answered by the same signal. It is very interesting to encounter fellow beings after being many days and nigh[ts] on the trackless deep.

Thurs. 22d. Calm. Capt. quite discouraged, weather getting warm as we go south, make slow progress.

Friday, 23rd. This evening, Samuel J. Mills, one of the Sandwich Islanders, lead in prayer at family worship. Seldom have I been so much interested. How I wished opposers to Missions could have heard that prayer, with what warmth he plead for his *poor* countrymen, that were worshipping idols, as he had done, that their *dark* hearts might be enlightened. To hear him pray thus and know that but a few years [ago] he too was enveloped in heathenish darkness and had no knowledge of God, was indeed affecting. Even now his breast is covered with prints of heathen absurdities and superstitions.

Sabbath 25th. Service on deck to my great satisfaction. Mr. Gulick appeared to feel his subject very deeply and addressed himself directly to his hearers. Text, "Without faith it is impossible to please God."

Monday, 26th. Saw a number of whales. They played about the ship two or three hours often throwing their enormous bellies quite out of water, a clumsy, ugly creature. They were too small to be dreaded. Conversed considerable with Capt. Taylor, seemed more softened than at first and often introduced religious subjects.

Tuesday 27th. High sea and several sea-sick again. I have been looking over the railing and admiring the sublimity of the scene. The whole Atlantic seems to be in a foam. The wake of vessel a flame of Phosphoric light. Clouds scud over the moon with great rapidity. I usually stay on deck till eleven. I have not learned to sleep on board ship. It tires me exceedingly.

Thurs. 27th [*sic*]. Wind from the north east. Capt. says it was never known before in this latitude. In danger of being driven ashore on Cape St Roque. Capt. says must be some Jonah aboard. Seen a whole school of flying fishes, look like white birds fly out of water to escape larger fish which prey upon them. Crossed the Northern Tropic this afternoon.

Friday 30th. We should meet the north-east trade wind at the Tropic, but no appearance of it, but head one continues which prevents us from getting far enough to east to clear St. Roque. Capt. says if it continues three days longer it will lengthen our voyage forty days at least.

Sat. Dec. 1st. I suppose friends in America are gathering round their fires to keep warm, while we are uncomfortably so with our lightest crepes on and in the coolest place we can find.

Sabbath 2nd. Weather very boisterous, worship in cabin. Mr. Andrews preached from Matthew 22. 25. Some of the officers and crew attended. Been by far the pleasantest Sabbath we have had. Capt. has never attended worship. But he read the Bible and I heard him enjoin it upon one of his men.

Mon. 3rd. A flying fish last night came on deck, in his speed to escape pursuers. Wind more favorable. We are but twelve degrees north of the Equator. This evening will be monthly concert. I hope the little Mission family on board the Parthian will be remembered in all the Christian churches, that our hearts may be prepared for the great work before us.

Thurs. 6th. A delightful shower today, a most ludicrous scene. Ladies were on deck writing. Capt. cries out, "a squall coming." "Ladies put up your desks." "Some of you boys aft here, and down with the hatches." "Stand by the main top gallant sail halyards," etc.etc. In an instant all was apparent confusion. Shower soon overtook us. The method devised for saving fresh water is to spread the awning (which we have for a shade in the sunshine) put weights on different parts of it, and set the tubs and pails under. The first is always salt but soon gets washed and the water very pure. It was laughable today to see us one with a bucket, a wash basin, stone jar, mug, pitcher, tumbler or anything we could find running about to save the precious drops. We feel the value of water after being kept on allowance as we do at sea. We have 3 quarts a piece a day which is none too much for our cooking and drink in these warm latitudes. Lat 7° North Lon 26° East [*sic*].

Friday 7th. Every variety of weather today, rain, sunshine, wind and calm. Seen a variety of fish. Dolphins, Nautilus, Porpoises etc. Very much amused with little Peero, as I am every day, says, "Dr. Judd pickenninny, (small). Mrs. Judd stand up too much." I am very tired of sea-bread, but nothing I want so much as milk. I can hardly drink tea and coffee without it. Water is very bad.

Dec. 10th. Awakened this morning by a great noise on deck. I threw on my *old green* morning dress in great haste, and soon made one of the noisy number. Mr. Taylor had harpooned a shark, and hauled him in. He was flouncing about violently. We all jumped about and mounted the highest places we could to keep out of danger and yet see him. Soon the carpenter came with his axe, knocked him in head and he became quiet. It was but a small one, 6 or 7 feet long. There was a little parasitical fish, fast on his back which they call a sucker. We preserved it in rum to send home. It has rained all day. Caught several hogsheads of pure water, beside some for washing dipped off deck. Ocean alive with fish. We have tried to wash pocket handkerchiefs etc., but no place, or hot water, or tubs, and no place to dry them when they are washed.

Tues. 11th. Suffer extremely with the heat. Rained after noon, head-winds and calms alternately for several days. Gone only 160 miles since last Friday, very uncommon in this latitude. Killed the last of our fowls.

Wed. 12th. Very light breeze, but fair this morning. Sun shines very warm indeed, fear the Dr. and myself have not saved out changes enough for our voyage, as we need more than I expected. A ship is a filthy place, and some degree of cleanliness is necessary both for health and comfort. Another flying fish came on board last night with such force as to break his little back. We saved one wing for a curiosity.

Thurs. 13th. My health is very good and I never enjoyed myself better, tho' I find sources of distress. O the wickedness of the ship's crew and then my own unbelief in the promises of God.

Fri. Dec. 14th. Crossed the Equator, nine o'clock this morning. A visit from "Old Father Neptune," as is his custom, but we did not see him. He left his compliments and said he would call on the "Strangers" when we cross the line again, in the Pacific.

Sab. 16th. A quiet day. The Sabbath is indeed a blessing even here, it is distinct from every other day.

Mon. 17th. Struck the South East Trade wind, pleasant sailing.

Thurs. 20th. Just raised our colours to an American Brig homeward bound. Could not get sufficiently near to spea[k] her which we regret extremely. It is the first American sail we have seen. Going 8 knots an hour.

Sat. 22nd. Heat very oppressive. My feet swell very much. It is now seven weeks since we sailed. All well, tho' languid and suffer for exercise. Do not go on deck much till evening. I skip rope a little.

Sab. 23rd. Mr. Gulick occupied us this morning from those solemn words of our savior, "What do ye more than others?" He applied it to us as a mission family, showed there was more expected of *us* than of others. I feel as the Psalmist did, "Let the righteous smite me it shall be a kindness." We have many temptations to worldly mindedness, to love the creature more than the creator. Our hearts need breaking every day.

Christmas Day. 1827. The warmest Christmas I ever knew. The[r]mometer 84° in shade, sun vertical. Gentleman stood in the shadow of their hats. We are but four or five hundred miles off the coast of S. America, pass Rio Janeiro this evening. Crossed the Tropic of Capricorn five this afternoon, lost the trade wind. A Christmas dinner of stuffed boiled ham, it was very salt. Cannot help thinking of the friends and comforts of our native land, and hope our friends remember us.

Wed. 26th. Ship rolls violently this morning. You would laugh [?] to us in the cabin. Every few minutes we find ourselves in a promiscuous heap, with chairs, boxes, etc. I was making some salt risings for fresh bread (which we have occasionally) in a small jar, had it on the floor, with a pitcher of hot water and a keg of flour, which Mrs. Clark was holding for me. Suddenly the ship heaved, and away we went to the opposite side of the cabin. We left a path of flour behind us. But I held fast to my yeast and hot water. At breakfast one held the coffee pot, another the cup, both in danger of being burned. I tried to help get away the dishes and tumbled about till nine o'clock, and then went to bed, which I have not yet been able to leave. Have had one of those very distressing turns I have been subject to. I thought of home, and the friends that used to take care of me, and I

[Page missing from MS. The next paragraph is in G. P. Judd's hand.]

know how comfortable and happy Laura is. The Lord is more to her than father, brothers or sister. She expects to meet you in a little while. A few more fleeting years and our work will be finished, well or ill done. How insignificant it makes all our selfdenial when we look upward when we *really think* of God and Eternity.

[The next paragraph is in L. F. Judd's hand.]

Jan. 2d. A sail in sight. Hope to send letters to America. We are now off the River La Plata, all engaged in preparing packages to send, with hearts beating high in the happy expectation of letting you hear from us.—Alas! Alas! our ardent hopes are all blasted. The sail already begins to grow very dim in the distance. Capt. thinks it a whale ship from the Islands, says if it was not so near night we would tack towards it. How often we are reminded that disappointment is [the] lot of all men.

[The next paragraph is in G. P. Judd's hand.]

Saturday 5th Jan. 1828. The writer of this journal being busily employed in making nut cakes and pie (domestic cares I might say) the person whose name she has adopted takes the liberty of writing a little for her. He has only to record however that the weather is calm and an Albertrose [*sic*] has been seen at a great distance from the ship, which is south of the River La Plata. Although he never saw Laura's Dear sister yet he feels an affection for her on account of her relation to his dear companion. May we meet when our work is done.

[*The next paragraphs are in L. F. Judd's hand.*]

Jan. 5th. The cry of Porpoise! Porpoises!! called us all on deck in great haste this afternoon. A school of them surrounded the ship. Capt. Taylor harpooned one. It was quite a curiosity. The lungs and heart resemble swine, blood warm. They breathe air and remain under water but a few minutes at a time. Flesh tastes some like fresh pork, but dryer like venison. It was not at all like fish. The smell of fresh meat, made the cat and dog crazy. Poor Lion was tied up with a rope to keep him within bounds. The Steward had a dish of it cooked and was devouring it in a most voracious manner, in less than fifteen minutes. Others seemed to crave it very much. For myself, I do not suffer for want of fresh food, tho' have been sixty three days at sea.

Sab. 6th. Today being the first sabbath of the year Mr. Andrews gave us a New Year's sermon. Text from Prov. "Teach us so to number our days as to apply our hearts unto wisdom."

Mon. 7th. Heavy sea, fair wind, nine knots an hour. Sun goes over to the north, and casts our shadows to the south. Days very long. Sun rises half past four, sets half past seven. This morning there was a beautiful rainbow formed in the spray before the ship. It is very grand to see the Parthian move along, as the white waves part, and comb up each side of her. Been mending clothes for my dear Companion, an employment as delightful as new. I am more and more sensible every day of the blessing of an affectionate friend, in whom we place confidence, and whose bosom is ever open to receive and participate in all our joys and sorrow.

Jan. 8th. High winds and heavy seas all night. Waves frequently break over deck. This afternoon it thunders. All hands are called on deck, preparations for a storm. God Almighty be our refuge. We are now in the most dangerous part of our voyage. O! how dreadful the rumbling of the thunder! and the flashes of lightning are very vivid.

Wed. Jan. 9th. "Sail O!" sail O! was the cry that awoke me this morning. It is close by. I have been looking at it with Capt.'s spyglass, can see two men on the masts. Delightful! delightful! Sorry I have not more letters ready, but you must take my journal in the place of them. Love to all relatives and friends.

Farewell
L. F. JUDD

Afternoon. The vessel proved to be the whale ship Galatea from New Bedford, five months out. We spoke it, but did not put letters

on board, as it will not go home till spring, and we hop[e]
sooner. It is impossible to describe the animation the events
morning have produced. A dear little American dove left the
ship and came to ours. It seemed sensible of its mistake, but did n[ot]
know the way back. We fed it with rice and water, and it is getting
more reconciled. We are very near the Fal[k]land Islands. The
storm yesterday did not prove to be as bad as we feared. After the
thunder and rain, the wind diminished to our great joy. On sound-
ings, for the first time since we have been out, fifty fathoms. Very
foggy tonight. Cannot see an inc[h] before you since dark. In
danger of running against vessels, as they are more likely to meet
here than any where else as they generally go between the F. Island
and the coast. We caught the Dove and put [it] in a work-basket to
sleep. It was quite chilled.

Thurs. 10th. Calm foggy weather, quite chilly. Carpenter made
a house for the Dove on deck. You will excuse bad writing for we
are buffeting the billows of Cape Horn. Sometimes I write sitting
up, sometimes lying down, depends on the steadiness of the ship.
Now it rolls continually. Very cold. I have sat with my feet in my
berth all day, reading Miss Jane Taylor, with only one interruption,
the cry of whale O! This is their region. They are around us spout-
ing at a great rate.

Mon. 14th. Passed the Falkland Islands yesterday. Did not see
them. The Ocean is covered with birds. Penguins are numerous. The
Albertross is the largest.

Tues. 15th. Am almost froze. Sat in my berth all day, and sewed
while Dr. J. read to me. The sea is rough, and we are subject to
sudden and violent commotions.

Thurs. 17th. A large wave broke over us today, and several hogsheads came down upon us in the cabin and dining room. Capt.
presented us with a box of raisins. We have no potatoes or vegetables
of any kind. Head-winds, 75 fathoms water.

Jan. 18th. "Land O!" "Land O!" was the joyful cry that saluted
our ears. The rugged peaks of Staten Island appeared to the west
of us. I have sat the live long forenoon feasting my eyes. It seems
to give us all new life. The mountains presented numerous and
pointed peaks, resembling volcanos. As the smoke and clouds brush
away I can discover something like snow, and in one place a tor-
rent running down from the top of the mountain. Little Peero is
very much animated, says, "Cape Horn kau kau kanaka" (eat-men)
"mamooly kau kau wahinas" (bye and bye eat the women). I told
him bye and bye they would eat Peero. No! he says, Me black, they
no like, kau kau you. I suppose someone has told him of the
cannibals inhabiting Cape Horn. Evening. The Land is 15 miles
distant, very little wind. In danger of dashing against those porten-
tious rocks. We have all been on deck to see the glorious sun go
down once more behind the hills. After seeing it set in the water
77 days, it is a pleasure indescribable. As I came below I heard the

Capt. tell the man at helm to bear off from the Land much as possible. A strong current is setting us toward it, but I retire to rest quietly myself under the protection of the mighty God of Jacob. He has saved me in six troubles, and in seven he will not forsake.

Jan. 19th. I arose this morning at 4. The sun already half an hour high. The surface of the Ocean is unruffled, the land still in sight. No wind. Been driven back by the current all night. The sky is clear excepting a few white clouds. I never before I never beheld so beautiful a prospect. It does not seem possible that it can so soon be thrown into turbulence and disorder. Got along very little today current still stronger than the wind.

Sabbath 20th Jany. O how I long to be freed from sin, to be no longer in bondage to the appetites and corruptions of an unsanctified heart. O for grace to overcome the love of this world. Who would think a missionary could love the world. He has literally resigned its riches and pleasures, is freed from its flatteries and etiquettes. What! And love it yet? Strange inconsistence, but so it is. I fear I shall make an Annanias [sic] and Sapphira work of it. But I must go often to the ["throne" crossed out] fountain, and drink more freely of that never failing source which is as a well of water springing up to everlasting life. I must feel more for sinners, realize more of the value of souls, of God's glory, and of Eternity.

Monday 21st. The current still drives us back. Meeting with the waves makes bad seas. Staten island still visible at the north of us. We dread the struggle with Cape Horn, but hope to triumph over it in the end. Many good ships have been lost there, others have been detained mid storms and tempests for many weeks. But we cast our burden on the Lord. He that led, guided and protected the wandring children of Israel through the wilderness will surely be our Guide and Protector.

Tuesday 22nd. The land still in sight. We have been driven back by the current all night. Captain says we shall be at Falkland Islands again pretty soon unless the wind changes, says if we do he will not come back nor go to Boston, but run into some harbour in Patagonia, sell or burn the ship, and establish a colony. We know him too well to think him in earnest.

Just after tea a squall struck us suddenly and unexpectedly. All hands on deck in a moment. The sun still shone in his usual brightness and I took my station in the Companion way to witness the interesting tho' terrific scene. There always seems to be a stimulus in a gale of wind, that excites men to exertions almost incredible. I counted fifteen men on the main mast furling the sail. Waves rolled the highest I ever saw them, their dashing and [ ]ing and roaring reminded me of what is said in the Bible, "The noise of many waters." In a short time, all was done that could be, the deck quiet, no one to be seen but the man at the helm, one mate and the Capt. pacing back and forth, with all the anxiety in countenance you would expect a man to feel in a station so responsible. It was our usual hour for worship, and we assembled around our family altar and poured out our evening oblation with feelings of no common interest.

Wed. Morn. The last night has been a sleepless one to most of us. The winds raged in all their fury. Capt. up all night, said he feared the decks would be swept and the masts carried away in spite of him. Waves so high as to be seen above the foreyard, must have been 40 or 50 ft. The Parthian is a noble sea boat and was so well managed as to ship very little water. The exertion requisite to keep in my berth has fatigued me exceedingly. Wind today high as ever.

Sat. 26th. Twelve long weeks we have been residents of the Parthian. Many and dreadful have been the dangers thro' which the Lord has brought us, and we will trust in him for help in every time of trouble, but no one can realize the tediousness of such a voyage unless they have tried it. Not yet around Cape Horn.

Tuesday Jan. 29th. Becalmed. Uncommon here. Lat. 60° S. Lon. 75 West, so that we consider ourselves in the Pacific Oce. and pacific it is indeed. I never saw so beautiful a prospect. The whole expanse of water visible as smooth as glass, and if it does not reflect the trees, it does the clouds the sun, the ship, and the large beautiful birds that sail about continually. The colour of the clouds varies from the purest white to blue and red, all in curls, and with the most splendid embroidery. We are so far south and the days so long that the twilight meets the morning. Caught an Albertrose. [sic]

Friday Feb. 1st. The months glide away strangely, anxious as we are to reach our desired haven. We have been out 90 days, are 11,000 miles from our native land. It is indeed true now that mountains rise and oceans roll between.

Sab. Feb. 3d. This has been a peculiarly interesting sabbath. Mr. Andrews preached in morning upon the incarnation of the Savior. Young Marshall and Mr. Thompson (2d mate) attended. *Some troubled,* as the impenitent always are, with the truths of the gospel.

Tues. 5th. A fair wind. Caught a Cape Horn porpoise. Dined on it. I like it very much.

Wed. 7th [sic]. Observed as a day of Than[k]sgiving, as proposed by the Prudential Committee, after passing the dangerous goal, Cape Horn in safety. We have encountered no gales equal to the one in the Gulph-Stream. Our provisions have kept well, and our health's good. We have not all the conveniences we could wish, but then the safety of the vessel and our confidence in the management of its officers is something towards compensation. Capt. been attentive, and often doing something to make us comfortable. Oh if I could say he was a Christian! It is three weeks last sabbath since we passed the Falkland Islands. Now we are nearly opposite the Island of Chiloe. We have much to be thankful for, and I hope I feel it.

Mon. 11th. Concluded to double my diligence, being so near the place of destination, and so much yet to be done. We make rapid progress, seen a school of black fish.

Wed. 13th. About 2 o'clock last night Capt. Blinn discovered [we] were but a few miles from ["the I discovered were but" crossed out] the Island of Massafuero, heading directly towards it, before a strong breeze. I awoke with the cry, "All hands on deck." The sails were furled, the ship's course altered, and soon all was quiet again. I fell asleep and did not awaken till Phelps called us at daylight, saying Land! Land! The Island of Massafuero was in full view to the Eastward. It is covered with sandal-wood, but very difficult of access from its bold shore. There is a pond of water on it, in which, they say a Spaniard threw a vast quantity of money on being pursued by an enemy. Large sums of gold have been got out but more remains.

We shall not see Juan Fernandes which lies still farther eastward. This the Capt. says if we were in want of water or provisions he would make it, as it contains excellent water, cattle, goats, etc. with thousands of peaches and all kinds of fruit, without a claimant. Mr. Thompson (2d mate) says, he landed there the last voyage he made. That one street is paved, the houses of stone and a nice stone church. It rises into mountains in the interior which are covered with wild oats and cattle, the beach strewed with fire arms. The Spaniards settle on it and the Patriots drive them off, establish themselves, and in their turn are routed by the Spaniards, so that the Island in all its beauty and fertility is left uninhabited. I feel a great desire to see it, as it is associated with so many pleasant recollections of childhood as being the residence of Robinson Crusoe. I suppose the Island we passed this morning is the one from which he obtained his good man Friday.

Sat. 16th. Sailing ten knots an hour before a fair wind. Twenty seven sails spread on the little Parthian. O I wish you could see how proudly she marches along thro' the deep. I rejoice, tho' she is bearing me farther and farther from my kindred and native land, yet she is bearing to a part of the Lord's vineyard, where my heart has long been. Evening. Our prayer meeting this evening has been unusually interesting. Mills (one of the natives) made the first prayer, Says, "we pray for our friends in America. We thank thee, O our Father for kind friends in America who teach *us* who were born in darkness the way of salvation." Phelps made the concluding prayer spoke as he always does, with so much clearness and propriety. One could hardly believe, he had but a *few* years enjoyed religious instruction.

Sabbath 17th Feb. We have a prospect of a quiet day. The bitterness of spirit, manifested for same past, seems in a measure softened. I rejoice for I know it is the restraining grace of God.

My heart, this holy morning is with the children of God in my own dear Land. I can think of many, with whom I have taken sweet counsel and walked to the house of God in company. O how little have I valued [w]hat I should now deem inestimably precious.

Thurs. 20th. [*sic*] The sisters enjoyed a very sweet season of prayer this afternoon in our little cabin. It seemed as if the promise was verified to us, "Where two or three are met together in my name there am I in the midst of them, and that to bless them." We confessed our faults with eyes wetted to tears and I hope contrite hearts. At the close, we sang, "When I survey the wondrous cross."

The heat is very oppressive, as we have less wind than in the Atlantic.

28th. This morning I used the last of some sewing silk wound on paper. I opened it and recognized Egr Royce's writing and figures. This is nothing remarkable to be sure, but then it brought up so many associations of the secretary in the middle parlour where I used to see him write, and the middle parlour brought along with it so many other associations. It cost me *one sigh*, but no matter it was not the sigh of regret.

Sat. March 1st. I write this by the light of a full moon, shedding her rays in a streak of sparkling light across the waters of the broad Pacific. I look upon the glittering path it makes, and think could I follow it could lead me directly to that favored spot I once called home. We are all on deck, some walking, some lounging on the settee, others viewing the moon thro' Capt's spy-glass, while here and there one leans pensively over the railing, med

[*A page or more is missing. The rest of the MS is torn and almost illegible. Passages impossible to read are indicated by three dots.*]

Thurs. 20th. We have struck the North East Trade which blows very strong. Ship rolls. Dr. Judd and myself up all night with Mrs. Green, suffered extremely. Relieved this morning about nine o.c. She has not been well since a fall she got at Cape Horn, which was the occasion of her *untimely confinement.*

March 21st. Observed as a day of fasting and prayer, that we may be prepared for anything that awaits us at the Islands. May be the Foreigners have prevailed, and the young king and chief[s] [a]re against the Missionaries, and we may not [be] permitted to land. But, "Trust in God," is my motto. "I count not my life dear unto myself." I am willing to lay it down if it be the will of God.

Wed. March 26th. All busy in making arrangements for landing. To morrow we expect to see Owhyhee. What my emotions are, I cannot tell, but I was never happier. Our dear Sister Mrs. G. is better, sat up a little this morning. Hope she will be able to land with us.

March 29th Sat. To our inexpressible joy we find we are in sight of Owhyhee this morning. The lofty h[ei]ghts of Mouna Kea, [*sic*] feet above the level of the [sea] reared themselves above the clouds that encir[cle] its middle. The summit is covered with [one line missing from bottom of page]. The natives are much animated. We shall probably reach Oahu tomorrow.

March 31st. Just at the close of service this afternoon, a salute was fired, colours hoisted and anchor cast. We are off a point of land called Diamond Hill. The shore all along is lined with native huts peeping thro' the cocoa nut and kou trees. The beach or plain extending half a mile or mile in width is backed by a range of hills and mountains. Some are sandy and [some are] covered with verdure . . . heights and hues. The [huts] of the natives look for all the world like straw bee hives. Phelps points out encl[o]sure that once contained [a] heath[en te]mple where [hun]dreds perhaps thousands [of] huma[n be]ings have bee[n] sacrificed. I think I [can] dis[ti]nguish the Miss[ion house]. There are thir[ty] large vessels in port. Upon one, the . . . is hoisted. A sea . . . has come to us in a boat manned by . . . . . . says th[e] Missionaries [are] all well. The young . . . . . . [v]isit Owhyhee. Nothing remarkable he . . . . . . Oh [how] strange it seems to see new faces after seeing the same for 148 days. . . . other boats have arrived. Several natives in each dressed as sailors and belong to ships. . . . give us very inquisitive looks. Another bo[at co]mes with intelligence that Mrs. Bishop . . . . . . I . . . . has come

APPENDIX B

Some Common Hawaiian Words

As STANDARDIZED by the missionaries early in the nineteenth century, the Hawaiian language has seven consonants (*h, k, l, m, n, p, w*), pronounced as in English. The five vowels are pronounced as follows:

a—ah, as in c*a*r
e—eh, as in v*ei*n
i—ee, as in mar*i*ne
o—oh, as in *o*wn
u—oo, as in r*u*le

In addition, there are a number of vowel combinations which resemble diphthongs:

ai—eye, as in m*i*le
ao and *au*—ow, as in h*ow*
ei—eh, as in v*ei*n
oe—oy, as in b*oy*

Otherwise every letter is sounded separately. Generally each word is lightly accented on the next to last syllable, but some words have no accent.

The following are some common Hawaiian words, many of which have replaced their English equivalents among island residents:

Aina, land
Akamai, clever, expert
Alii, chief
Aloha, love, hello, good-bye
Auwe, alas
Hale, house
Hana, work
Hao, iron
Haole, white man, foreigner
Hapa, fraction, part
Hapai, pregnant, carry
Heiau, place of worship
Hikiee, couch
Holoku, gown, often with a train
Hoomalimali, flattery
Hoomanawanui, take it easy, patience

Huhu, angry
Hui, union, society, syndicate
Huki, pull
Hula, dance
Imu, underground oven
Imua, forward, in front of
Kahili, royal standard
Kahuna, expert, priest
Kai, sea
Kamaaina, native-born, old-timer
Kanaka, man
Kane, man, male
Kapakahi, crooked
Kapu, forbidden, sacred
Kauka, doctor
Keiki, child

211

Kiawe, algarroba (tree)
Kokua, help
Kona, south
Koolau, windward, north
Kuhina nui, premier
Kuleana, a right, property
Lanai, porch, terrace
Lauhala, pandanus leaf
Laulau, bundle, especially of food
Lei, necklace, usually of flowers
Lomi Lomi, massage
Luau, feast
Luna, foreman, overseer
Mahalo, thanks
Mahele, division
Maikai, good, beautiful
Makai, seaward
Malihini, stranger, newcomer
Malo, loincloth
Mauka, inland
Mauna, mountain
Mele, song, chant
Menehune, dwarf, elf
Moe, sleep
Muumuu, gown, mother hubbard

Nui, big, great
Oe, you
Okole, posterior
Okolehao, Hawaiian liquor
Opu, stomach
Paakiki, stubborn, hard
Pake, Chinese
Palapala, writing
Pali, cliff
Paniolo, cowboy, Spaniard
Pau, finished
Pehea, How? How are you? How is it?
Pikake, jasmine
Pilau, stench, smelly
Pilikia, trouble
Pipi, beef, cattle
Poha, gooseberry
Poi, taro paste
Puaa, pig
Puka, hole
Punee, couch
Pupule, crazy
Ukulele, stringed instrument, literally "jumping flea"
Wahine, woman
Wiki, quick, hurry

APPENDIX C

Some Basic Books About Hawaii

ALLEN, GWENFREAD, *Hawaii's War Years, 1941-1945*. Honolulu: University of Hawaii Press, 1950.

DAY, A. GROVE, *Hawaii and Its People*. New York: Duell, Sloan and Pearce, 1955.

————, and STROVEN, CARL (eds.). *A Hawaiian Reader*. New York: Appleton-Century-Crofts, 1959.

JUDD, GERRIT P., IV, *Dr. Judd, Hawaii's Friend*. Honolulu: University of Hawaii Press, 1960.

KUYKENDALL, RALPH S., *The Hawaiian Kingdom, 1778-1854: Foundation and Transformation*. Honolulu: University of Hawaii Press, 1947.

————, *The Hawaiian Kingdom, 1854-1874: Twenty Critical Years*. Honolulu: University of Hawaii Press, 1953.

MORGAN, THEODORE, *Hawaii, A Century of Economic Change, 1778-1876*. Cambridge: Harvard University Press, 1948.

NORBECK, EDWARD, *Pineapple Town: Hawaii*. Berkeley and Los Angeles: University of California Press, 1959.

RADEMAKER, JOHN A., *These Are Americans: The Japanese Americans in Hawaii in World War II*. Palo Alto, Calif.: Pacific Books, 1951.

STEVENS, SYLVESTER K., *American Expansion in Hawaii, 1842-1898*. Harrisburg, Pa.: Archives Publishing Co., 1945.

TEMPSKI, ARMINE VON, *Born in Paradise*. New York: Literary Guild of America, 1940.

INDEX